Your Sexually Addicted Spouse

Your Sexually Addicted Spouse

How Partners Can Cope and Heal

By Barbara Steffens, Ph.D., LPCC,
and Marsha Means, MA

New Horizon Press
Far Hills, New Jersey

"In Terror's Grip: Healing the Ravages of Trauma," by Bessel A. van der Kolk, M.D., from Cerebrum, Winter 2002, reprinted with permission of Dana Press, a division of the Dana Foundation, www.dana.org.

Quotations from the ISO-COSA Web site are reprinted with permission from the ISO-COSA organization.

Reprinted with permission from *Psychological Trauma* by Bessel A. van der Kolk, M.D., copyright ©1987, American Psychiatric Publishing, Inc.

From *Waking the Tiger: Healing Trauma* by Peter A. Levine with Ann Frederick, published by North Atlantic Books, copyright ©1997 by Peter A. Levine. Reprinted by permission of publisher.

Requests for permission should be addressed to:
New Horizon Press
P.O. Box 669
Far Hills, NJ 07931

Steffens, Barbara and Means, Marsha
    Your Sexually Addicted Spouse: How Partners Can Cope and Heal

Cover design: Robert Aulicino
Interior design: Susan Sanderson

Library of Congress Control Number: 2009923751

ISBN-13 (paperback): 978-0-88282-309-6
ISBN-13 (eBook): 978-0-88282-357-7
New Horizon Press

Manufactured in the U.S.A.

2019   2018   2017   2016   2015   7   8   9   10   11

Dedication

This book is dedicated to the many courageous women and men who openly shared their experiences in the hopes that others might receive the help and support they need. I'm grateful for the privilege of serving as a witness to your journey through such difficult places. I have learned much from you. I also dedicate this to my husband who is the bravest man I know, and my daughters who are my delight. Ultimately, this work is dedicated to the glory of God; He is the one who can make all things new.

—Barbara Steffens, Ph.D.

To my mother, "Rusti" Eloise Farnworth, who rolled up her sleeves and helped me in practical ways, such as listening as I dealt with my own trauma and grieved my painful losses. She continues to be my biggest fan and my prayer warrior extraordinaire. Lord, what will I do without her when you take her home?

—Marsha Means, MA

Authors' Note

This book is based on our research, a thorough study of the available literature and experience counseling patients, as well as our clients' own real life experiences. Fictitious identities and names have been given to certain characters in this book in order to protect individual privacy and some characters are composites. For purposes of simplifying usage, the pronouns his/her and s/he are sometimes used interchangeably.

The information contained herein is not meant to be a substitute for professional evaluation and therapy.

Table of Contents

Introduction

U nlike most books written for partners of sex addicts, this book is not written to help you understand the addict and his or her addiction. Rather, it is written to help you survive, recover and thrive, no matter what your partner does with his or her addiction.

Another distinct difference separates this book from others written for partners of sex addicts:[1] Nowhere between these covers will you encounter information that automatically labels you a co-addict or a codependent. And nowhere will we tell you that you have a co-addiction, simply because you married a person you have since discovered struggles with sexual addiction.

These terms are often automatically used to label you by those who believe that you, along with your partner, have a problem or even an addiction from which you need to recover simply because you chose your partner in the first place. In past sex addiction literature, if partners of sex addicts compulsively check up on their spouses, become emotionally numb, feel anger or rage, placate their partners or isolate themselves, among a long list of other behaviors, many view them as showing signs of their own addictive tendencies and loss of self.

Nevertheless, we categorize your pain, confusion, distress, reactions and fear as natural responses to trauma. As the authors of this book, our deepest desire is to help you understand how you have been wounded and most likely traumatized so that you can bravely begin to heal. After years of experience and research, we believe that healing the pain from the trauma provides the shortest route to emotional and physical health and wholeness. We know many of you will comment, "Finally, someone is saying what I've intuitively known all along!"

We hope that, in time, these observations will empower and equip professionals hoping to provide alternate ways to understand

and aid you in processing your pain so they can help you completely heal from its effect in your life. While not all partners of sex addicts are female, most of those who seek help are women married to male sex addicts. Little research exists that focuses on the male partner of a female sex addict. We believe that the material and suggestions found in these pages will help, encourage and bring healing to both men and women who are so deeply affected by the reality of sex addiction in their spouses. Even as we write, other mental health professionals incorporate Barbara's study on the relationship of trauma and sexual addiction into their Web sites and practices. We believe that true hope, help and change will come, though it may come slowly.

In the meantime, information is power and we hope this information will empower you to recognize your needs and find help to heal your ongoing pain so that you can once again experience true joy in your life. This is our prayer for you.

PART I

WHEN YOUR PARTNER'S SEXUAL ADDICTION SHATTERS YOUR WORLD

Chapter 1

What is Trauma and Post-Traumatic Stress?

The deep relational trauma Katherine experienced in her relationship with her husband is evident in her story.

Sitting there on the narrow staircase with a blanket wrapped around me, I couldn't stop shaking. The sergeant and a female officer had just spent an hour and a half grilling me about my husband, Neil.

Unable to move, I listened as they repeated the whole process with my seventeen-year-old son. Only moments before he had returned from band practice and walked into this bizarre scene. Numb, I heard my son asking the same questions I had.

"How is any of this possible?"

"If this is true, wouldn't I have seen it?"

"Why can't I stop shaking like this?"

The sergeant and five others arrived to our home at 8:00 P.M., April 1. Ironically, April Fools' Day. I thought it was a prank at first—a cruel prank—but as three of the officers began to scour our home computers as the sergeant and the female officer focused on me, I realized they weren't joking. I took my youngest son to his room and turned up his television set.

My husband had been missing for twenty-four hours. He was on his way home from a business trip, but he never showed up.

"Your husband was arrested as he entered the country," the sergeant said. "He's been charged with possession of child pornography and he's in jail."

He was relentless as he began to grill me. As time went on, I think he must have realized I was going into shock and attempted to be gentler, but it didn't change anything. What he said—what I heard about my husband—was not gentle.

The female officer never said anything. She just kept watching me, never taking her eyes off of me. Watching me intently.

I felt myself dissociating from reality. It felt like I was having an out-of-body experience, as if I was observing the whole scene, rather than participating in it. But mostly I was numb. Cold and numb.

What will this do to my children? I kept wondering. My two older kids were on their way to the house only to be told news about their father that was going to devastate them. They needed to know, but what was I going to say? How could I break the news that their father was in custody?

Eventually, the officers left. I went to bed, but I couldn't sleep, even though I was exhausted; more tired than I've ever been. I curled up in a ball and cried and prayed all night. I couldn't think. I just cried and prayed.

Neil's actions wounded Katherine deeply and left emotional scars—scars she must integrate into her life if she wants to completely heal from the experience.

Although trauma and post-traumatic stress have been recognized as common occurrences in the human experience for over a century, the acknowledgment of *relational trauma* evolved later as researchers began to note the extreme emotional pain and psychological damage we experience when betrayed or victimized by someone close.

As researchers studied relational trauma, they observed that its intensity increased when inflicted by someone we believe we can trust—someone we believe we can go to for support, like a parent, friend or romantic partner. In those times, the person we trust becomes our source of pain, as did Neil in Katherine's life.

To gain a better understanding of trauma, let's begin by looking at its general forms: trauma, post-traumatic stress and post-traumatic stress disorder (PTSD). We'll look at what comprises these diagnoses of clustered symptoms and how they impact our ability to cope. Then we'll take a closer look at relational traumas, the trauma category we believe partners of sex addicts fall into.

What is Trauma and Post-Traumatic Stress?
Trauma Defined

Two kinds of trauma exist: physiological trauma and psychological trauma. Each involves an injury that takes place during an extrinsic (or external) event. Physiological trauma damages our bodies and our psyches. In this section, we will focus only on the psychological form and its impact.

Reports and vividly colored photos and video footage of traumatic events fill our newspapers and news shows every day of our lives. All who watched as airplanes crashed into the Twin Towers in New York City on September 11, 2001, know how a traumatic event looks and feels. Our awareness that thousands of family members with loved ones trapped in those buildings experienced unspeakable horror as *they* watched the same drama unfold inflicted us with a measure of their pain. But only a measure.

For the family members themselves, the trauma was far more devastating. Author Abigail Carter was among them. She writes:

> The phone rang. It was my husband telling me that he was at Windows of the World in the World Trade Center.
> "There's been a bomb!" he said. I had been preparing my six-year-old daughter for her second day of first grade, balancing my two-year-old son on my hip, and I was distracted. "Okay . . ." I managed to say. It was 8:49 A.M. on September 11, 2001. He never came home. [1]

Before 9/11, Abigail believed she had everything she wanted in life, including a loving husband and two precious children. But in one destructive moment her life was forever broken into two starkly different chunks: before 9/11 and after 9/11.

Though we felt her faceless, nameless pain from a distance that morning, our lives were not irreparably altered forever. Abigail was at the personal epicenter of that traumatizing event. Our secondhand observations could never enable us to grasp the extent of what she endured that day or in all the days that followed it. Trauma remains a very personal experience.

Though psychological traumas don't generally involve blood, their wounds can damage and cripple us just like those that wound our flesh. Actually, in many ways, their damage can be more severe and less likely to heal, because psychological trauma wounds remain invisible. They are often overlooked, mislabeled or misunderstood.

Psychological trauma frequently accompanies natural disasters and catastrophic events, but it also accompanies personal and relational traumatic events, such as sexual abuse, rape, domestic violence, ongoing emotional and verbal abuse, long-term extreme poverty and sexual betrayal. Such events cause intense psychological pain and overwhelm our ability to cope or to readily integrate the violations and emotions produced by these experiences.

When traumatic events invade our lives we feel shocked, rocked to our cores and no longer safe in our world. Like a boulder dumped into a still pond, trauma generates ripple-like symptoms that move outward from the point of entry, ultimately impacting multiple areas, just as it did in Katherine's and Abigail's lives.

Trauma's Symptoms and its Long-Lasting Effects

The symptoms experienced following emotionally traumatic events may vary from person to person depending on several factors, including personal history, the type of traumatic event experienced, the amount and kind of support available to help one grieve and heal and whether the "victim" remains in an unsafe environment or relationship. But regardless of these factors, a long list of typical symptoms flood into our lives, some immediately and others delayed in their arrivals. These symptoms can include the following, among others.

Hyperarousal	Helplessness	Sleeplessness	Immobility
Reliving the event	Hypervigilance	Anxiety	Nightmares

Intrusive Images	Withdrawing	Avoidance	Mood Swings
Panic Attacks	Phobias	Flashbacks	Denial
Oversensitivity	Depression	Restlessness	Confusion
Dissociation	Inability to Eat	Overeating	Rage
Health Problems	Chronic Fatigue	Immune/ Endocrine System Problems	

On A Personal Note: Which of these symptoms have you experienced as you've struggled to deal with your partner's sex addiction?

Examining this list, it becomes clear that traumatic events in our lives need to be taken seriously. When traumatized, we need support and helpful resources in order to heal and avoid long-term chronic trauma symptoms. Without help and support, trauma can weave its way throughout an entire life and create patterns that can have crippling effects. In many ways, trauma's threads wove their way through every strand of Lenore's life. Note them as she shares:

I first experienced sexual abuse at the hands of two teenage boys when I was four or five years old. And at four I also recognized how unclean we were—our clothes, our house, our bodies. That same year, my parents put me on a bus—alone. I was sent to stay for a while at a relative's house several hours away. I remember at five wishing I had clean, pretty dresses like my younger cousins wore.

At seven, I realized our family wasn't like "normal" families. At eight, my embarrassment grew. My shabby, dirty clothes, my shoes with holes in them, the two-room shack without running water or a bathroom where we lived all became a source of great embarrassment.

At age eight, the live-in nanny told me about her sexual escapades with my father and the other men in her life. By the time I was nine, I began to shoplift, usually grooming supplies: shampoo, toothbrush, toothpaste, fingernail file, bobby pins. I "ran away" on my bike at ten, but as darkness fell and fear came with it, I decided to ride back home.

As I grew older, I realized that I was never played with, held, hugged or kissed like other children. I began to realize how strange it was to have a nanny sleeping with my father, while my mother turned her head and looked the other way.

My teens were filled with many geographical moves and school changes. In one place where we lived, rats ran across my bed at night; in another, my sister and I slept under the carport, covered by a plastic sheet to protect us from the leaking roof in our rainy, northwest environment.

There were sexual violations, including waking up in terror one night in the tent while on a family camping trip as a relative was sexually assaulting me.

At eighteen, I married my boyfriend, totally oblivious to the fact that my childhood history affected my choices. I did not know it then, but that day I made a choice that set me up for many more years of heartache and trauma.

As Lenore's story illuminates, trauma can have a lasting impact on our lives, often changing its shape for years to come.

Post-Traumatic Stress and Post-Traumatic Stress Disorder
Nearly all of us who live through a traumatic event experience post-traumatic stress—trauma stress that hangs around for a time even after the traumatic event has passed. Yet for some, post-traumatic stress symptoms take on a chronic nature and develop into a serious, long-term condition known as post-traumatic stress disorder (PTSD).

PTSD can last a lifetime. Long-term PTSD sufferers develop painful coping mechanisms that burden their lifestyles and become ingrained in their personalities, or they may develop physical symptoms. Often they develop both. Post-traumatic stress that becomes chronic can take a terrible toll on our bodies. We take an in-depth look at the frequent health responses to trauma in chapter 5.

PTSD has strict diagnostic criteria that must be evident in a person's life before he or she receives a PTSD diagnosis from a mental health professional or medical doctor. These criteria include:
• Exposure to a traumatic event: "...the person experienced, witnessed, or was confronted with an event or events that involved actual or threatened death or serious injury, or a threat to the physical integrity of self or others." Their

response to the event must have involved "intense fear, helplessness or horror."

- Persistent re-experiencing (of the event).
- Persistent avoidance of stimuli associated with the trauma.
- Persistent symptoms of increased arousal (such as difficulty falling or staying asleep or hypervigilance).
- The symptoms last more than one month.
- Significant impairment in social, occupational or other important areas of functioning. [2]

Though rigid and technical in nature, the above list of symptom criteria weighs down the people experiencing them. In a very real way, PTSD can restrict and restrain its victims no less than heavy anchors and binding chains. Extreme PTSD can restrict one's personality and make life nearly impossible to live. Such was the case for Deborah, another woman whose life has been shaped by the effects of ongoing, unhealed trauma.

I am the oldest of three children and my earliest memories include my parents treating me with love and delight until I was four and my brother was born. It seemed that once they had someone else to love they almost forgot about me. And that pattern held true when my sister was born when I was seven years old.

Because I was the oldest, I was expected to take care of my younger siblings, especially my sister. When she was a baby, I had to push her around the block in her buggy almost every day. And if I wanted to go play at a friend's house, my parents made me take my baby sister so I could watch her while I played. That embarrassed me so much that I chose to stay home rather than have to drag my little sister along with me. The rides my dad gave me on his scooter stopped, too, just as soon as my brother was old enough to go in my place.

I grew up believing my parents only wanted me if they needed me or if they could use me to clean the house, do the dishes or watch my brother and sister. I was shy and quiet, stayed in my room alone a lot and learned to try hard to please my parents—something that trained me to be a people-pleaser even at my own expense.

And I felt lonely. Even at school I was alone and felt lonely, always having to sit all by myself at lunchtime. By then, I had grown so timid and quiet I simply didn't know what to say to people. Even when someone did try to befriend me, they didn't hang around for long, because I didn't talk. I simply didn't know what to say. One of my teachers told me I was the quietest person he had ever met.

I was fearful growing up and every year through the eleventh grade I threw up on the first day of school, as I dreaded being alone again every day for nine months. I began to dream of meeting my prince charming—a man who would love me for who I was.

I was drawn to seemingly fun-loving men and both my husbands appeared to be carefree and full of life before I married them. However, not long into both marriages I learned they were cruel, abusive men and womanizers.

A year after my first divorce, I was so afraid that I developed agoraphobia. I had two small children to raise with no money, no car and no job. I was a single mom for eight years and was actually surviving, even with agoraphobia, when I met my second husband. He made good money and I thought he loved me and that life would finally be better. It didn't take long to realize I had gone from the frying pan into the fire, but by then I felt so fear-bound and helpless I remained in that marriage for thirty-five years. Now, finally, at sixty-five, I'm breaking free and determined to become who God really created me to be.

Deborah's painful story portrays what can happen when we can't find a way to heal from events we experience as traumatic: Our trauma symptoms can become chronic. They can shape and color our choices and decisions and alter the course of our lives. When that happens, the list of symptoms grows longer and proves increasingly challenging to heal, like Deborah's impairments. No doubt you'll recognize many of her symptoms in the following list.

PTSD Symptoms

- Increased feelings of anxiety that result in behaviors like scanning the environment looking for any signs of potential danger or threat, paranoia, overwhelming terror, insomnia, inability to concentrate, agoraphobia or startling easily.

- Avoiding reminders or conversations of the event or not being able to remember some or all aspects of the event (blocking/denial).
- Re-experiencing the event through invading thoughts or memories that can't be held back, be it through flashbacks and/or nightmares.
- The person's distress grows so intense it impacts them in multiple areas of his or her life, such as the ability to work, take care of day-to-day responsibilities or participate in relationships.

On A Personal Note: Can you identify with any of the behaviors listed as PTSD symptoms?

Relational Traumas

Relational traumas, often called attachment injuries, occur when one person betrays, abandons or refuses to provide support for another with whom he or she has developed an attachment bond. One researcher found these traumas—or attachment injuries—to "…overwhelm coping capacities and define the …relationship, as a source of danger rather than a safe haven in times of stress." [3]

Research indicates that following a relational trauma we begin to focus our efforts to interact with others in one of two ways: We may attempt to get our partner to reconnect with us, or we may do the opposite and build emotional walls to defend ourselves from his or her lack of care. In doing either of these actions, it's likely we'll begin to display many of the PTSD symptoms listed above.

Betrayal in a committed relationship includes violating relationship norms. When your partner violates the standards you consider to be the norm in your relationship, you may experience it as a relational trauma. [4]

Strangely, few professionals have extrapolated relational traumas to include what we experience when we learn our partners act out sexually. Certainly, most partners of sex addicts report that *they* experience their spouses' behaviors perpetrated by sexual addiction as significant and damaging betrayals that threaten their relationships, as relational traumas are defined, yet very few therapeutic professionals examined this reality closely.

Two researchers did, however, study four Internet message boards where partners of sex addicts posted their feelings and stories. As the researchers studied 100 spouses' entries, they discovered several common themes. Three themes were included: experiencing the discovery of sexual addiction as a traumatic event, viewing the sexually addictive behaviors as betrayal or infidelity and feeling the need to reappraise their relationships as a result.[5]

The spouses sharing their feelings and stories on those four message boards perceived their partners' sexual addictions as *betrayal* or *infidelity*. We hear this response from many people we encounter in our work, too.

In Barbara's research for her clinical study of partners, she scoured everything written that reported on partners' experiences of betrayal and trauma. However, the only literature available within the therapeutic community discussing a partner's experience as traumatic was that which reported on *infidelity* in committed relationships. She found nothing that called sexual addiction within a committed relationship—within an attachment bond—relational trauma.

Infidelity and Relational Trauma
Within the community of professionals who focus their work on infidelity in committed relationships (rather than on *sex addiction*), trauma recognition abounds.

One researcher wrote that traumatic stress symptoms "...are the usual results of the discovery of the infidelity." Another reported that the news of a partner's infidelity "sends a jolt of adrenaline into the body that sets off a stress reaction." And others have written that in cases of infidelity they see emotional responses replicating those of other traumatic events, including shock, repression, denial, intense mood fluctuations, depression, anxiety and lowered self-esteem. They also report that healing from the pain of infidelity shares many similarities with healing from other kinds of traumatic events. [6]

And so we ask:

If counselors recognize that infidelity in a committed relationship creates trauma, why don't they recognize that sex addiction incites similar effects, especially for those who experience the sexual betrayal—whatever form it takes—as a breach of the marital promise? And what about the fact that sexual addiction generally involves multiple acts of breaking the marital promise? Why don't more professionals recognize how traumatic this is for committed partners?

We believe our questions should echo with validity and importance for those who hope to help individuals and relationships heal from the pain that sexual addiction produces in a committed relationship. Due to the absence of available help, many women and some men tell us that they feel misunderstood, invalidated, lost and alone in their efforts to heal their pain and the impact the addiction has on their marriages. Rebecca's story echoes the stories of so many with whom we've spoken. She emailed us:

> I am looking for help dealing with my husband's porn addiction. I've tried to find help in my city but I can't find anything. My husband is getting lots of help and support, and he's excited because for the first time he has tools to use to fight his addiction, but I don't have anything.
>
> We have a marriage counselor who is helping us as a couple, but he can't provide what I need for healing myself. I made the mistake of sharing my husband's addiction with my support system at church and they asked me not to come back until we got our life straightened out! Now I'm afraid to tell anybody else, but I desperately need to talk to other women who share my pain and I need some way to heal. Please let me know if you offer anything that might help me.

As in Rebecca's case, many partners' efforts to find help and hope leave them feeling lost and more alone in their pain.

On A Personal Note: Have you had difficulty finding the help that you need?

What We See in Our Work with Partners

We find that nearly all partners of sex addicts we encounter bear the symptoms, express the feelings and report the experiences described earlier as a result of the shock and pain disclosure of a sex addiction can bring to their lives. Yet few in the helping professions view a partner's pain and symptoms as coming from the *trauma* the partner has experienced.

Many recognize it as a traumatic event initially, but most soon try to turn the person toward forgiving, moving on and dealing with his or her own "stuff."

Other counselors encourage the hurt people to join their partners' addictive behaviors, which many say only adds to their confusion. They *know* what they feel in response to their spouses' sexual choices: It hurts. However, a professional is now advising them to participate, causing them to question their own instincts, needs and judgment.

Both of these responses leave women and men experiencing a partner's sexual addiction emotionally lost and without the validation they desperately need for their extreme trauma pain. This leaves the partners of sex addicts without the help and resources they need so they can heal and move on. Danelle shared feeling such difficult emotions during marriage counseling after discovering her husband's sexual addiction. Danelle told us:

I feel mostly misunderstood by our marriage counselor. The counselor said, "Danelle, the roots of your pain are coming from your childhood sexual abuse, not from what your husband did."

There *was* sexual abuse in my childhood, but that is not what hurts right now; right now, it's his addiction! The counselor doesn't address my husband's affairs as sexual addiction, even though they happened repeatedly. At our last session he asked me, "What would it be like to forgive your husband, Danelle? Why can't you move on?"

I finally said to him, "I feel like you're brushing aside the pain I've been through. It's only been a few months."

After that he apologized to me and said he hadn't meant to do that. But I still have no way to deal with my feelings. It's altered the way I see myself; it's affected my personality—I'm not free and fun like I used to be. I'm not even the same person anymore.

After we sent Danelle a handout about trauma in partners of sex addicts, she wrote back: "It's really nice to know that all of the things that I'm going through are normal and I'm not losing my mind. Thank you."

We've found that once the hurt partner feels heard, understood, validated, supported and equipped to deal with the current pain, in time we can help the person move through a process that will enable him or her to look at other areas where new growth and new skills would better equip the person for life with (or, if s/he so chooses, without) the sexually addicted partner.

While many who work with hurting partners do help them process their grief and loss, at least for a time, most simultaneously treat their symptoms and feelings from the commonly held perspective that the partner is a co-addict and therefore codependent to both the partner and that person's addictive behavior.

From that perspective, most mental health professionals prescribe changes in thought patterns, emotions, relational interactions and quite often 12-step program participation, none of which is bad. Indeed, those things can prove beneficial in everyone's life and they were enormously beneficial in Marsha's life. However, they weren't enough to help her heal and avoid long term stress or worse, post-traumatic stress disorder.

Sadly, when a partner "fails to follow" professional advice or symptoms drag on, ricocheting emotions and behaviors only reinforce the belief that he or she portrays the unhealthy co-addict condition.

However, we believe that while one is suffering from trauma symptoms, the hurt person will likely find it *impossible* to control thoughts, feelings and relational interactions as prescribed in codependency and 12-step literature *unless that person receives help to heal from the trauma first, or at least simultaneously.* We interpret the hurt partner's inability not as further evidence of codependency, but instead as likely being natural human reaction to relational trauma.

Complicating life further, the trauma *may still be taking place in the person's life, because the other partner's addictive behavior continues. Or the addicted partner may continue to disclose new information about past (or current) addictive events as the person recalls them or gains the courage to share with the partner.* Elena talks often about the pain that reality has caused her.

It's been four years since my husband told me about his addiction. At first it was so hard, but I found a wonderful counselor for the two of us to work with and in time I began to heal.

But just as I would be starting to make progress, my husband would disclose he'd acted out sexually again, and my pain would start all over again—right back at the beginning. That cycle has happened several times and it's going on again right now. I feel like a basket case.

I love my husband so much and I know he really loves me, but I don't know how much longer I can do this. It's gotten to where if he grows quiet or doesn't share his thoughts and feelings for a while, my imagination goes crazy. I end up right back on the merry-go-round of internal pain without knowing for sure if I have a reason to be there! I hate it!

As we listen to women and men share their experiences and feelings, we hear them use words and phrases that paint vivid pictures of reverberating emotions that endure throughout their lives. These pictures and emotions replicate those of people who've survived traumatic events.

Partners' intense feelings of terror, anxiety, helplessness and hopelessness in coping with their painful situations mirror those of people who have survived violence, assault and other kinds of psychological traumas. Nothing prepares a person for this surprise in life: not a stable childhood, not a good education, not adequate training—not even a breadth of life experience can prepare the hurt partner for the intense pain encountered when this addiction surfaces in a marriage.

Maria, an ER surgeon, describes the sense of utter hopelessness she felt at times as she and her husband plodded through their healing experience.

I'm a very emotional person and I need to talk about what I'm feeling. If there's a problem or a wall between us, I need my husband to engage with me, to talk it through until we work it out.

But for several months he didn't seem to be able to meet that need for me. I might spend fifteen minutes describing my feelings and end by asking him to share his, but he'd sit there like a stuffed animal staring back at me! He said he didn't like talking about this all the time.

There were times I saw myself going to the kitchen, pulling a butcher knife out of the cutlery drawer and using it to gut myself. That's how bad the pain felt. I just wanted it to stop, and my husband didn't seem to be able to help with that need back then.

I was still experiencing severe PTSD symptoms six months after I learned about the problem. There were moments of total hopelessness, even after six months of knowing. Nothing in my fifty years of life prepared me for those tumultuous times in our lives.

Partners describe intense emotional and even physical responses to the discovery that the people they love act out sexually, whatever form it takes. Many partners of sexual addicts demonstrate such intense and enduring responses that they meet the diagnostic criteria for PTSD, just as Maria described.

Some women and men have told each of us that discovering their partners' sexual addictions proved more devastating to them than hearing their doctors say, "I'm sorry, but you have cancer."

Kelly, a trained psychotherapist, shares the traumatic impact her husband's addiction had on her compared to the impact of battling incurable ovarian cancer.

At the time I unexpectedly discovered my husband was acting out sexually, I had been diagnosed with Stage 3 ovarian cancer for three years. I'd been through four major surgeries, one cancer recurrence and two cycles of intense chemotherapy. I had spent three years giving my attention to healing my body so that I could live long enough to be at my sons' high school graduations. It was painful and difficult work.

My immediate reaction to the discovery of his infidelities was the loss of physical control of my body—I fell to the floor, numb and breathless. I could not believe that my life had come to this place after fighting so hard to survive my cancer a few more years. After two days spent trembling in bed, unable to eat or sleep, I realized I needed to contact my oncologist. He wanted to see me immediately. There was a deep concern that the stress would trigger another recurrence, not to mention the possibility that my husband might have given my already compromised immune system a sexually transmitted disease.

I couldn't bring myself to schedule an appointment. My entire being was in complete shock. I spent the next days/weeks trembling on the floor in my darkened closet, moaning. I wasn't able to swallow or eat. From a distance, I watched myself live the life of a wounded animal.

There was no part of my cancer journey, even hearing I'd likely not live five years, to compare to the pain of my husband's betrayal. Gradually, cancer seemed to be the way out of the pain. I couldn't see how I'd have any energy to give to healing a marriage so damaged while healing from cancer. I looked forward to the release of death.

Partners' Descriptions of Their Betrayal Experiences

If a listener has the ability to empathize with another's pain, hearing partners of sex addicts describe their pain upon discovering their spouses' sex addiction actually *hurts*. We could fill thousands of pages with partners' words alone, but we share only a few here. Read them out loud and as you do, listen to what *you* hear.

- It left me shell-shocked.
- I threw up, couldn't sleep, couldn't eat and cried constantly. I felt horror, anger, rage, terror, fury at God.
- I loved my husband and I wanted his comfort, yet he was the source of my searing pain.
- I frequently had disturbing dreams and nightmares.
- I couldn't read; nothing made sense. I totally lost my ability to concentrate. I got lost a lot.
- My initial reaction was to shake uncontrollably. I've had this reaction before to someone's death. It *was* a death.
- It's hanging upside down, trying to right myself. It's being stabbed in the back and trying to find solid ground under the slippery pool of my own blood...most of the time it's lying in a shallow grave as a part of me dies.
- It was like someone ransacking my house and I was left with all the pieces.

- I'm cycling through emotions like crazy. This is worse than when my mother was killed in a car accident.
- I never felt so betrayed in my life.
- It was devastating; traumatic.

When women and men talk about what they felt and experienced during their partners' disclosures (or the discoveries they made of spouses' secret lives), they often say they felt assaulted by the information they heard or saw. In their own words, hurt partners describe life-changing, world-shattering events in their lives.

Events of such magnitude are normally considered traumatic.

On A Personal Note: What do you think about when you read the list of partners' betrayal experiences? With which feelings or experiences do you most identify?

Chapter 2

A Study in Contrasts:
Is it Co-Addiction or is it Trauma?

Thank you, God, for this meeting and for this amazing group of women who breathe new life into me every Monday night, I thought as I entered the church basement where we held our weekly support group meetings. I felt thankful I had survived another difficult week and made it back for this special time with sisters on the same journey.

Some evil monster continued to slowly devour my personal world, one bite at a time. Monday nights had become my emotional and spiritual blood transfusions. This was the "hospital" I returned to every seven days as I watched and felt my marriage, my ministry—my life—slowly bleed to death. I seemed helpless to save them, in spite of the fact that thousands of others were asking us to help save theirs.

"My name is Marsha and I'm a co-addict to a sex addict," I began, after steeping in what I heard others share long enough to have gained the emotional strength to take a turn. Those words always left a bad taste in my mouth when I said them, but this was a 12-step meeting for partners of sex addicts and these were the rules. And I *was*, after all, the partner of a sex addict.

From around the large circle, thirty women's heads turned my way, most of their eyes filled with their own pain and sadness. Though my position with the organization kept me from being completely vulnerable in what I shared, I drew sustenance from the love, the "sisterhood" and the courage and strength modeled by these beautiful women who fought and worked so hard to save their marriages, often in vain.

However, it was the readings we repeated every week that provided the greatest nourishment to my aching, weary heart. They had grown familiar and offered a prayer-like mantra: an anchor in the tumultuous sea of chaos and confusion that my life had become. Plus, according to 12-step literature, they also offered a yardstick of sorts—a measurement of "health" if one is married to a sex addict. Hearing them every week helped to "reset" my pain-clouded thinking.

Tonight, our meeting was using step 1 as the foundation for our sharing. "I am powerless over sexaholism and the sex addict, and my life has become unmanageable," I began. By repeating step 1 out loud, it helped me remain focused on my "stuff," not his, though the excruciating pain I felt had marred my perspective and self-awareness. But even in the fog of my pain, it was the 12-step process that enabled and empowered me to maintain the slippery level of detachment I intermittently grasped.

Even then, during the design phase of our ministry, I was keenly aware that the 12-step process didn't provide everything these hurting women needed. It didn't provide everything *I* needed during my draining, slow bleed. *But what would? What could?* I wondered.

I had searched repeatedly and still hadn't found anything better for partners of sex addicts during the months—and often years—of maintenance that follow the stages after early grieving and healing. So I felt deeply grateful for the strength I gained from our weekly 12-step process.

Yet in spite of all its value and benefits, it was the 12-step model that birthed the widely held view that partners of sex addicts suffer from their own disease—the disease of co-addiction.

THE CO-ADDICTION PERSPECTIVE

Let's begin our examination of the co-addiction perspective by first examining the addiction model itself.

Addiction Model

The world in general—particularly families and partners of alcoholics and addicts of every variety—owe much to the 12-step movement. For untold millions, it has provided the only consistent road map to freedom from addictive, destructive self-indulgences and behaviors for those who've worked its program into their lives.

Lois Wilson, the wife of Bill Wilson—one of the two founders of AA—first recognized addiction's impact on spouses. Each week, as men struggling with alcoholism gathered in her home, Lois remained out of the way in another room so she wouldn't disturb their meeting. Then one day she noticed that other wives were doing the same thing *outside* her home as they waited for their husbands in their cars.

Lois seized the opportunity to talk to them and soon recognized that other wives felt the same ricocheting emotions she felt. It wasn't long until she had transformed their weekly waiting into a support group that gathered in her kitchen, the birthplace of Al-Anon, the now global organization for family and friends of alcoholics. Lois had accidentally struck upon two truths: Alcoholism and addictions of all kinds *do* impact family and even friends, and family and friends need support for how it impacts them.[1]

And from that sprang the 12-step community's belief that addiction is a "family disease." Certainly, we agree that addiction of any kind *affects* the addict's partner and other family members.

The Birth of the Co-Addict Label

When early mental health and addiction specialists began to recognize the problem of compulsive and destructive sexual behavior in people's lives, they naturally turned to the model that had provided the only broadly helpful road map for society's other destructive habits: the addiction model. From that model, they coined the term "sex addict."

However, the 12-step sex addiction model takes it one step further: not only are partners of sex addicts *affected*, those partners are also *addicted*. They are addicted to the *sex addict*. In his early writings, author Patrick Carnes stated that our personal histories and personality characteristics are "mirror images" of the addicts themselves. [2]

Hence, we bear the label "co-addicts" in this model, even though this perspective is *only* applied to partners of sex addicts. Partners of alcoholics, drug addicts and gamblers are labeled only as codependents. They are *not* labeled co-addicts.

The current operative sex addiction model uses a sort of a one-size-fits-all approach to dealing with a partner's strong emotional reactions to learning that the spouse he or she loves seeks sexual gratification outside of the marriage. If he or she has no traumatic and dysfunctional past, that's beside the point. The person loves a sex addict, so he or she is a co-addict. [3]

In *Back from Betrayal,* Jennifer Schneider, MD, a psychiatrist who is also the former partner of a sex addict, wrote:

> Although it is tempting for the co-addict to feel like a victim and to cast all the blame on her straying spouse, the fact is that her choice of partner is no accident. The co-addict's core beliefs do not begin when she marries an addict, and the men she selects tend to follow a pattern....The seeds of the future co-addict can be found in her family of origin. [4]

Never mind that the partner feels betrayed and that in his or her mind the other partner has broken his or her wedding vows; the partner is encouraged to stop focusing on and trying to control the sexually addicted spouse and to work his or her own 12-step recovery program to control codependency—his or her co-addiction. As the partner does, so he or she is told, the sexually addicted spouse's behavior will no longer affect his or her peace.

While many writers and professionals in the sex addiction treatment community recognize that this kind of a person is catapulted into crisis and they respond as they would following any crisis in a client's life, they simultaneously work to encourage their clients to enter their own 12-step recovery programs for their own disease—their co-addiction to their partners and their partners' sex addictions.

The partner is told there is no cure for his or her disease or for the sex addict's, and the best he or she can hope for is remission.

Remission, as with cancer, is achieved when there are no longer any relapses. Therefore, to achieve and maintain remission, he or she must attend meetings and work within the confines of the 12-step program, possibly for the rest of his or her life.

Additionally, the partner learns that the spouse's sex addiction is not about him or her. However, the partner also learns that his or her disease contributes to the continuation or deepening of the sexually addicted partner's disease and that attempts to "fix" the other partner are symptoms of co-addiction disease. The partner can demonstrate growth by detaching from the addict to reduce the obsession with the afflicted's life and behavior.

Generally, the partner hears that trauma experienced early on in life contributes to his or her distress; because the addict's sexual betrayal triggers old emotional wounds, which, of course, it does, if there is an earlier trauma history. Fresh trauma of any kind nearly always hooks old trauma, even when we've done great recovery work. Just as a formerly broken bone will remain susceptible to future breaks and arthritis, so, too, will an old trauma wound leave emotional vulnerability.

On A Personal Note: Do you have earlier life trauma that your partner's addiction has hooked? If so, how has it complicated your healing?

Two Heat-Seeking Missiles Theory
Partners receive the label of "co-addict" automatically, simply because they love sex addicts. It does not matter that many partners knew nothing of the other person's addiction prior to making a commitment. Nor does it matter that the partner may not have seen recognizable signs of the addiction's existence. The theory holds that partners develop co-addicted traits and characteristics over time due to the fact that they are in relationships with addicts.

Like "two heat-seeking missiles, these two sick people found each other," a partner is told, evidence that he or she is just as sick as the sex addict, because he or she married the addict in the first place. A partner's co-addicted beliefs and behaviors, he or she learns, include:

- Neglecting his or her own needs

- Attempting to control the addict's behaviors
- Holding the same core beliefs as the sex addict, including the beliefs that his or her most important need is sex and that if people really knew him or her they wouldn't love him or her

Early sex addict researchers also recognized that partners of sex addicts experience intense emotional pain in response to the sexual betrayal they feel and that partners often react with emotionally-driven behaviors they find difficult to control or heal. In an attempt to understand and help these men and women, researchers questioned them about their feelings and reactions and studied and recorded what they heard and observed. And from those recorded observations grew a list of common emotions and behaviors broadly experienced in partners' lives.

Thus it was that early pioneers in the sex addiction field—Patrick Carnes and a researcher named Carmak—came to view the partners' responses as a *parallel addiction to the addict's addiction*. From that parallel addiction mindset they coined the term *co-addict/co-addiction*.

Since they viewed partners as co-addicted (addicted to the addict) they logically believed partners need treatment and recovery for their addictions, just as the sex addicts do.

It's a fact that we, the partners of sex addicts, need help and often treatment because of the tremendous pain that addiction creates in our lives. Without help, our trauma can become chronic and result in PTSD and can keep us and our marriages from healing. Many of us need help to overcome our enabling behaviors as well. As partners of sex addicts, we owe a huge debt to those who care enough about our pain to search for ways to help us. Yet as authors, we believe that this view leaves most partners feeling misunderstood, unheard and often invalidated by automatically labeling their painful emotions and erratic behaviors as their own illness.

We believe that the partner's emotional and behavioral responses to living with a sex addict are better framed and understood as attempts to find safety and security following the most devastating of all traumas: the betrayal of trust.

On A Personal Note. Does the word "safety" resonate with you? Do you find yourself looking for ways to feel safe again, only to find that it remains elusive?

We also believe partners of sexual addicts often get lost in their own attempts to survive and to protect themselves from further injury. Susan's story reflects how panic—a by-product of the trauma in her life—swamped her and then trapped her on an island of fear as she considered the possibility of future pain if she did not leave her husband. Stranded, she was unable to find hope or receive help.

Lauren had just finished sharing how, during the twelve years since she confronted her husband's sex addiction, he has experienced two brief relapses. She explained how she chose to deal with those relapses and talked about the written Boundary Contract she has with her husband and his accountability partner. Although Lauren and her husband now have a happy marriage, minister to other couples who need help with sex addiction and have successfully navigated the challenges sex addiction catapults into a couple's life, all Susan could hear was hopelessness.

"It sounds like you're just waiting around for him to screw up!" Susan commented loudly.

"Oh, not at all," Lauren replied calmly. "My husband demonstrates his love for me every day in dozens of little ways, including letting me know he's working his program."

"Can you guarantee me my husband won't screw up again?" Susan interjected, her emotion building to a crescendo. When she heard Lauren's "No" response, she came right back with a determined, "Then I can't spend the next ten years in this marriage only to have him screw up later! I think it's time for me to get a separation!"

Rather than believing Susan and other partners demonstrate characteristics of addiction, we believe partners of sexual addicts engage in attempts to seek what they can no longer find: safety in unsafe relationships with sex addicts to whom they feel their deepest attachment bonds.

Our personal and professional experience, along with Barbara's research study, has led us to our alternate view of partners of sex addicts. We believe that, yes, partners are very much affected by their spouses' addictions. And yes, like all human beings, many of us have work of our own to do. However, not all partners are co-addicts/codependent or have co-addiction. Rather, we have found many partners experience natural responses to trauma in their lives.

Yet in spite of what we perceive to be its shortcomings, the 12-step model has provided help, support and recovery for millions of sex addicts and many of their partners. The 12 steps are rooted in solid, life-changing principles that, when applied, truly can—and often do—change a person's life for the better. The 12 steps have added greatly to Marsha's healing and life. Even now, in the aftermath of enormous personal loss, she knows that, in part, it's the work she did to integrate the spirit of the 12 steps into her thinking and their foundation in strong spiritual principles that enable her to live life with peace and joy each day, no matter what future days may hold.

On A Personal Note: Have you been part of a 12-step group for partners of sex addicts? If so, how did it help you? Are there areas that were not helpful? What are your thoughts about the 12-step model as a tool for healing your betrayal wounds?

Under-Treated Trauma

We believe the automatic co-addict or codependent labeling, along with the "two heat-seeking missiles theory" and the view that "she's just as sick as the sex addict," minimizes a partner's trauma. While the addiction model might focus on *past* trauma in a partner's life, it overlooks and misses the fact that disclosure/discovery is a traumatic event in itself and that many partners report they experience ongoing trauma at a myriad of other times as they share their lives with sex addicts.

In our experience, many men and women do not find the addiction model helpful, particularly early in their healing. Instead, they find it deeply hurtful. And many partners express feeling offended by the automatic co-addict labeling they receive, even when the labelers know nothing about their personal trauma histories. That was Ashley's experience:

> I went to a COSA meeting, a 12-step recovery program for partners of sex addicts, to seek support and encouragement from other women going through circumstances similar to mine. The first thing we had to do was state our name and say to the whole group that we were co-addicts. I felt like I had been labeled as a "sick" person who needed recovery and they didn't even know anything about me!
>
> According to the group, I needed to figure out why I chose to pursue a relationship with a sex addict. But I'm just a wife whose world got flipped upside down when my husband disclosed his porn addiction and his attraction to other men. I felt scared, frustrated, confused and hurt by that meeting. I knew it wasn't where I belonged.

We hear from many partners who, like Ashley, never find the help they need within the 12-step process to move beyond their raw trauma pain. Such was the case for Sue, a woman in the large 12-step group Marsha helped start in Seattle, Washington, (1999) for partners of sex addicts. Marsha tells of Sue's search for help:

> Sue's story was filled with pain. An older couple who appeared to have it all, she and her husband sought help from the best treatment the world had to offer for his flagrant, out-of-control sex addiction. But nothing seemed to help. Then they stumbled onto our work in Seattle, hopeful that they had finally found the tools that would free them from the torture this addiction had created in their lives.
>
> I wish I could say they did. Hundreds of times I've seen Sue's pain-filled face in my mind's eye, even now, nearly a decade later. I gave her the best I had to offer at that time, which, besides twelve weeks of early healing meetings in a small support group using my workbook, was the 12-step group meeting we held each Monday night for spouses.
>
> She couldn't seem to focus on "working her own program," but instead recounted his latest sexual encounters every week. It saddens and embarrasses me to admit that I soon began mentally labeling her "hopelessly codependent." Sitting across the circle, I listened as she

shared and watched as hurt and anger contorted her countenance.

Won't she ever get it? I wondered. My mental solution for what she needed to do was to "draw a line in the sand" with her husband—most likely via a marital separation—then quit enabling him and focus on recovering from her own co-addiction. I failed to recognize that those of us who live with the fresh trauma Sue lived with each week as her husband participated in new and degrading sexual encounters live in constant states of panic, especially late in life when aging makes loss of security an even greater fear. No human being is exempt from responses to trauma when he or she lives with that kind of pain and abuse, year after year. Nor is he or she exempt from the learned helplessness that often develops because of dissociation and freezing responses to such trauma.

Sadly, Sue was one who never found the help she needed to move beyond her raw trauma pain, because nowhere in the 12-step program in which she participated was her trauma dealt with in a way that would enable change to take place in her life.

THE TRAUMA PERSPECTIVE

We view the partner as a person in a relationship with a sex addict; someone with human reactions and behaviors in *response* to discovering his or her most intimate relationship is not what it originally seemed. In one moment of life, security is replaced with betrayal and the death of life-long dreams. Such a discovery causes adrenal glands to dump cortisol into the body's system, triggering the "fight/flight/ freeze" response to danger, in this case the inherent danger of loving a compulsive liar. At that point, the partner knows that the person with whom he or she lives, sleeps and invests time and feelings in participates in hidden sexual behaviors that jeopardize his or her finances, safety, health and even her life, not to mention their children.

Prior to this discovery, the person believed his or her partner loved only him or her and remained faithful. Suddenly, their relationship holds danger and dark secrets. Discovering that much of your life is built on lies proves traumatizing and destroys one's sense of safety and security. Vicky struggled hard with that reality as she searched her soul for the strength to forgive her husband so she could return to peace and joy in her life. As she shared her story, her voice broke and tears began to flow:

> I'm having trouble with the whole forgiveness thing. I can't seem to stop reacting to what he did, even though he's doing everything right now to get help and truly change. My thoughts get out of control and I can't seem to stop them. And when they do, I yell terrible things at him and I throw things. I know my anger crosses a line and becomes abusive. My greatest losses in all of this are my innocence and my long-held belief in the sanctity of marriage. I'm cycling through emotions like crazy. This is worse than when my mother was killed in a car accident.

That loss of safety and security often presents a host of safety-seeking behaviors. These might include checking the partner's pockets, wallet, cell phone and computer history, trying to verify the person's whereabouts when not home and even utilizing GPS tracking devices to monitor the addict's location throughout the day. The addiction community views such behaviors as evidence that the partner is indeed addicted to the other spouse's addiction.

Rather than label traumatized partners as co-addicts for their safety-seeking responses, we see them searching for ways to keep the traumatic event from occurring again. If one lives through a terrible earthquake, he or she will feel terrified when the ground shakes again, even if it is only a minor tremor.

Just as living through a bad earthquake produces trauma, so, too, does living through the discovery that one's partner is a sex addict. Sex addiction produces a *life*-quake, leaving traumatic effects on a relationship and on lives. When new tremors—or even *perceived* tremors—occur, an already traumatized partner almost always has a stress response, just like an earthquake survivor does. Ironically, Rusti had both kinds of quakes happening in her life simultaneously and she felt the similarities between her inner and outer worlds:

> I live near the epicenter of an ongoing series of earthquakes that have been rattling our home and town for three long months. Today we were once again jolted in the

middle of the night by earthquakes big enough to wake everybody up, make the coyotes howl outside our window and our dog curl up right by my husband. Quite a slumber party between 1:00 and 4:00 in the morning! Though most of the quakes are small, they have left our family and other residents nervous, fearful, anxious and traumatized. We feel constantly on edge, not knowing when the next one will occur or what damage it will produce to our already damaged home.

Concurrently, I am living through a "personal quake" because of my husband's sex addiction. There never seems to be an end to the earthquakes and aftershocks in this process, either! I start to heal from a disclosure of betrayal or relapse, only to have him disclose another one a short while later. Every time there is a new quake my pain and trauma returns and with it comes depression, anxiety, fear and a mix of other emotions.

It seems I can never stay on level, solid ground long enough to heal. I often wonder if this pattern will ever end. The continual "unknown" dramatically slows the healing I need and my ability to move on.

Looking at Rusti or the other partners' stories we share here, someone could mistake the symptoms and responses for those of a co-addict or codependent. If one has been trained to evaluate a partner's responses by looking at the person through a co-addiction lens, it's going to prove challenging to view the partner any other way. However, we propose a shift in the way mental health professionals, clergy, loved ones and most of all *you* look at partners of sex addicts so that true healing becomes possible in their lives. Let's take our comparison between the co-addiction perspective and the trauma perspective one step further before moving on to our proposed shift in focus.

Next, we present a chart that compares the similarities in behavior between the responses of the partner viewed as a co-addict by the addiction community and people's natural responses to trauma. Note how many ways the responses mirror each other.

Co-Addiction and PTSD Comparison Chart
The list that follows compares and contrasts Patrick Carnes' co-addiction characteristics with the symptoms experienced by people with post-traumatic stress disorder. [5]

Look at the following "co-addiction" traits listed. After each of the traits, we give its definition and beneath the definition we've placed post-traumatic stress symptoms that mirror the co-addiction trait above it. After each pairing of a co-addiction trait and a trauma symptom, we list an example of an illustrative behavior.

Co-Addiction Trait: **Collusion** – Helping perpetuate the person's addiction (colluding with him or her in it) by using behaviors such as helping to keep it a secret from others or by participating in addictive behaviors

Trauma Symptom: **Avoidance** – Avoiding activities or other reminders of the trauma event

Example: To avoid being told that YOU have sexual problems because you're too "straight-laced," you may choose to look at pornography with your partner to avoid conflict, hoping that if you do he or she will turn to you sexually instead of the porn. Or, avoidance can cause you to avoid sex with your partner because it triggers painful memories and feelings you're not yet healed enough to handle. Such avoidance is about trying to feel "safe" in the relationship.

Co-Addiction Trait: **Obsessive Preoccupation** – Persistent thoughts of the addict and that partner's behaviors

Trauma Symptom: **Re-experiencing** – Recurrent and intrusive recollections, thoughts and memories that you can't control or stop

Example: You go through your day and you can't stop wondering what he or she is doing. Is the person acting out online? Cheating outright? These thoughts consume your energy, and you may find difficulty paying attention to other things. Your lack of safety and vulnerability to more pain create constant anxiety.

Co-Addiction Trait: **Denial** – Avoiding evidence of the partner's addiction; *or* the belief that you can control the addict's behaviors

Trauma Symptom: **Avoidance & Arousal** – Ignoring your "gut" or new evidence that your partner is acting out again; *or* the opposite— attempting to control the environment; hypervigilant behaviors (we believe both behaviors are an effort to control further pain)

Example: Perhaps at times you felt sure something was wrong, or you found a phone number or Web site that was suspicious. Then, you remembered that your partner had told you repeatedly that he or she loves you and would never cheat on you. Even though you have some kind of evidence, you talk yourself out of thinking or believing the worst, so you can avoid the source of more pain.

Co-Addiction Trait: **Emotional Turmoil** – Feeling anxiety, shame or that life is out of control

Trauma Symptom: **Arousal** – Intense psychological distress

Example: This can demonstrate itself in your life in dozens of ways. Most partners experience depression and anxiety. Perhaps you are nervous and fearful—you may have panic attacks. Even though you didn't do anything wrong, you may feel shame. You may wonder: What's wrong with me that causes my partner to go outside the relationship? You may believe that you can't let anyone know, because it is too embarrassing and shameful.

Co-Addiction Trait: **Manipulation** – Efforts to control the addict's behaviors

Trauma Symptom: **Arousal** – Efforts to control the environment

Example: This one can also demonstrate itself in dozens of ways, from your choosing where he sits in restaurants to prevent him from looking at a certain woman you spotted as you came in, to staying up very late so you can keep him away from the computer. In another scenario, you may threaten that you'll leave if he acts out again, but never follow through when he does.

Co-Addiction Trait: **Excessive Over-Responsibility** – Self-blame; keeping the addict dependent upon you to avoid future pain

Trauma Symptom: **Avoidance** – Trying to avoid future pain by attempting to control the partner's addiction, engaging in recovery activities, numbing your feelings or choosing denial (We believe each of the symptoms is an attempt to avoid more pain.)

Example: You may attempt to avoid the pain by seeing your partner's addictive behaviors as your fault and setting out to do more to make the other person happy. You might schedule counseling appointments for your partner, set the addicted person up with a sponsor or accountability colleague and give him or her all the latest books on sex addiction to read. You may believe that if you do enough, the addicted partner will stop and you will be safe.

Co-Addiction Trait: **Compromise or Loss of Self** – Changing yourself to please the addict

Trauma Symptom: **Avoidance** – Feelings of detachment, numbness or denial, avoiding activities or other reminders of the event, resulting in loss of self. Many men and women tell us, "I'm not even the same person anymore."

Example: In order to avoid facing your partner's addiction, you may attempt to change him by changing yourself. You may alter your looks, the way you dress or style your hair. You may engage in sexual acts that leave you feeling uncomfortable or dirty. You may shut down and not tell him how you feel, because when you do it produces conflict and painful memories that you want to avoid.

Co-Addiction Trait: **Blame and Punishment** – Anger, blame

Trauma Symptom: **Arousal** – Intense psychological distress, irritability, efforts to control the environment

Example: Your rage is stronger than anything you've experienced before and it doesn't seem to end. You use your anger as a weapon to hurt your partner or shame him/her into faithfulness. You blame him/her for everything wrong in your marriage, even areas where you share responsibility.

Co-Addiction Trait: **Sexual Reactivity** – Impulse to shut down sexually

Trauma Symptoms: **Arousal** – Hypervigilant behaviors, attempts to control one's environment, intense psychological distress

Re-experiencing – Recurrent, intrusive recollections and thoughts

Avoidance – Avoiding activities and other reminders of the event

Example: You don't want to be sexual with your partner. When you engage in sexual relations with him or her, you imagine that he or she has been with people in the pictures he or she has viewed. You have difficulty with nudity in your partner's presence, even though before your discovery of the addiction you found it easy to undress in front of him or her. You find it difficult to watch television programs or movies together, because you fear a sex scene will appear and your partner will act it out in his or her mind or use it later when he or she has sex with you.

The addiction model says that when a partner checks the computer for new evidence, he or she is attempting to control the addict's behavior and could be considered a codependent. A trauma perspective says the partner is scanning his or her environment for signs that the source of the previous trauma has returned and he or she is in danger. This is akin to searching for strangers in the backseat of one's car in the weeks after being carjacked. Doing so is a normal response to such trauma. No one would label a carjacking victim's behavior as signs of disease. They would say the crime victim is reacting in predictable, under-standable, safety-seeking ways following a traumatic and fearful event.

The addiction model says that when a man or woman no longer feels comfortable having sex with his or her addicted partner, he or she is "shutting down" sexually. The trauma model says the person is seeking to avoid uncomfortable memories of the traumatic event and is working to regain a sense of control over his or her own body and choices. This is like a sexual assault victim avoiding places or situations similar to the place where he or she was assaulted. Again, this is a normal trauma response as one seeks to remain safe in a potentially dangerous situation.

The addiction model says that when a partner continues to fixate on the addict's behaviors, he or she is obsessively preoccupied with the addict. The trauma perspective sees the same thought patterns as intrusive thoughts and memories of the trauma. Imagine a sexual abuse survivor who has trouble controlling his or her memories of the abuse being told he or she is obsessively preoccupied with the abuse, when in fact he or she is experiencing unwanted memories or flashbacks that remain beyond one's control!

In the trauma model, we choose to view the partner as one who has experienced significant life trauma due to the discovery that a loved one has sexually betrayed the partner and the partner responds in ways common to trauma survivors. The partner's behaviors are his or her best attempts to regain a sense of safety and control in life (although these attempts may or may not actually work). Later in the book, we'll talk about how the partner can shift from actions that don't help to those that do.

On A Personal Note: What are you feeling and thinking as you compare your "symptoms" with those of someone with post-traumatic stress? What behaviors or symptoms do you see in yourself that you now understand may stem from your trauma?

A New Definition of Codependency

We define codependency in this manner:

I'm codependent when I feel driven to control you, another person or a situation for *my gain*; or *to control who holds the power*; or *to project a better self-image so I feel better about myself and how others view me*. However, when those same behaviors follow a traumatic emotional or physiological injury and are used to prevent further harm to one's self or to maintain one's safety, we label those behaviors as natural responses to trauma.

It's as if we are looking at the same behaviors or feelings in *two different ways*. We've come to see it as having two pairs of glasses on our desks. If we wear the co-addiction glasses, a partner will appear co-addicted. However, if we wear the trauma glasses, he or she will clearly be experiencing post-traumatic stress.

Simply put, we reframe your symptoms as responses to the trauma you've experienced as a result of your partner's sexual betrayal. Viewed and worked on from this perspective, true healing becomes possible for the partner who has been traumatized by the addiction. We believe this view also increases the potential for marital healing and restoration if the sexual addict has the capacity to empathize with his or her partner, is committed to his or her own recovery and is committed to the restoration of the relationship. We've encountered this change in sex addicts and heard their spouses' relief at finally being understood.

Michael shares how finally understanding his wife's trauma helped change his perception of her pain and his responses to it.

When you e-mailed Katrine a copy of chapter 1 of *Your Sexually Addicted Spouse* and I read the page where partners describe how they feel—where they describe the pain created by their partners' sex addiction—it really hit me. I started to visualize them and the deep hurt they felt. It made me cry to realize I'd done that to Katrine and it softened my heart. Because it helped me understand what she was going through, I was able to let her talk about what she was feeling and cry, even when it happened over and over again during the early months of her healing.

So is it Co-Addiction or is it Trauma? Why We Ask This Question

We plead this case for several reasons:

- To offer an alternative theoretical framework for understanding and helping the partner of a sex addict following the disclosure or discovery of the addiction in a relationship with a loved one
- To be a "voice" for the partner
- To let the partner know that he or she is *heard* and that we understand and care
- To help the partner cease attempts to find safety in someone who is not safe and to look to his or her own resources and power
- To give the partner a perspective that can enable him or her to begin to heal
- To enable sex addicts to understand what their partners feel and to enable them to empathize with their pain

The idea that partners of sexual addicts demonstrate symptoms similar to those surviving significant traumatic life events began for us after listening to partners describe their experiences in counseling sessions, support groups, in letters or emails and as trauma-induced health problems (often auto-immune in nature) afflicted many clients. For Marsha, it also grew out of her own trauma as her personal world fell apart following the re-emergence of the sexual addiction in her marriage. But it was Barbara who had the courage to act on what she heard by returning to school to earn her doctoral degree so she could do valid research on the topic.

Evidence We Cannot Deny or Ignore

Barbara asked the female participants in her research study with partners of sex addicts to complete trauma symptom tests. In compiling the results of their tests, it became clear that the characteristics of "co-addicts" read like the description of symptoms common among those who suffer from post-traumatic stress following traumatic events.

Trauma victims of all kinds respond in predictable emotional, behavioral and physiological ways as their minds and bodies attempt to survive and adapt to a shattering and/or dangerous situation. Trauma, as we noted in chapter 1, can produce some of the following symptoms, among others.

Hyperarousal	Helplessness	Sleeplessness	Immobility
Reliving the event	Hypervigilance	Anxiety	Nightmares
Intrusive Images	Withdrawing	Avoidance	Mood Swings
Panic Attacks	Phobias	Flashbacks	Denial
Oversensitivity	Depression	Restlessness	Confusion
Dissociation	Inability to Eat	Overeating	Rage
Health Problems	Chronic Fatigue	Immune/ Endocrine System Problems	

Attempts to avoid painful stimuli and scan the environment for dangers are common reactions among trauma survivors and it's no different for partners who've experienced sexual betrayal. A partner becomes hypersensitive to any indication that the threat may have returned, whether those indications come from the other partner's behavior or from the partner's own reaction to a reminder of the painful past event. Something the sexual addict does or something in the environment, such as a movie scene, a particular person in a restaurant or walking past a lingerie store in the shopping mall, can trigger flashbacks, suddenly throwing the hurt partner into an as-if-it-is-happening-all-over-again alternate reality. Such was Beth's experience whenever she went shopping.

> For months after I discovered my husband's compulsive pornography use, I felt so triggered and anxious that even a simple trip to the mall felt like I was entering a battle zone. Every walk down the corridors brought new assaults: stores with displays of women's lingerie, glossy photos of women looking as if they were in the middle of a sexual encounter and seductive photos of beautiful, young women used to sell perfume, bras and clothes.
>
> Even a trip to the grocery store proved daunting with the checkout aisles lined with magazines touting stories of "What every man wants" or with photos of gorgeous, large-breasted, scantily-clad women. Each time I saw one of these "triggers", I felt the sudden and now familiar tug of a fearful, heart-racing, on-the-edge-of-panic sense of anxiety. Tears welled up and I felt fresh pangs of shame and grief. Flashes of memories of the initial discovery of porn on our home computer invaded my mind. All I wanted was to be able to peacefully go out in public again! I began to wonder: *Will going shopping ever feel "normal" again?*

Obsessive and intrusive thoughts of the partner's sexual betrayal can continue to occupy the other partner's mind and energy as the person seeks safety in what is feared may remain an unsafe situation. And if the loved person continues to act out sexually, dismisses or denies the pain and damage produced by his or her betrayal or does not take action to help restore safety in the relationship, the partner will feel perpetual threat until he or she is removed from the situation and can develop adaptive ways to manage the anxiety and stress produced by the addicted partner's unsafe behavior.

It's Time for a Paradigm Shift
Both of us have encountered *some* therapists who recognize that partners suffer from trauma and post-traumatic stress. However, as we've noted and Barbara's research indicates, a complete review of all sexual addiction literature available about partners of sex addicts

does not yield research focused on treatments and healing from a trauma perspective. And nearly all the partners we hear from find that most therapists they turn to for help automatically label them as co-addicted and refer them to 12-step groups.

We believe the evidence indicates the time has come for a paradigm shift.

The Much-Needed Shift is in the Air
We are excited to tell you that the needed shift has begun! Presenting her trauma material to the Society for the Advancement of Sexual Health (SASH) in the fall of 2006, Barbara's research was well received.

And at the SASH 2007 conference, Stefanie Carnes, Ph.D., facilitated a workshop entitled *Trauma Survivor: Codependent or Crazy?* Dr. Carnes cited Barbara's study as she began her talk, and she included participation by a panel made up of sex addiction treatment specialists who shared their experiences and thoughts on the topic.

Well-known sex addiction expert Robert Weiss, MA, was among the panelists. Dr. Weiss shared that much of his thinking about *partners* of sex addicts had formerly been based on what he learned as he worked with *sex addicts.* He said he compared the "out of control" behaviors he sees in addicts to the "out of control" behavior in partners:

> My thought was when I first started doing the work [with partners] was, *Well these spouses are out of control. They're doing detective work, they're eating, they're spending his money, they're furious—they need confronting, containing, managing, too.*
>
> That's my lack of empathy…and that's why the trauma issues weren't addressed: because we just wanted to control all that anger and didn't really understand it.
>
> I think collectively that they had a right to it. And I think it's really good news to have the experience of both in our clinic for the last year…because I see spouses de-escalating, you know—feeling validated, feeling supported, feeling understood, being given the space to do what they need to do to take care of themselves and not be called "crazy" because they are so *out-of-control* [italics added].

We hope that reading Robert Weiss's words gives you hope, as it does us. Change is coming. Though paradigm shifts typically take time, this means our children and grandchildren will be met with greater understanding if they, too, are faced with this terrible pain. And it also means that in time husbands and wives will be taught how their addictions have impacted their partners, thus helping couples communicate and attempt to heal together.

Another psychologist, Dr. Omar Minwalla, has also come to believe that partners of sex addicts, those who have experienced significant sexual betrayal, are trauma survivors. He articulated his beliefs at the 2008 Society of the Advancement of Sexual Health conference. Dr. Minwalla said:

> Why we as a profession lack awareness of trauma among partners…is really confusing to me…I just don't get why this is so hard to accept or integrate into treatment. It just seems obvious. The [traditional] model is narcissistic and based in male entitlement. Unfortunately, this has been demonstrated by the fact that by being a male and having a male voice, I opened up dialogue around this issue in the midst of female voices who have been talking about this for a very long time. Any healthy sexual model that does not clearly acknowledge [the issue of trauma] is limited at best, and most likely re-traumatizing and inappropriate. I would also like to say personally, my journey began in a place of cluelessness and I have finally worked my way to a place of clarity and recognition. It really helped me work with partners and couples once I made that shift. I'm personally no longer willing as a professional to endorse the existing model that continues to neglect a very wounded population and I'm committed to challenging this patriarchy.[6]

Viewing partners through a trauma lens not only fits the experiences men and women report, it also validates and offers understanding of their pain. And validation and understanding are essential ingredients in helping partners create the safety, support and empowerment they desperately need in order to deal with and begin to heal from the trauma in their most intimate relationships.

And safety, support and the empowerment to heal are essential liberties we all seek for ourselves, for other individuals and for relationships damaged by sexual betrayal.

On A Personal Note: After reading this chapter, what do you feel? Has there been a shift in the way you view your reactions to your partner's sex addiction? What would you like others to know about your experiences?

Chapter 3

Why Your Partner's Sex Addiction Hurts So Much: Attachment Bonds Betrayed

Marissa reveals the pain that every person who experiences sexual betrayal feels:

Three years into our marriage, I found out about my husband's emotional affair with my best friend. He also told me he had engaged in a one-night stand. Those disclosures broke my heart. A few years later, I still occasionally had nightmares that woke me up in the middle of the night and left me wide awake in emotional pain.

Then, just a few weeks before our twelfth wedding anniversary, my best friend's husband called me.

"Marissa, I love you like a sister," he began. "And I hate to tell you this, but I just found a bunch of emails on our computer. They prove that my wife and your husband have been having sex for all of these years. It was never over like they said it was, and it was way more than just emotional!"

I couldn't believe what I had just heard! I was shocked; I was numb. The greatest fear in my life was that my husband might be living a double life like so many men in the news. I confronted him with what my friend's husband told me, and he denied the affair with my best friend. He lied and said they had only kissed. About twenty-four hours later, after I spoke with my friend's husband again, my husband admitted he and my best friend had had sex.

"But only a few times," he said. Then he reassured me it was long over. It wasn't until a day or two later—after I got new information about a phone conversation between the two of them a few months earlier—that he finally admitted these painful words: "Your worst fears have come true. I use call girls; I've used porn; I've had cyber-sex." But even then he didn't tell me everything. There were more disclosures a few days later.

We arranged for a three-day couple's intensive with a sex addiction therapist who requires complete disclosure plus a lie detector test as part of his program. My husband worked hard to make sure he disclosed everything prior to that test. And in those final disclosures, I learned he had participated in group sex, he'd had sex with co-workers and he'd had sex with a woman he met at the mall! And on top of everything else, he had told my supposed best friend that she was the one he truly loved, not me. Of everything I've lost, that piece of information has been the most painful and damaging.

All of us who've lived through the discovery of sexual betrayal remember in razor-sharp detail the agony, shock and overwhelming loss that ripped through our lives in that one earth-shattering moment in time. From that moment on we instinctively knew nothing would ever be the same again.

There are many reasons why sex addiction's impact on a partner severs the past from the future. And many reasons it cannot be compared to the impact other addictions have on a partner's life. In this chapter we discuss those reasons and in that discussion lies the answer to the question: *Why does your partner's sex addiction hurt so much?*

Our Deepest Attachment Bond and Trauma
Attachment Bonds: What They Are and Their Meaning in Our Lives

When we develop relationships, we establish what psychologists call attachment bonds. We form expectations of how we will be treated in the relationship, and the connections grow as we share experiences. As they do, we begin to look to the relationship for a sense of safety, security and fulfillment. Brook Feeney and Nancy Collins, respected researchers on attachment, tell us attachments share four specific qualities:

- *Proximity Maintenance*—the attached individual wishes to be in close proximity to the attachment figure.
- *Separation Distress*—the attached individual experiences an increase in anxiety during unwanted or prolonged separation from the attachment figure.
- *Safe Haven*—the attachment figure serves as a source of comfort and security such that the attached individual experiences diminished anxieties when in the company of the attachment figure.
- *Secure Base*—the attachment figure serves as a base of security from which the attached individual engages in explorations of the social and physical world.[1]

In an intimate relationship—or bond—if something threatens those four elements we've grown to believe the relationship provides in our lives, we fear that we may lose the important connection we've come to enjoy, expect and depend on. The more significant the relationship, the more intensely we feel the fear and threat to the relationship. That fear is called "fear of abandonment."

Fear of Abandonment: The Fundamental Human Fear

"Fear of abandonment is the fundamental human fear," Dr. Tim Clinton and Dr. Gary Sibcy write in *Attachments: Why You Love, Feel & Act the Way You Do.*

They explain:

> It is so basic and so profound that it emerges even before we develop a language to describe it. It is so powerful that it activates our body's autonomic nervous system, causing our hearts to race, our breathing to become shallow and rapid, our stomachs to quiver, and our hands to shake. We feel a sense of panic that will not be assuaged... until we regain a feeling of security. This attachment system is not just part of human behavior; it's evident throughout the animal kingdom.[2]

When Attachment Bonds are Betrayed: The Impact of Relational Trauma

When our fear of abandonment becomes our reality in our most intimate relationship—when the one we love betrays our trust—we suffer betrayal trauma and we're thrown into crisis mode. For some of us, the betrayal is relatively short-lived and we can begin to heal. For others, years, even decades can pass without lasting change. That's the way it was in Mikki's case.

I married my high school sweetheart. I knew from the beginning something was absent in our marriage; something important was missing. He physically abused me during the first five years before our first child was born. Because of the abuse I started divorce proceedings, but when he pursued me and it seemed like he was changing, I decided to stay.

But he didn't change. We'd go to parties and he'd disappear, and I wouldn't know where he was. I tried to be okay with that, but I had recurring dreams of him walking away hand in hand with someone else. After my second pregnancy, I decided to try to focus on being the perfect wife and mother, hoping that would make a difference in our marriage.

After a few years he went into ministry, yet he remained aloof, angry and withdrawn from me. When I caught him masturbating he simply said, "All guys do it," and closed the door to his office and on the subject.

The years passed and, eventually, our last child left home. And there we were, looking at each other. I confronted him again when I found porn, but he lied his way out of it. I didn't know what else I could do.

Finally, I drew a line in the sand and said I was done unless he sought help and made changes in his life. So he sought joint counseling, went to Every Man's Battle and returned a different man. He confessed to numerous affairs and a one-night stand, along with all the porn. I joined a wives' group for me, and we continued individual and joint counseling.

After thirty-five years of a horrible marriage, we were on our honeymoon. But it was short-lived. The months following his miraculous turnaround have been one long rollercoaster ride filled with spine-tingling emotional and spiritual intimacy that suddenly gives way to deep plunges into his dark rage and emotional separation.

These cycles have left me physically and emotionally wrung out, and I've developed post-traumatic stress disorder and some difficult health problems as a result. Trauma has filled the thirty-five years of our marriage; I'm not sure I can go on in this kind of relationship and survive.

If the attachment bond you felt for your partner has been violated and broken as it was in Mikki's life, you have a relational trauma wound as well. When that happens, all the warmth, safety, joy and comfort that the relationship formerly held can no longer be counted on. The relationship now becomes a source of danger, because you've discovered that much of what you believed about the one you love was a lie.

On A Personal Note: What do you think about the concept of relationship trauma following a betrayal? Do YOU feel unsafe with the person you most expected to be there for you?

The Destructive Effects of Repeated Relational Trauma

If we experience relational trauma in a one-time event during which we hear our spouse's full disclosure of sexual betrayal, it devastates us and healing requires time and effort. However, when relational trauma recurs—when your partner acts out again sexually or discloses new sexual information in a delayed manner—healing is interrupted. If you've just begun to believe that your partner has finally come clean and then he or she produces another heart-piercing disclosure, it slashes through the fragile, early stages of healing taking place in your mind and soul. That was Annie's experience.

Although the past several months have left me reeling, I was beginning to heal and felt hopeful again. Then my husband was sent abroad by his company. When he came home he confessed that he purposefully toured the red-light district in the city he was in and almost gave in to the sexual temptation that seemed to overtake him when he saw the girls standing on street corners.

When he told me, he seemed devastated. He was crying, and he said, "I'm never going to get better! I might as well give up!" He went to bed inconsolable, lost in the shame he felt.

When I laid down beside him he was already asleep. I could feel myself sinking into a black hole. Part of me was angry, yet I knew it wouldn't do any good to condemn him. I also knew I needed space to deal with my feelings, so I moved to the sofa for the night. Lying there, I cried and prayed for hours. All the pain started over again. I'm struggling with my own self-esteem. I'm getting older every year and I know I'm never going to be one of those beautiful young girls that he looks at. Sometimes I feel like just letting go and giving up!

Just as fresh blood oozes when the scab is ripped from a deep wound, so too, does fresh, raw pain gush from yet another trauma injury when new sexual betrayal or, as in Annie's case, near sexual betrayal is disclosed. With each new revelation that your marriage is not secure, healing must begin anew. And as it does, hope of returning to "normal" often slips further and further out of sight.

New disclosure not only creates a delay in your healing, it can also set up a new set of problems. When fresh disclosure interrupts the re-establishment of safety, which is so essential to your healing, it can set up a cycle of chronic trauma pain—post-traumatic stress. And with post-traumatic stress comes the potential for post-traumatic stress disorder to develop in your life. Trauma expert Tana Slay, Ph.D., explains it this way:

> When the natural healing process is interrupted or interfered with, then the pain of the trauma can intensify and become chronic. The chronic nature of trauma pain can develop into severe emotional disorders.[3]

And as we've said earlier, post-traumatic stress disorder can cripple a life, and it can trigger complicated, long-term health problems.

On A Personal Note: *The image of a scab ripped open is a powerful and painful one. What image would you use to describe your pain after repeated disclosures?*

The Painful Effects of Delayed Reconnection

Even when no new betrayal occurs and no new disclosures are revealed, if months pass and a loving emotional reconnection does not take place between you and your partner, your trauma can extend, dragging out your healing process. Again, that extension holds the potential to set up a cycle of chronic trauma pain. Jessica shares how she experienced such a delay in her marriage.

> I never dreamed that we would be dragging this drama out. I thought that the "truth would set us free" from this secret. I thought we would pick up the pieces, mend and go on. I thought that we would be okay by now, months after his revelation. I had no idea that the childhood wounds at the heart of his addiction were so deep and that I would be a "nut case" regarding all of this. Right now it looks hopeless.

Each of the reasons discussed so far—the depth and expectations of our deepest attachment bond, the piercing pain produced by betrayal trauma, the universal fear of abandonment generated by sexual betrayal, the threat of repeated incidents and the isolation and loneliness created by delayed emotional reconnection—provides part of the answer to the question: *Why does your partner's sexual betrayal hurt so much?*

But there are other, simpler reasons this addiction slashes right through the core of our hearts and souls. Let's look at these reasons next.

The Betrayal of the Marital Promise

Shelly told us about how her views of marriage and commitment were shattered.

> "This is *not* what I signed up for!" Shelly almost shouted. The deep pain and disappointment seeped from her words, even over the phone line.

> "When I married my husband, I expected to be treated the way my father always treated my mother. He loved and adored her right up until the day he died. By their example, I was taught that marriage was a promise—a commitment to complete faithfulness for the remainder of our lives. And those were the words he spoke to me on our wedding day!

But that's *not* what I got!"

Shelly's beliefs about the institution of marriage and the meaning of wedding vows sounds typical of those we encounter in our work with partners of the sexually addicted. We've yet to meet a person who is happy that his or her spouse betrayed vows of emotional and physical faithfulness. Meanwhile, researchers' findings correlate with what we hear from men and women.

"Infidelity or extramarital sex is considered by many as a betrayal of the marital promise…a form of deviant or immoral behavior" one study found.[4] Even in this era of high divorce rates, partners—especially those in faith-based communities—hold on to the belief that their life partners will remain emotionally and physically faithful.

Your Partner Held Secrets and Locked You Out of a Part of His or Her Life

Discovering that the person you think you know so well—the one you snuggle up to every night—has locked you out of a secret part of his or her life is shocking and repulsive. Suddenly, every valued memory and belief about your life vanishes into a black sea of questions with unknown answers. One such instance was the horrific discovery Alice made after her husband of thirty-five years died while having sex with a prostitute.

My adult children and I buried my husband a month ago and I'm still trying to determine what I am grieving: the loss of the wonderful, caring man with whom I've shared my entire adult life and thought I knew so well or the discovery that the last thirty-five years of my life were nothing but a lie.

Until my husband died suddenly of a heart attack, I only knew him as the perfect husband and father. Then police officers came to my door and told me he had died of a heart attack while having sex with a prostitute! They gave me his watch, his wallet, his wedding ring and the other personal belongings he had with him at the time of his death. In that moment, time stopped and all sense and order vanished from my universe.

"How could this possibly be?" I wondered aloud. Everyone who knew him adored the wonderful, faithful husband, father and friend they believed he was.

However, as my adult children went through his wallet with me, we found several credit cards that I knew nothing about, women's names and telephone numbers I had never heard or seen before.

After weeks of trying to untangle the mysterious plot these new pieces of information have been revealed: I now know he left me with at least $100,000 worth of debt—debt he accumulated with the call girls represented by the newly found names and numbers in his wallet. These, I now know, comprised the "little black book" carried by the man I loved, adored and with whom I raised my children.

How is it that anyone can so completely fool those who share their lives with him and think they know him best? I can't imagine that I will ever completely thaw from the frozen shock I'm presently encased in.

Though Alice's story far exceeds the horror most of us are forced to face because of our partners' sexual betrayals, even the more "minor" evidences that our partners hide secrets and lock us out of their innermost worlds run counter to our closely held beliefs about what marriage means in our lives and in theirs. The discovery of these secrets can be devastating.

Relapse Potential and the Possibility of Future Betrayals

Another reason your partner's sexual addiction hurts so much stems from the very real threat it imposes on your partner's future faithfulness. Men and women ask us again and again: "How do I know my partner isn't going to do this in the future?" One relatively young woman recently sobbed during a support group meeting, "I'm getting older every year and there is always a fresh crop of ripe young beauties for him to ogle. There is no way I can compete with that!"

The truth is that no one can guarantee a sex addict won't repeat his or her sexual betrayal sometime in the future. Over the years we've heard hundreds of partners say, "If it happens again, I'm out of here!" And a few honest sex addicts express the sadness and concern recently expressed by one man as he talked about his wife's pain.

He told us how she keeps asking, "How do I know you won't do this again?" She needs and wants to know she has security with him, to know that this won't happen to her again. And though he desperately wants to promise her it's over, that it'll never, ever happen again, as he hears other men share about their relapses in his Sex Addicts Anonymous meetings, he knows he can't honestly make that promise. He believes the best he can tell her is, "All I can do is be honest with you, go to my meetings, walk in accountability, call my support people, go to my counseling sessions and live it out one day at a time."

He's right: He can't make a 100 percent guarantee that he'll never fail in this way again. Yet we know sex addicts who have decades of sexual sobriety. These men and women have made a commitment to themselves and God to stay mentally and physically pure, one day at a time; their characters, lives and marriages bear the fruit of their faithfulness to their sexual purity. Sexual sobriety is *not* an impossible goal for the sex addict who wants it and seeks it with his or her whole heart, soul, mind and body.

HIV and STD Risks

The risk of HIV and other sexually transmitted diseases (STDs) add additional pain and trauma to every partner's life. Because we can never know beyond a shadow of a doubt that we have heard total disclosure, sex addiction leaves us with at least a shred of uncertainty. We recommend every partner be tested for STDs, no matter what his or her partner says.

It isn't fun; many partners of sex addicts have said that asking their doctors for these tests produced painful humiliation and shame. However, because STDs show up frequently in sex addicts' lives, this step becomes a must for each of us.

Security Risks as You Get Older

Sharing your life with a sex addict automatically places your older years in the path of possible financial hardship. If a sex addict returns to his or her addiction later in life—or worse, never leaves it in the first place—the risk remains that your partner might abandon you in search of freedom or yet another sexual fling. Add to that the fact that sex addicts often prove to be financially irresponsible across adulthood and you have a setup for possible poverty as you face the final decades of your life. Such is the case for Irene.

> We've been married for over thirty years. I've always known my husband was a womanizer, but it was my second marriage, I had children to support and his business enabled us to live a very affluent lifestyle. Somehow it was easier to put up with his flirtations and stay. Now, after my youth is long gone, I've uncovered the extent of his behavior.
>
> I've discovered that he's had affair after affair and spent hundreds of thousands of dollars on those women. I've finally filed for divorce, but my attorney discovered that my husband conducted a lot of his business under the table, making it impossible to trace and locking me out of my share. So far my husband's doing everything possible to make sure I never get a dime. I'm not even sure I can keep the house. I'm sixty-five, in poor health and I haven't worked in years. Without a miracle, my future looks bleak and frightening.

Though most people aren't as selfish and uncaring as Irene's husband, her story holds an important truth for all of us: Life holds no guarantees. It behooves us to take part in our family finances and to *know* that our futures are well planned for, regardless of what happens in our marriages.

On A Personal Note: As you read Irene's example, what thoughts or fears do you have about your financial security? What steps have you or CAN you take to begin the process of self-protection in your finances?

Unique Reasons for Hurt Felt by Those in Faith-Based Communities

Some partners in faith-based communities have told us that their spiritual beliefs and deep faith enable them to survive, even through the worst possible betrayal scenarios. One woman's quite simple yet beautiful statement describes this well:

> "At times I think I can feel God hugging me," she said softly into the phone as she shared her story. "Even though this is the most horrible trauma I've ever endured, my faith and my children are keeping me alive."

Her faith and sense of being loved and cared for by God represents thousands of other stories we have heard. Yet some of the teachings and beliefs in faith-based communities bring added expectations of spouses to be emotionally and physically faithful when, in fact, these partners are fallible human beings and battle with sex addiction, too. People in such relationships struggle to make sense of the clashes in their two most important and personal worlds.

Spiritual Leadership, Submission and the Husband's Authority in Marriage

In some sects there are the oft-taught concepts that the husband has spiritual authority over his wife and she must submit to his leadership. These frequently cause a woman to surrender her total trust to his care. If and when a man betrays that trust sexually— and abuses the position of authority his wife has given him in her life—she encounters an additional betrayal and accompanying relational trauma.

Sometimes a man will use his spiritual leadership position to deflect attention away from himself by hounding his wife for not reading her Bible enough, for wearing makeup or for not living a "spiritual" life. At times these behaviors flow from his own feelings of guilt, because *he* is living a double life and violating his own standards. Ultimately the woman realized a guilty conscience was behind her husband's overbearing behavior, unkind words and volatile attitude, as her testimonial suggests.

> My husband ragged on me for spending money on anything extra, especially if it was for me. If I colored my hair, he made it about my lack of spirituality; if I had my nails done, same thing. Man, he even told me that taking my antidepressants proved I didn't have enough faith in God. Now I know all that time [he was criticizing me and questioning my faith] he was using prostitutes! Go figure!

Many Churches Fail to Respond With Care and Educated Understanding

In our work, we have found the following experience is not uncommon in some faith-based communities. Penny had silently struggled alone for years, afraid to reach out for help, when we met her.

Several years into my marriage, I was diagnosed with an STD. Though it shocked me, I already knew something was wrong, because my husband didn't seem to want to be with me sexually. Following the diagnosis, I asked my husband if he had been with another woman. He lied and said, "No."

I was terrified of hearing something that would destroy my family, so I wasn't disappointed when he offered no explanation for the STD. I just tried to put it out of my mind.

Then, I accidentally found porn files on our home computer, and porn videos began to turn up when I did a deep clean of the house. With our five children in the home, I became nervous that they might stumble onto these things, too, and I knew that would devastate them.

So I decided to turn to a religious leader for help. When I told him what I found and what I feared, he condemned me for suspecting my husband and not trusting God to take care of me and my family. With a raised voice he said, "Your husband is a leader in the church. How can you even think such things?"

Now, years later, I still find new porn files and my husband still isn't interested in me sexually. He really doesn't even seem to like me very much! But I'm scared to reach out for help in our community again. I thought they would support me emotionally and spiritually and help me confront my husband when I tried years ago. I was shocked and devastated by the way I was treated back then. After so many pain-filled years, I don't think I can endure that again.

Penny's failure to receive the help and support she sought and expected from her church added spiritual trauma to her life, in addition to the relational trauma inflicted by her husband's attitude and behavior. Many people share Penny's experience

when their faith-based communities fail to recognize their
spouses' betrayals, provide emotional and spiritual support for
their healing and/or help them confront their spouses' addictions
to provide an opportunity for change.

Having a Sense of "Responsibility for His or Her Soul"
Generally, many women and some men shine at nurturing others
and taking care of loved ones' needs. But this beautiful quality,
rich in faith-based communities, can imprison a person in a cage
of distorted thinking. When a partner feels so responsible for a sex
addict's soul that he or she continues to live with the sexual
acting out, he or she overlooks many serious risks. The partner, in
turn, fails to face the facts that accompany sexual addiction, both
inside and outside the church. Let's examine those facts and risks:

- Risking health and life due to the very real danger of STDs
  since one cannot *know* a sex addict's truth.
- Risking the damage that living with ongoing trauma can do to
  one's health.
- Risking financial difficulties often created by the secrets of
  addiction.
- Risking the children discovering their parent's addiction,
  which we've seen devastate a child to the point of attempting
  suicide.
- Risking the sex addict participating in more hazardous sexual
  behavior with the passage of time.

Yet in spite of the risks, many men and women in faith-based
communities experiencing partners' sexual addiction often hold
on to beliefs like those expressed by Sue:

> Life calls for sacrifice, doesn't it? I have to make my
> husband's soul my highest priority. Aren't we supposed to die to
> self? I believe I need to continue to trust God to meet my
> emotional needs, because my husband refuses to meet them. And
> I trust God to protect me from sexually transmitted diseases. If
> He wants me rescued, *He* will rescue me. I plan to steer clear of
> any selfish motivation.

However, after years of sifting through the ashes of burned-
out lives and marriages, we've come to believe that, in all cases,

confronting the addiction and requiring a plan for help provides the least selfish option available to the partner of a sex addict.

It does not come without risk of great loss, which the addiction has created in our lives already. Yet the risk of confrontation places the highest value on *each life* represented in the family. It provides the shortest route to the highest possible outcome for everyone involved, if your spouse chooses to seek help.

Easy? No. *Nothing* about living with sex addiction proves easy.

On A Personal Note: What aspects of faith have helped you? Where in your journey have people of faith helped or hurt you in their responses to your pain? Is there something you'd like to communicate to God? Take a moment and tell Him.

Life Factors that can Influence Trauma Severity
Length of Time Married

Nearly every person to whom we've talked who has faced sexual addiction in a committed relationship has also experienced agonizing trauma. Yet the severity of trauma experienced can vary depending on certain factors in partners' lives. We encounter these differences daily as we hear stories filled with pain.

In her study, Barbara sought to determine how the length of time a woman had been married before her husband's addiction was discovered affected her trauma symptoms. The results suggest that the longer the secret continues to be undisclosed and unaddressed, the greater the impact it has on the addict's partner.

One woman in the study had been married for twenty-five years before her husband's sexual addiction was revealed and can no longer look at her wedding album, because now the pictures only represent "a lie" to her. In addition, she had begun to question everything about their marriage.

Another woman married for many years discovered that while she recovered from having their first baby, her husband was on a trip acting out sexually. And even though the baby was a teen at the time of the study, she found it still hurt to look at his baby pictures, because they reminded her of her husband's betrayal.

The study results suggest that with the passage of time and the compiling of cherished memories, partners tend to feel they have more to lose at the discovery of addiction.

Earlier Life Trauma

Because earlier life trauma generally predicts the susceptibility and intensity of future trauma, Barbara also examined the trauma histories of the women in her study. And indeed she found that the number of traumatic events in the participants' life histories heightened the trauma they experienced upon the discoveries of their husbands' sexual addictions.

We often see this in our work with partners as well. A young woman married only a few years describes horrific childhood abuse that has left painful emotional scars. It's not surprising that the discovery of her husband's addiction—even though they've only been married a few years—flooded her with fresh trauma. The result? She smashed all of her wedding memorabilia and threw them away and she beat his computer to bits with a hammer.

Her childhood trauma includes a mean, unloving father who told her she was ugly and that she'd better get good grades, because no man would ever marry her! Old trauma becomes a magnet for fresh correlating pain.

The Behaviors a Sex Addict Engages In

The stories we hear in our work, as we have said earlier, indicate there is indeed a connection between the kinds of sexual behavior in which an addict engages and the partner's trauma. While we find that even people whose spouses "only" use pornography and masturbation suffer trauma and often post-traumatic stress, trauma levels seem to increase in severity when the addict's risks and behaviors are considered extremely deviant.

Most partners suffer devastating and often crippling trauma, post-traumatic stress and symptoms of PTSD when their partners have engaged in sex with women, men or prostitutes, in group sex, in child pornography or in other lacivious behavior.

Yvonne's case presents one example.

Yvonne is a young woman married only a few years and has had no previous trauma. She has beautiful childhood memories, holds a master's degree that enables her to be financially independent and has extremely high self-esteem. Yet she often finds herself derailed by trauma symptoms, even though her husband consistently attends Sex Addicts Anonymous (SAA) meetings and uses a sex addiction recovery program. He had shockingly disclosed that he'd always been more attracted to men than to women and that he chose homosexual pornography.

The myriad heartbreaking stories bear out an important truth: neither people nor trauma fit neatly into studies or charts. Nonetheless, more research is needed to help us all better understand the trauma partners of sex addicts face and how we can best help ourselves heal.

What We Believe this Means for Partners of Sex Addicts
That Many People Don't Understand the Impact on Partners

Clearly, many people—even many counseling professionals—don't understand or recognize the impact sex addiction has on partners. Along with the automatic co-addict labeling partners generally receive, other unfair labels and diagnoses get noted in their files.

The theory of collusion provides one primary example. The professionals in two researches Barbara cited in her study noted their belief that many therapists *wrongly* see partners as "colluding" in the betrayal by ignoring it.[5] But even when partners suspect something is amiss, ask questions, check computers, phone bills, credit card and bank statements—basically do everything they can short of hiring a private investigator—their mates simply lie. This leaves them with continued suspicions, but with no concrete evidence and thus no way to prove what they only fear.

Does that mean they collude? In our experience the answer is rarely; they simply don't know what else they can do to uncover what they fear may be the truth.

That the Negative Impact on Partners is Enormous

Barbara explains:

> While existing sex addiction literature acknowledges that discovering your partner is a sex addict produces a life crisis and a traumatic event, I wanted to look more closely at the hurt partners so that we could study and explore new methods to help them heal.
>
> Rather than just stating that women experience any number of emotional or behavioral symptoms following

disclosure, I wanted to identify a specific *type* of symptomatic response and measure it.

Because I repeatedly heard women describe disclosure in word pictures filled with violent imagery, I knew they must be experiencing trauma and even PTSD. I heard women say disclosure left them "shell-shocked," "violated," "totally disoriented," "emotionally raped" and it was "like being stabbed repeatedly." Such destructive descriptions generally accompany traumatic events.

So I assessed the women in my study for symptoms consistent with a traumatic stress response or symptoms of *post-traumatic stress disorder* (PTSD). As we described in chapter 1, PTSD is a condition that often follows the survival of a traumatic life event—an event like a devastating earthquake, a rape or losing a loved one in a fire. Such events leave survivors with extreme levels of anxiety, hypervigilance and recurrent memories or flashbacks. They find themselves obsessing about what happened, and even small environmental reminders can "trigger" a "reliving it" response accompanied by such strong reactions that they feel as though it's happening all over again. These symptoms are generally so strong they interfere with daily functioning, leaving a woman emotionally wrung-out and often unable to cope.

I think the most startling outcome of my study was that 70 percent of the women met the symptomatic criteria for PTSD in response to the disclosure of sexual addiction. This is not to say that they have PTSD, but that the level of symptoms is consistent with those in someone exposed to a natural disaster or sexual assault who went on to develop PTSD as a result of that event. To me, that is significant information for the spouse and for those who seek to help him or her heal.

That Healing is Hard Work

Healing proves to be especially hard work for the partner who remains in the relationship even though the sex addict chooses not to embrace healing and growth.

Even when a sex addict fully embraces the recovery and healing process, the other partner's recovery journey may have many bumps, potholes and twists and turns. All of us continue to live in a sexually charged world filled with triggers that often stimulate flashbacks, nightmares and intrusive or obsessive thoughts in us. It can take time for these trauma symptoms to be calmed and for our sense of feeling secure in the world to return.

To someone who has never experienced the relational trauma that results from the discovery that your most significant attachment bond cannot be trusted—that it is indeed *dangerous* to your safety—these reactions may seem out of proportion, even bizarre.

However, they replicate in millions of lives every year as new women and men discover their partners have betrayed them sexually.

Another reason healing is frequently hard work is that pornography *prevents* true intimacy. Because the porn or other sex addictions a user has learned to substitute with the quick, easy fix such vices provide for the emotional and relational work, which true intimacy requires, the addiction *blocks* both a secure attachment bond and authentic intimacy.

So even when a partner lets go of sexual addiction habits, building the ability to provide security and intimacy takes time. Moreover, if the addict has old emotional wounds that block true connection and intimacy with a partner, those wounds must be healed with the help of a professional *before* the sexual addict can hope to establish a long-term, intimate connection.

Trauma's Echoes
These words and stories all reverberate with echoes from other traumatic life events encountered by people. Rather than view these partners as addicted and pathological, we believe that when we recognize their symptoms and behaviors as attempts to adapt to destructive information in their lives, we can help them more quickly gain what they desperately seek: renewed safety and the empowerment required to make decisions for their own lives and those of their children. Then healing can begin to happen.

On A Personal Note: You have just read a lot of difficult and probably painful information and stories. You have also read some new ways of thinking about or responding to your pain. Take a moment and consider how you are feeling right now. Sad? Heard? Validated? Confused? Angry? Encouraged? Whatever you are expressing, we encourage you to feel it, express it and then find a way to share these feelings with someone you trust.

Chapter 4

How the Addiction and Trauma Models Differ in Helping You Heal

Many partners say they feel their world is shattered by sex addiction when they're told *they* have a problem and need weekly treatment via a 12-step program for *their* issues.

Many partners of sex addicts we've worked with do not seem to harbor codependency or co-addict traits. Rather, they demonstrate healthy boundaries, a strong sense of self and intolerance for their spouses' extracurricular sexual activities once they discover them. *Wait a minute!* they seem to say. *My heart is broken and my life is a train wreck. Can't you give me time and help to process my feelings and allow me to grieve over my losses instead of skipping ahead to my role in this chaos, assuming I'm to blame as well?*

Many Partners Do Not Enable Once They Discover the Reality

Fran provides one strong example of a non-enabling partner. Her response to her discovery of her husband's pornography addiction was to calmly draw a firm, clear boundary. She realized she needed space and time to gain greater emotional safety, to seek the whole truth, to think things through and to begin getting the help and support she needed to determine her long-term decisions and plans. Listen to the spirit with which she approached her situation as she shares her feelings:

Amidst the shocking discovery of my husband's compulsive pornography use, I recall feeling very sure of what I needed to see my husband do to not only get help for himself, but to help restore the sense of safety within our home. I told him that I needed to know that my home was free of sexual material. I could not control what he chose to do outside, but I could demand to live in a place that was clean from pornography. I made it very clear that if he chose to bring pornography into our home again, he would need to leave. I had the right and responsibility to our family to draw a firm line to help restore a healthy place for our daughters and for myself. Out of some place of strength I didn't know I had, I also told him that I would be watching to see if he chose health and recovery for himself. I knew I could never be reason enough for him to choose health; he had to choose to do this for himself.

A Messy Exterior Does Not Equal Codependency

Though not all partners of sex addicts project such strength and clarity about their worth, in our experience, neither do all partners project codependency. *We believe it can be extremely difficult for any professional to clearly assess a partner's personal empowerment, because his or her post-traumatic stress can trigger such extreme responses that the person may* <u>*appear*</u> *to demonstrate codependency and erratic mental health.* Such a person may look panicked, unkempt, hysterical, angry, depressed, impatient and even abrasive as he or she sees his or her marriage, dreams and life crumble, lost to a spouse's sexual addiction.

Yet we have found that if we look under the surface presentation of a sex addict's partner and seek to understand the *motivation beneath* his or her behavior, we can begin to more clearly understand where the person is coming from. Only then can we help her determine what he or she needs to feel safe again, empower him or her to act in his or her own best interest and help him or her begin to heal. Once this early "ER" treatment and the beginning steps of healing take place, we find that most partners are able to look at personal issues on which they need to work.

We'll talk more about motivation later, but first let's take a closer look at what the 12-step perspective offers partners of sex addicts for their healing journeys. We'll examine its strengths, as well as those things we believe get overlooked in this model. Then we'll discuss motivation in more detail. Lastly, we will ask the question: *Can a partner of a sex addict benefit from using both the trauma model and the 12-step model as he or she seeks healing?*

The Addiction/12-Step Approach to Treatment

The addiction model and the 12-step groups they prescribe—groups like S-Anon and COSA—do help many, many partners of sex addicts grow and learn to deal with their situations. This approach can enable partners to learn how to live with the addictions present in their marriages if they choose to stay with spouses who don't want growth and change. It can also empower them to draw boundaries and remove themselves from the relationships if they opt for separations or divorces. In addition, it provides support from others on the same journey, as well as a pathway for personal growth. As we've said in earlier chapters, Marsha utilized this approach as one aspect in her own healing process.

Strengths of the Addiction/12-Step Approach

The 12-step approach provides much strength. We turned to the COSA Web site so we could utilize their own descriptions of all they have to offer.

The 12-Step Approach Provides a Community of Hope and Help

From the COSA Web site:

> COSA offers hope. In COSA, we begin to experience relief from our isolation, in the safety of an anonymous gathering with others who share our stories. During every meeting—little by little—sanity, clarity and our own truth begin to emerge.[1]

The 12-Step Approach Provides a Well-Established, Broadly Available Community

Because this model has been in operation for much longer than other forms of healing for partners of sex addicts, groups can be easier to locate. The S-Anon Web site can be read in Dutch,

English or Spanish, there is no cost for attending a 12-step group and a central Web site for each organization not only assists one in locating support groups, it also has newsletters, an online store to buy 12-step literature and CDs, information about retreats and conventions and COSA even has info about the tele-meetings they make available to men and women. In addition, S-Anon provides community outreach to make professionals, the media, institutions and the public aware of this resource via download-able posters and flyers, letters for newspapers, materials to public libraries and packets to professionals. COSA provides a letter to mental health professionals as well.

The 12 Steps Offers the Benefits that come from Working the 12 Steps in Our Lives
From the COSA site:
> Working the steps is the foundation of recovery in COSA; they are a set of spiritual practices COSA members use for personal growth and recovery; based on the Twelve Steps of Alcoholics Anonymous....

> COSA follows the 12 steps and 12 traditions of Alcoholics Anonymous (AA). These steps have helped COSA members become aware of their own codependent behaviors in relationships with friends, family members and partners. Admission to ourselves allows us to acknowledge our own patterns in addictions and sexual codependency.[2]

The 12-Step Approach Helps Us Change *Us*
From the COSA Site:
> In COSA, we learn that the only person we can change is ourselves....In defining our own sobriety, we make a list of those behaviors we engaged in that made us, and the situation, worse. We choose, one day and one situation at a time, not to engage in those behaviors.[3]

What We Believe Gets Overlooked in the 12-Step Approach
The Addiction Model's Presumption of "Disease" in Partners of Sex Addicts
While we value and feel grateful for the wealth of help and resources S-Anon and COSA bring to partners of sex addicts, we

believe the addiction model unfairly represents all partners as unhealthy people with their own diseases. Listen to that reality in the following excerpt from the COSA Web site:

> Whether we choose to call it sexual codependency or co-sex addiction, our problem is a serious and progressive disease—as harmful to us as sexual addiction is to the sex addict.[4]

The Addiction Model Reinforces Feelings of Powerlessness Over Our Own Lives

Trauma specialists recognize that if you are traumatized, your greatest needs include the need to feel safe again and the need to feel empowered to direct and manage your own life—to *not* feel afraid that the traumatic incident could occur again at any moment. These needs reflect the *opposite* of accepting your powerlessness over the chaos that produced your trauma, which is what we find in the 12-step approach, as the following excerpt reflects.

From the COSA site:

> What brings us to COSA? Before recovery, we are unable to admit our powerlessness over compulsive sexual behavior; either someone else's behavior, or our own obsession with the sex addict. We attempt to control, losing regard for our own well-being in the process. [5]

The Addiction Model Misinterprets Your Trauma Symptoms as Codependency

As you've read the earlier chapters in this book, you've become aware of the types of behavior that could indicate you or someone you care about suffers from trauma, post-traumatic stress or PTSD. And you've probably begun to recognize how important accurate diagnoses and help becomes if you want to win over possible long-lasting effects of trauma in your life.

However, within the addiction/12-step model the thoughts and behaviors symptomatic of trauma are *automatically* labeled as indicators of a partner's own disease. Note the evidence of misinterpretations found in the following excerpt from the COSA site:

> Lying, covering up, explaining away or ignoring compulsive sexual behaviors are some of the unhealthy ways

we may cope. We stifle the inner voice telling us something is wrong. We accept promises like "it won't happen again" many times over, and in effect, enable the addiction. With the denial of reality, our lives become increasingly unmanageable.

Our efforts to control escalate in an attempt to alleviate the strain. We tell ourselves that if only we could somehow change—for example, be more (or less) attractive, provocative, intelligent, competent—we could change another person's sexual behavior.[6]

S-Anon states:

We tried every known method to control it. We lied and covered up, spied at doorways, listened to private conversations, checked up on the sexaholic's whereabouts, read through journals and personal papers, begged, pleaded and threatened... No matter how we tried to struggle against it, deny it or minimize its effects, the failure of our efforts to cope with sexaholism brought us to the point of despair.[7]

While we recognize that such behavior can produce a disintegration of its own, we understand that it's a partner's desperate need for truth and efforts to prevent further pain that fuel searches for signs when changes in a spouse's attitude and behavior cause fear that he or she is back into the sexual addiction.

The Importance of Knowing the Whole Truth

The addiction model not only labels a partner's need to know the truth as a "disease," but in doing so it also minimizes the urgency a trauma victim feels to prevent further pain. Partners of sex addicts need to know the truth; they need to know what the one they love has and has not done sexually. Until he or she deciphers the truth, a partner can't know the loved one, what STDs he or she might be carrying or what activities he or she is forgiving when he or she is finally ready to forgive. Nor can the partner decide if he or she wants to leave the relationship or stay and try to rebuild the marriage if the other partner is willing to do the hard work that entails.

Partners Seek Truth, Not Control

Partners seek *truth,* not control, though many fail to understand this. A partner's motivation for truth stems from the need to once again feel safe—to keep the environment safe to prevent further trauma and pain. Like a typhoon victim, he or she seeks higher, drier ground.

For that reason, some counselors and psychologists who specialize in sex addiction *require* the sex addicts they work with to take a lie detector test (polygraph test) in the beginning of treatment.[8] Some require follow-up polygraphs as well. These helpful professionals know from experience that addicts struggle with truth; they find it much easier to deceive, or at least omit certain elements of their stories, in their efforts to hold their lives together. These sex addiction professionals also know that healing cannot begin until everyone is operating from a foundation of truth.

But the use of polygraphs remains controversial in many people's minds. Yet even though they cannot be deemed 100 percent fail-safe, police departments and prison systems continue to use them, because they provide the best technology available to decipher fact from fiction. As for partners of sex addicts, the polygraphs can play a huge role in establishing a foundation of truth on which to begin to build a new marriage based on honesty and a slow-growing sense of trust. A polygraph test—and the knowledge there will be more tests in the future—turned Annette's story into one of hope and new beginnings. Annette shares:

When sex addiction erupted in my marriage a second time, I was devastated that I was being dragged through it again. To try to save our marriage we spent three days in an intensive, which meant just the two of us in all-day-long therapy with a therapist who specializes in sex addiction. A polygraph test for my husband was a part of the deal. What we gained from the three days was amazing, but what I personally got from the polygraph turned my world around. Before the test I was very depressed, I cried a lot, I felt mad at the way things had turned out and I isolated myself, which is not like me at all. I didn't even answer the phone. But after the polygraph and the intensive, my depression lifted. I knew I had learned the whole truth because of the test; all the dark things were now in the light and my husband had nothing more to hide. It felt freeing for him to tell. Knowing what was real and what wasn't freed me to start over again, because I knew what he was saying to me was the truth. What he said now had merit in my mind—it could be believed. And that gave me a lot of strength and hope. And there are follow-up polygraphs coming in future sessions we scheduled with our therapist. Just knowing they are out there on the calendar has released me from the feeling that I need to try to control his recovery in order to protect my children and myself from a third round of his addiction. It seems to be helping my husband, too, because he's taking more responsibility for building in the safeguards that protect his recovery.

Annette would probably tell you that attempting to control the addict in order to gain safety never worked for her, that it always fails. Partners need new methods. In addition, they need help from others. On these principles, the trauma model and the addiction/12-step model agree. But when a partner reaches out for help, will he or she find true empathy and understanding for the trauma and loss that was experienced? Or will he or she quickly be labeled "as sick as the sex addict" and considered to be a co-addict?

One sure way to gain an accurate perspective on a partner's true condition comes by examining motivation. Simply listening with an empathic heart and a sincere desire to recognize true motivation can boil it all down to basics and provide clarity in our confusion, whether we are doing a self-examination or seeking to understand a client.

> *On A Personal Note: As you read about the differences between codependency and trauma, what are your thoughts? Does the term "codependency" describe your behaviors or do you identify with the idea of safety-seeking behaviors? Do both instances make sense to you?*

Recognizing and Understanding a Partner's Motivation

Motives drive us to take certain actions in life; they form the reasons we do the things we do. Thus, motivation presents a good place to start when we feel confused about co-addiction and codependency. Here is some advice we believe invaluable when used as a tool for self-evaluation. Ask yourself: Is your motivation to boost your power over others or is it to seek the safety you need in an unsafe situation to prevent further trauma and pain?

Why We Believe it's Important to Re-Frame a Partner's Reactions as Trauma

It Acknowledges the Partner's Symptoms as Predictable Reactions to Traumatic Stress

Even months into the healing process, trauma can continue to create difficulties for a partner struggling to heal and regain emotional footing. Myra still felt its effects fourteen months after learning about her husband's sexual addiction:

> I've been thinking about my reaction yesterday. I don't know much about PTSD, but I feel like this anxiety reaction could be because of my trauma. I still feel unsettled this morning. I feel sick to my stomach and very nervous, kind of shaky inside. My husband hasn't done or said anything today that should be upsetting. In fact, he's been loving and considerate. Even when he told me he had been tested for STDs it didn't upset me, yet I can't shake these feelings. I feel like such a flake. I just want to feel normal again. My disorganization is driving me nuts. I need to pull myself together and get some order inside me. To others I appear together, but inside I feel like I'm losing it!

It Validates the Partner's Pain

Unless those helping partners recognize and validate a partner's deepest pain, a partner can never truly heal. Yet once he or she receives the gifts of empathy and validation from those who seek to help, the door to healing slowly begins to open.

It Encourages the Partner to Share His or Her Story in Safe Settings and a Guided Format to Ease the Pain

The trauma model honors the retelling of the partner's story in various ways to externalize the problem and let go of the pain. Seen through a trauma lens, a partner's story becomes the thread woven through several stages of healing and trauma recovery.

It Places the Responsibility for the Addiction on the Sex Addict, Not on the Partner

The trauma approach does not blame the victim, but empowers him or her. And once a partner tastes his or her own empowerment, she can feel as strong as if she was backed by an army.

The Partner Becomes Responsible for Setting Boundaries if Choosing to Stay in the Relationship

A part of healing in the trauma model involves increasing the partner's sense of personal power or choice, so he or she can exercise his or her own choice and control in important areas of life. We seek to find the areas where the partner is *not* powerless and build on those to empower him or her to make further changes.

It Provides Diagnostic Understanding for Partners with Learned Helplessness

Learned helplessness is a condition that follows repeated attempts to affect change in one's life without adequate *power and support* to produce the needed change. Learned helplessness often becomes evident in abuse victims—people stay in destructive relationships, simply because over time they've come to believe they are helpless or powerless to make change, so they give up on trying.

Living with repeated, long-term sexual addiction can produce this effect, especially in those who have lived with abuse during childhood or in previous relationships. Yet when a counselor, minister or doctor recognizes this as a side effect of his client's trauma rather than of a disease, change and renewed personal empowerment becomes possible.

The Trauma Model Seeks to Connect the Partner to a Support System for Healing

Both the trauma model and the 12-step model recommend support through connection with others who understand your pain as the cornerstone healing. None of us can do it alone.

Is 12-Step Recovery Work a Good Adjunct in Your Healing Journey?

Let's let Carol answer that question for us. After several years in her 12-step group for partners of sex addicts (which she remains active in), Carol joined one of Marsha's *Partner's Healing Journey* telephone support groups. Before long, it became apparent that her years of hard 12-step work and growth had transformed her life. Here Carol shares a part of her story:

By the year 2000, my marriage had grown so bad that it felt horrible. I consoled myself by thinking, *At least he isn't having an affair.* But simultaneously I knew my frustration and unhappiness was fueling impatience and shortness with the kids, and I didn't like it. That's when I decided to get help for my own issues. I shared with safe friends—some of whom had lived through their own marital problems. As I listened to their experiences, I began to realize that *something* must be going on with my husband. So I prayed for truth.

At that time, my husband and I had a mutual e-mail account. One day, I saw some odd emails from other men in the inbox and I decided to check them out. It was then I discovered he was involved in unknown activities of a possible homosexual nature.

Again I prayed, this time asking for clarity as I waited. Three months later my husband admitted to me that he believed himself to be a sex addict. I was numb. I was in a fog. I struggled with horrible anxiety. I did crazy things like forgetting appointments for the kids; my mind was just overloaded with pain and pressure from the fear and uncertainty about my family and future. The anxiety was so bad that in the afternoons I had to take brisk walks before picking the kids up from school so I could be the mom I needed to be for them.

Fortunately, I had a neighbor who got me started in a 12-step recovery group. It was there that I first began to realize my father was a sex addict as well. I came to see that I grew up in a sex addict's home and now I was married to one, too! During that time I began to feel rage about all of it. I also became aware of my codependency.

The group educated me about all of this, and it gave me tools to do something about what I needed to fix in myself. I got a sponsor and, with her help, I worked the 12 steps, which enabled me to begin tackling my character defects. I learned about detachment, I utilized the slogans and I had the support of the other women in my group. There I learned an important lesson: If you are hit by a truck driven by a drunk, you don't lie in the road waiting for the truck or its drunk driver to help you. You know you need the help of others if you want to heal. And so it is when we live with a sex addict: We need to make sure we get the resources to help *us* heal, no matter what the addict does or does not do.

Yet with the wealth of tools, skills and health I had gained—and continue to gain—from my 12-step codependency recovery group and friends, healing the deep pain and trauma of my shattered dreams came from the work I've done with my gifted counselor. I'm so grateful that she understands sex addiction and its impact on me and my life. She understands that I get triggered, because I'm in an intimate relationship with a man who often does not consider my needs. Where some in 12-step circles would say that if I'm triggered I need to "step up my program," she recognizes that the triggers are not my fault. Rather, they are a by-product of the trauma of being in an intimate relationship with a man whose sex addiction has deeply wounded me and, at times, continues to wound me.

If a woman looks messy it doesn't always mean she's a co-addict. Instead, it usually means she would benefit from work with a counselor who understands her trauma and anger; one who can help her deal with the pain, in addition to having a sponsor if she's already working the 12 steps.

We agree with Carol: If a partner looks messy, it does not always mean he or she is a co-addict. In nearly every case we discover a traumatized partner in desperate need of help under the messy exterior. And without that help, far too many partners develop long-term trauma complications and untreated trauma eats away at their emotional and physical health. We'll examine the health aspects of trauma in the next chapter.

Self-Check: You've read a lot of information about trauma and a need for safety as a motivator or drive for your behaviors. Take a look at the following list of behaviors. Which behaviors do you find yourself engaging in? Are you looking to feel safer, or are you trying to control the addict? Place a check under "safety" or "control" to identify your motivation/reason for the behavior. (You may have some, all or none of these behaviors.)

Behavior	Motivation (what am I seeking)	
	Safety	Control
1. Checking (Internet, wallet, cell phone, etc.)		
2. Calling partner frequently		
3. Angry outbursts		
4. Obsessing about the addict's behaviors		
5. Avoiding sexual intimacy		
6. Keeping secrets about the addiction		
7. Trying to forget about the problem		
8. Threatening to leave (or did leave)		
9. Participating in the addict's behaviors		
10. Changing my appearance		
11. Giving up things I enjoy doing		
12. Shutting down emotionally or physically		

Chapter 5

Trauma Impacts on Every Level: Potential Physical and Mental Health Side Effects of Trauma

Toni tells her story, vividly describing the shock and pain of discovering her husband's sexual addiction:

It all began one Saturday in July, one month before our twenty-eighth wedding anniversary. I walked into the den and there on top of the shredder were instructions for deleting our computer history. When I asked my husband about this, he mumbled, "I don't know." But within a few minutes he suddenly blurted out: "I like to look at naked women!"

Though his face showed anger—or maybe it was frustration—I don't remember if he said any other words. My mind had gone numb and everything became a blur when I heard the words "naked women." I was in total shock. This was not the man I knew. He showed no remorse or compassion at how his news affected me.

During the next three months, my husband told me he looked at pornography on the Internet and watched pornographic movies while I was away. Instead of giving me a full confession at one sitting, he revealed bits and pieces of the truth, dribbling it out over time. And each time he told me more details, it felt like he was stabbing me in the heart with a knife, plunging it in again and again. I begged him to stop leaking the disclosures out slowly, but he didn't seem to care how it impacted me. At times the pain was indescribable and I could hardly breathe. I spiraled into a deep pit of depression and I couldn't stop crying.

To make matters worse, I was unexpectedly laid off my job. My boss said it wasn't personal—but it was very personal to me. It felt like a slap in my face. Between my husband's revelations and my job loss, some days I found it difficult to even get out of bed. My life as I knew it was shattered and I had no idea what to do or how to start over.

My emotions bounced all over. At times I was angry. I didn't want to know anything about sex addiction; this was not supposed to be a part of my life! Even though it was my husband's problem, it had changed my world forever! At other times, I was so consumed with sadness, because my heart had been so broken that I thought I was going to die. The pain was so intense and deep, but I always woke up in the morning. I hurt so bad that I didn't think I'd ever smile or laugh again.

Over the next several weekends, my husband made more disclosures. One in particular blasted me into an even deeper depression and brought a new flood of tears. He confessed that for the last thirteen years he had only fantasized about and masturbated to the thought of one person: a lovely young woman who is one of my closest relatives; someone whom I love like the daughter I never had. I learned that for thirteen years he had been raping her in his mind, and some of these fantasies happened while she was a guest in our home!

Within a few days, my lower back and sciatic nerve began to hurt. I had herniated four disks and experienced two agonizing days eight months earlier, but why was the pain suddenly back? Each day the pain grew increasingly intense as I felt the muscles in my back tighten up more and more. We were scheduled to fly to Texas for a marital intensive with a sex addiction specialist. As our departure date drew closer, I could hardly sit or walk; how could I possibly fly?

I made an appointment with the doctor who was treating my back. I told him I hadn't done anything to re-injure my back; I also told him what had happened to my marriage. He examined me then gently said, "Toni, it's the marital stress that is causing your terrible pain." He gave me prescriptions for pain medication and a muscle relaxer then said, "Your pain will go away eventually."

Somehow, I made it to Texas and through three days of intense therapy—including my husband's complete disclosure, followed by a polygraph test—and back again without dying. I felt certain that once our trip was over my pain would go away, because those three days changed our lives and gave me hope for our marriage as I saw and heard my husband take responsibility for his choices and his behavior. However, the pain only continued to get worse. Soon I couldn't sit for even a few minutes, because the white-hot pain from my sciatic nerve radiated across my buttocks and down my leg with such intensity.

It's been two months now since the trip to Texas and even with lots of medication, there have been many days when I could find no relief. But lately, little by little, I'm beginning to experience days when my pain level stays in the low range and the pills I need to take are few.

During this time, the pain's pattern has become clear to both of us: it obviously parallels the relational cycles in our marriage. As we do better, my body seems to be able to relax little by little and I'm beginning to hope that one day before too long I'll be free to try to rebuild and live my life again. I know it won't be easy and it won't happen all at once, but for today I feel a little hope.

Toni's story echoes the realization behind the famous words of microbiologist Rene Dubois, a French-American Pulitzer Prize winner who wrote, "What happens in the mind of man is always reflected in the disease of the body." Even before Dubois's time— nearly 100 years ago—Harvard physiologist Walter Cannon realized that when confronted by a threat, including emotional threats, the body responds by increasing blood pressure, heart rate, muscle tension and breathing rate.

Increasingly, science and medicine have come to see that the mind and body function as a single unit. Breakthrough research illuminates formerly unknown truths of human anatomy including the theory that such "traumas may temporarily or permanently alter not only people's capacity to cope, their perception of threat, and their concept of themselves and the world, but their very biology."[1]

We now know that the body's response to stress and trauma involves hormones and inflammatory chemicals which can foster everything from headaches to heart attacks, particularly in chronically traumatic lives. These medical realities can wreak havoc on both the physical and mental well-being of partners of sex addicts when their circumstances don't change or when they develop PTSD.

The risks these realities pose to the quality of our lives deserve our focused attention and well-thought out action, not only as individuals experiencing them in the present, but also as friends, family members and mental health professionals who will likely confront an opportunity to help someone else through the pain that comes with sexual betrayal. Learning how to respond proactively in the face of deception can mean the difference between a life filled with emotional and physical pain or one invested with good health and the joy of being alive.

Trauma, PTSD and Your Brain

To begin to understand the emotional and physical ramifications sex addiction can launch in a partner's life, we first need to understand the physiology and neurochemistry of trauma and what it does to our bodies, including our brains. Only then can we begin to learn how to care for ourselves and others in betrayal's dark shadow.

Fear Activates the Amygdala

Let's discuss the amygdala as we examine how trauma affects the brain. The amygdala, an almond-shaped structure just one inch in length that sits a few inches from either ear, has long been known to play a major role in a person's mental and emotional state. Only in recent years has science begun to uncover what really takes place in the amygdala when we experience stress, fear and trauma, and why humans can prove impotent to counter the automatic responses launched by our brains as they commandeer systems throughout our bodies.

Fear activates the amygdala, propelling signals throughout the body long before the rational mind can begin to grasp what's taking place. In fact, research shows that your alerted amygdala can get the word out to every region of your anatomy in microseconds.

As the amygdala goes into overdrive, it sends messages to the hypothalamus, which in turn signals the pituitary and adrenal glands to flood the bloodstream with epinephrine—better known as adrenaline—as well as norepinephrine and coritisol. These stress hormones take charge in commando-like fashion, sending orders throughout the body and shutting down non-emergency systems, including digestion and immunity. Simultaneously, "The amygdala tells the rest of the brain, 'Hey, whatever happened, make a strong memory of it'," says James McGaugh, a neurobiologist quoted in Geoffrey Cowley's *Newsweek* article. [2]

As everyone who has ever lived through the discovery of their partner's sexual betrayal knows, our brains do indeed make indelible memories of the traumatic events; events that, for some, continue to replay like old home movies, even after they tire of the scenes that run and rerun in the theaters of their minds. Wanda, a young wife struggling against that pain, emailed in the dark hours of a difficult night saying:

> I'm having a terrible night. I can't stop crying. The movies in my head keep portraying what he's done and the deep pain from his betrayal won't quit. It's all so relentless. Please tell me I won't hurt like this forever.

Where Does Stress End and Trauma Begin?
We've all felt the panic of stress as chemicals dump into our systems and anxiety overwhelms us. But does that equal trauma? No, there are understandable differences between stress and trauma. Trauma generally hits you suddenly, like an avalanche. It leaves you feeling powerless, helpless and paralyzed. The effect is longer lasting and, like that avalanche, it buries you, robbing you of life functions. You lose your ability to think, to plan, to cope, even as you're forced to attempt to figure out how to survive. Trauma clinician and researcher Bessel van der Kolk, M.D., tells us, "The critical difference between a stressful but normal event and trauma is a feeling of helplessness to change the outcome....As long as people can imagine having some control over what is happening to them, they usually can keep their wits about them." [3] An excerpt from Marsha's journal, written during the

years when sex addiction slowly deteriorated her marriage, reflects
the important distinction between everyday stress and trauma that
Dr. van der Kolk explains.

A part of me feels disconnected from my body—as if
my thoughts have become a separate observer of what is
unfolding in the unspoken space between us, something so
everywhere it silently fills every cubic inch of our home. A
silence so heavy that at times it's almost physically painful, like
breathing air with too little oxygen.

Life is getting harder and harder. I can feel myself dying
and letting go. It's more than I can bear—the pain, the loneliness, the never knowing what will happen in the next
moment, the hot then cold, the love then hate, the closeness
then abandonment.

I'm sinking and can't seem to save myself. I feel flat,
directionless and without zeal for anything or anyone. I'm
sure the DSM IV would say that I am depressed, although I
don't feel the blackness of death sucking me into its swirling
vortex, a sucking that generally accompanies my depression. I
guess I've given up…on life, on him for sure, on dreams and
plans, hope and a future.

There is no point in breathing right now; no point in
waking up in the morning. No energy to get out of bed, to
hurry through the morning ritual of preparation to face the
world and run out into my day and move through it with
plans and goals. It's as if I'm in a stupor and can't determine
how to make my mind and body work together.

I remind myself of the main character in the movie *The
Pianist*. During the destruction of Warsaw, which looked like
a-hell-on-earth place and experience, he sometimes stumbled
from blown building to blown building, starving, sick, lonely,
with no real direction, except survival, remembering only that
he was trying to somehow stay alive, often while cannon fire
was blowing apart the walls and ceilings around him. Like
him, I am often discombobulated, lost, without direction.
And it's so unlike me. I'm usually so goal-oriented and able to
accomplish what I need and want over enough time to make
it happen. Now, all the parts of me are at war with their own

members, and I feel so many conflicted feelings at one time.

I'm so tired. So very, very tired. A part of me wants to just go to bed tonight and never wake up. The pain is agonizing and so exhausting. When will it ever end? Or will it? Tell me; will I carry this deep, "knife-through-my-soul" feeling with me until I die? If so, God, how can I bear it?

Action's Countering Force

When faced with overwhelming fear, threat or loss—such as the loss of attachment, security and safety in your most intimate relationship—the long-term impact it will have on you hangs *in part* on whether or not you believe you can exert some control over your own life and the shape of your personal world. In other words, if you believe you hold some power over your own safety and destiny and act on that belief, you increase your chances for healing earlier.

Dr. van der Kolk reports that if one can stay "...focused on problem solving, on doing something, however small, about the situation—rather than concentrating on one's distress—[it] reduces the chances of developing post-traumatic stress disorder."[4] Concurrently, David Baldwin, Ph.D., writes that "PTSD is also more likely if passive defenses, such as freezing or dissociation, are used—rather than active defenses such as fight or flight."[5]

Unfortunately, when you are suddenly railroaded by a traumatic event, you rarely have the chance to choose whether or not to take action rather than freeze or dissociate. The overall impact of the event, plus your personal trauma history, more or less determines what your response will be in those moments. Yet information is power and it can only better equip you to face your own pain as a survivor, rather than a victim.

Principle 1: If I believe I hold enough power to do something about my situation and act on that belief, my efforts will help me survive and heal.

However, this action-oriented approach is easier when a trauma victim truly believes he or she has some power over the circumstances. Feeling helpless—or powerless—in the face of tragedy and loss creates a setup for PTSD. In a word, action—or empowerment—can help you escape PTSD in many circumstances. The opposite of action in this case is dissociation. Dr. van der Kolk explains: "...spacing out (dissociating) during a traumatic event often predicts the development of subsequent PTSD. *The longer the traumatic experience lasts, the more likely the victim is to react by dissociating (separating those thoughts away from the rest of the mind). Once a person dissociates, he becomes incapable of goal-directed action* [italics added][6]."

As Heather, a counseling professional, looked back on her experience with a sexually addicted husband and shared it with us, she clearly saw how her lack of belief in her power to induce change in her situation contributed to her own PTSD.

I remember how very early in the downward spiral of my marriage, we sought help from a counselor who worked with our health insurance plan. After having each of us share during that initial session, she gave me a homework assignment that I was to bring back the following week.

She said, "Heather, I want you to write a story. In it you are the main character. You are an eight-year-old girl and you have just moved to a new city and today is the first day at your new school. You are outside for your first recess and you're wearing a red coat. It's cold and you love that red coat. But two boys who are bullies begin to taunt you and soon they rip your coat right off you and threaten to hurt you the next time if you tattle on them.

"Now Heather, I want you to finish the story and bring it back next week. You are in a tough situation and faced with some difficult choices. How are you going to get your coat back without risking further harm and making more enemies?"

I'm embarrassed to say I never went back. "Why?" you might ask. I didn't go back, because I couldn't figure out how to get that coat back without making things worse! I felt just as stymied in the make-believe situation as I was in my marriage. I knew I couldn't actually *change* those boys—or my husband—and I let that realization block my ability to find ways to help *myself* in a difficult situation. I had already dissociated from my personal power when it came to men, a by- product of another traumatic experience that happened decades earlier. While this wise counselor sought to empower me through a metaphor, I remained trapped in my feelings of helplessness and I failed to accept her offer. Sadly, many partners of sexual addicts exhibit similar behavior.

Principle 2: Taking action to help myself early in the situation can help me prevent PTSD.

The Power of Powerlessness

Unfortunately, many partners of sex addicts cannot find ways to change or escape their situations, especially if they still have young children at home and they can't earn enough money to seek outside help and support themselves. Often, older partners, too, feel restrained from challenging sexual betrayal because their retirement, old age security and savings are so intertwined with their spouses'. Compounding the dilemma, many sex addicts feed their partners' disempowering self-beliefs by maintaining economic control of household income and financial records.

Frequently, the addict also controls his or her joint support system; the addict tells family and friends stories that work in his or her favor, leaving the partner without the emotional and social support one needs, in addition to monetary challenges.

Circumstances like these present traps that many partners feel powerless to pry open under their own force. However, their power-lessness comes with a price: "The immediate effects of prolonged trauma...recur with each new wave of traumatic experience. The long-term effects include post-traumatic stress disorder, complex post-traumatic stress disorder and a variety of mental and physical illnesses."[7]

These marital traps can bind a partner indefinitely and fuel a cycle of trauma —> powerlessness —> more trauma —> increased powerlessness as he or she falls victim to an ongoing sense of powerlessness. In the face of their own powerlessness, many partners choose "emotion-focused" change instead.

The Mistake of "Emotion-Focused" Change

Some partners of sex addicts believe they can ignore the circum-stances that create their overwhelming pain and attempt to change their "...emotional state instead of the circumstances giving rise to it."[8] This method of dealing with—or rather *not* dealing with—trauma is called choosing an "emotion-focused" outlook. With such an outlook, we give up trying to do anything concrete and proactive about the negative consequences our spouses' sexual betrayals produce in our marriages, our families and our lives and try instead to change the way *we feel* about their actions.

A few partners do this by having affairs of their own, believing that if they "level the playing field" they will no longer care or hurt when their spouses act out. Others simply determine to harden their hearts like stone so that no emotional pain can possibly take root there. This, they believe, will eliminate any pain their spouses' behavior might inflict in the future.

However, this never returns our lives to health and balance and that lack of balance triggers further consequences to our health. We're cautioned that, "Failing to reset their equilibrium after a traumatic experience, people are prone to develop the cluster of symptoms that we diagnose as PTSD."[9]

Principle 3: Changing our feelings, rather than our unhealthy circumstances, fuels a sense of powerlessness that often leads to PTSD.

Neurochemical and Physiological Differences between Trauma and PTSD

Although a full discussion of what goes on in the brain and throughout the body in the face of trauma lies beyond the scope of this text, it remains important for us to catch a glimpse of the complex chemical responses trauma triggers, as well as the longer lasting threat the chemistry of PTSD thrusts into our lives. Only as we grasp and accept trauma's truths can we think and act proactively on our own behalves in the face of ongoing trauma and respond in grace, true helpfulness and support when people we know or serve face the personal disaster and loss that comes with sexual betrayal. So let's go one step further and attempt to understand the neurochemical and physiolgical ways PTSD differs from trauma.

Enter PTSD

While living with trauma feels excruciating and can convolute your life, PTSD can shatter your ability to cope and compound your pain. "Those suffering from PTSD can have trouble functioning in their jobs or relationships. ...*Many people with PTSD repeatedly re-experience the ordeal in the form of flashback episodes, memories, nightmares, or frightening thoughts, especially when they are exposed to events or objects that remind them of the trauma* [italics added]," the American Psychological Association Web site tells us.[10] These events or objects are known as "triggers." And because a trigger can cross your path suddenly and unexpectedly, PTSD can turn your world upside down without a moment's notice, sometimes years after the original traumatizing event has slipped into the past.

Old triggers nearly cost Tanya a second chance at happiness years after relational betrayal ended her first marriage.

By the time I met my present husband, Matt, I had lived through several traumatic life experiences, including betrayal trauma. I carried the remnants of those old wounds into our early courtship. However, from the time we met over eighteen years ago, Matt has played a big role in my healing.

It all started one weekend early in our dating when I drove several hours to his house for a visit. When I arrived, I found a note he'd left me. It said he was sorry but he had forgotten he promised to help some friends move that morning. But the time he said he'd return wasn't far off, so I thought, *No problem*, and I settled in.

But when that time came and went with no sign of him, I was suddenly overcome with a quickly-building, intense sense of panic.

Still, when he did arrive a short while later he seemed clearly happy to see me. However, by then I was shaking uncontrollably and my mind was racing with thoughts that were telling me how unsafe it was to trust him.

He was bewildered by my condition and couldn't understand when I explained, "I have to get out of here! I can't be in a relationship!"

Matt knew my history, but this was his first encounter with its impact in my life. Yet what he did at that moment couldn't have been more powerful for me if he'd planned it. With a very gentle expression on his face, he looked into my eyes as though I was a friend he cared for deeply, a whole person. "Tanya," he said, "you gave your former husband twelve years of your life! Are you going to give him the rest of it?"

Just as Tanya's PTSD was triggered by reminders of her betrayal experience, a large percentage of partners of sexual addicts suffer the same symptoms. Tanya and Matt's story has a happy ending, because she has worked hard to heal at every level of her being. But many partners aren't so fortunate. Often their PTSD triggers are misunderstood and mislabeled, quickly categorized as codependency and their PTSD remains untreated.

Principle 4: Things that remind you of your trauma can trigger flashbacks, panic attacks and more, leaving you feeling powerless to control your behavior and manage your life.

Clearly, PTSD's devastating grip can squeeze all hope of a normal life beyond the reach of its victims. But what internal and chemical changes account for the functional differences between trauma and PTSD?

The Chemistry Behind Indiscriminate Fight or Flight Responses

One difference involves cortisol levels. Studies have revealed that, unlike the high levels of cortisol seen in trauma cases, cortisol levels in people with PTSD are quite low.

Dr. van der Kolk explains:

Studies over two decades have shown that people with PTSD develop abnormalities in the brain chemicals (neurotransmitters) that regulate arousal and attention... while acute stress normally activates the stress hormone cortisol, people with PTSD have relatively low levels of cortisol.... In people with PTSD, increased arousal accompanied by low cortisol levels provoke indiscriminate fight or flight reactions.

...The vulnerability of people with PTSD to overreact to emotional and sensory stimuli shows up in their behavior as increased impulsivity and anxiety.[11]

For partners who have suffered with their spouses' sexual betrayals, this means that behaviors which might look and sound like codependency may indeed *actually* be generated by PTSD's indiscriminate fight or flight reactions.

Principle 5: Your behaviors that may look and sound like codependency may actually be generated by PTSD's indiscriminate fight or flight reactions.

On A Personal Note: Have you experienced the "fight or flight" reaction in response to your partner's addiction and behaviors?

PTSD's Impact on the Brain Can Skew Your Judgment

Another difference involves the prefrontal cortex. Daniel Sweeney, Ph.D., cautions that "...people with PTSD may experience a deactivation of the prefrontal cortex (which is responsible for executive function). This interferes with their ability to measure and respond to threats."[12]

This inability to measure and respond to threats with accuracy means our judgment about people, events and conversations can become skewed. And skewed judgment can create all kinds of trouble in our lives. No wonder we sometimes question our own realities and feel confused about what's true and what's not.

Principle 6: If your thoughts or actions seem out of sync with others whom you respect, it may be that your prefrontal lobe has been deactivated by PTSD and your judgment is skewed.

PTSD Interferes With One's Ability to Self-Sooth

To make matters worse, the normal human ability to ground ourselves and return to emotional homeostasis when we feel upset becomes affected by PTSD. "For traumatized people who develop PTSD...this capacity to sooth oneself is compromised."[13] Without that ability, PTSD sufferers often exhibit anxiety, insomnia, racing thoughts and other symptoms that only add to their pain and inability to cope. In addition, they frequently turn to replacement soothers such as food, alcohol or other unhealthy or harmful behaviors to self-medicate PTSD's tortuous emotional pain.

"Speechless Terror"

The high levels of neurochemical arousal that induce feelings of fear, anxiety, panic and terror wreak havoc on the important functioning of a region of the brain known as Broca's area, the area we rely on to translate our feelings into words. One study suggests that "...when people with PTSD are reliving their trauma, they have great difficulty putting that experience into words."[14] They suffer what Dr. van der Kolk refers to as "speechless terror."

This often exhibits in a partner's inability to tell even a counselor or support group his or her true feelings, because he or she does not know. The partner may know he or she hurts; the partner may know he or she is angry, but the road to deeper emotions remains blocked by PTSD.

Principle 7: If you have difficulty articulating your story or your feelings, it does not mean you are being codependent, you are being difficult or you're stupid. It likely means that the Broca's area in your brain has been affected and non-talk-based therapy will probably prove more helpful to you.

Nature's Just-As-If Response

Perhaps PTSD's most humiliating and most misunderstood component comes with the boomerang-like effect of its "just-as-if response." Dr. van der Kolk explains it this way:

> Confronted with an experience that includes elements of their original trauma, people with PTSD may react as if they were going through it again. Specifically, when enough of their sensations (such as being touched in a particular way, being exposed to certain smells, or seeing images that remind them of the earlier event) match imprints from the original

trauma, these people activate biological systems that make them react as if they were being traumatized anew [italics added]. In short, they have conditioned psychophysiological and neuroendocrine responses to reminders of the trauma.[15]

When a partner of a sex addict has PTSD, just being in a situation that brings back the memories of the original betrayal *can produce a response—such as panic, fleeing, weeping and often dissociation—just like the original event did.* This helps explain why a reminder of your sexual betrayal, even a sexy movie scene or a beautiful person in your spouse's presence, can trigger an old response that looks ludicrous to others, yet it remains outside your ability to stop or control.

Dr. van der Kolk goes on to say:

> The amygdala acts like a smoke detector to ascertain whether incoming sensory information spells a threat, and creates emotional memories in response to particular sensations, sounds, and images that it associated with threats to life and limb. When someone is exposed to stimuli that represents danger, signals calling for protection pass from the amygdala to the rest of the body. These emotionally labeled sensations are believed to be indelible, or at least extraordinarily difficult to extinguish. Once the amygdala is programmed to remember particular sounds, smells and bodily sensations as dangerous, a person is likely always to respond to those stimuli as a trigger for fight or flight reactions.[16]

Many partners of sexual addicts encounter this reality in their lives and when they do, the scene it creates can derail them at best, and at worst, it can leave them feeling totally humiliated and thrown back in time, caught up in their own traumas all over again. Rochelle shared such an event with us; one that she hopes never revisits her life.

> My husband loves thriller movies: the kind with cops and robbers, chase scenes—movies that are usually somewhat violent by my standards and usually include at least some sex. Because his sexual addiction hurt me deeply and because I lived through an abusive first marriage, I worked hard for

years to free myself from the dissociative disorder that resulted from my PTSD. To take care of myself, I had made it clear to my husband that I no longer wanted to accompany him to thrillers that might trigger any old response.

One evening, a new thriller he was dying to see was playing at our local cinema. He wanted me to go with him and make it a date night. He had already read the book the movie was based on so I felt fairly comfortable with his knowledge of what I could expect on the screen. But I asked him to read the movie reviews online to make sure it was one I could handle without being triggered. He did and he reassured me it would be okay, so off we went.

A lot of in-your-face-violence and some sex soon filled the big screen. This stuff is too much for me on a television screen, but on a bigger-than-life movie screen, it totally overwhelms and overpowers my ability to stay grounded and not dissociate. Sitting there, struggling to stay present, I was filled with anger at my husband for intentionally putting me in this situation yet again.

Within moments, it was as if I was back in time, trapped in my own pain all over again. I knew I had to get out of there. I leaned over and told my husband I had to leave, but he just kept on watching the scenes in front of him. Before I knew what was happening, I got up and hurried through the darkened room and out the exit door.

By the time I hit the cold, drizzly night air, I was operating on primal survival instincts. I might as well have been a wounded animal searching the darkness for safety. Home was five miles away. My husband had the car key. It was raining. None of that stopped the panic, the force that propelled me forward.

In an out-of-body experience, I began working my way through dark streets, up hills, to the highway and through neighborhoods, always trying to avoid being seen; always fearful of being caught, trapped, exposed again. Sensible? No, but that was beside the point in those moments. My need for safety pushed me onward.

It turned out to be a very long walk, and the next part is really embarrassing to admit. As I got closer to home, I knew enough time had passed for the movie to be over. That meant my husband could pass me on his way home. The thought of him seeing me walking home left me feeling exposed and petrified, even though he would never hurt me physically. Every time a car drew near I ducked into the darkness, hiding like a frightened animal. If the shape of the car could possibly be his, I ducked further into the cover of the night.

Suddenly, one of them *was* his. I darted into a housing development and crouched behind the corner of a stranger's home. The primal force within grew stronger still and my heart began to pound in my chest.

Then my husband turned into the development, too. Had he seen me? I wondered. I scurried to an island of dense shrubbery, crouched down and buried my form in its midst. My husband circled around slowly, with the window rolled down, calling my name into the night. But I stayed still, watching him as he drove back toward the quiet highway that took him home.

It's strange to look back on that night now, knowing how I behaved. To many and to myself—both then and now—it looks and sounds like pure insanity. Or at least co-addiction. Yet I know that if I were to place myself in a triggering situation—one that for me remains "dangerous"— and not do proactive self-care immediately, it could happen all over again. That will always feel both scary and strange.

Such is the fingerprint of PTSD on a life. Is it any wonder that those who don't understand trauma's impact may also misunderstand what it can do to the psyche and body and mislabel it?

Principle 8: Behaviors that may seem like outlandish or codependent reactions might very well be your body's PTSD response to triggers (information stored during a traumatic event in your life). Research shows that these automatic

physiological responses often extend beyond your conscious control unless therapeutic interventions can enable you, the PTSD sufferer, to integrate them into your larger story.

On A Personal Note: How have your responses to triggers affected you? Do you have a story similar to Rochelle's where your response was intensified? Talk to someone about your experience.

PTSD Can Interfere with Your Therapeutic Process

This motley assortment of symptoms—the "speechless terror," skewed judgment, inability to self-soothe and the indiscriminate fight-or-flight responses—can make navigating post-trauma life akin to driving at night without headlights in a foreign country without a map while drunk. Not an easy task to say the least.

Symptoms such as these can also interfere with the therapeutic process. While high levels of emotional and physiological arousal whirl within because of triggers they can't control, some partners find they are unable to use *words* to process all that whirling. As we discussed earlier in this chapter, their ability to articulate their pain may be handicapped by the Broca's area of their brains.

Your trauma can trap you in a catch-22: While your whole being is bound by the ropes of PTSD and screams for freedom, the language-generating region of your brain has been bound by the PTSD, too. You can no longer adequately *talk about and use words to process what you're experiencing.* Now the usual talking version of psychotherapy doesn't even help!

Earlier Life Trauma Can Set You Up for Trauma Later in Life

As we saw in Rochelle's story, trauma earlier in your life can set you up for later bouts with trauma by leaving you with an innate susceptibility to its influence and power. This tendency is often strongest for partners who suffered betrayal bond damage or trauma in childhood. A quote from the Healing Resources Web site explains this well:

> Children who fail to receive an adequate attachment bond with their primary caretaker because of abuse or unintentional neglect lack neurological means to calm, focus and soothe themselves. This lack of resiliency makes such individuals more at risk for traumatic experience in the future.

Without the ability to remain calm and stay focused in the face of painful, difficult and threatening experiences, we are overwhelmed and become traumatized.[17]

Events that can traumatize children include, among others, forced separation from their primary caregivers, poor care giving in general, living with physical or mental illness, depression or grief, extreme poverty, as well as emotional, verbal, physical or sexual abuse. Child trauma specialist Bruce Perry adds that "Simply stated, traumatic and neglectful experiences...cause abnormal organization and function of important neural systems in the brain..."[18]

As we search for ways to help ourselves and others, we need to take into account our childhood histories as well as our earlier adult life histories as we attempt to make sense of our trauma reactions and process and integrate them into our larger life stories. Seeking to heal from trauma without taking a look at our histories can severely handicap our healing process.

Principle 9: As you seek healing from trauma's impact on your life and health with the help of a professional trained in family-of-origin issues and trauma, examine and consider your childhood and previous adult-life experience for trauma that may play a role in your current reactions to new trauma.

Trauma's Body-Wide Damage

Sadly, both research and the everyday life struggles encountered by millions of trauma sufferers bear testimony to the all-encompassing impact that trauma can have on human health. One study reports that "Strong associations between betrayal trauma exposure and negative physical and psychological status were found in this sample of ill adults."[19]

Let's look at the ways trauma and PTSD can impact your health, both mentally and physically.

Trauma's Impact on Mental Health

Many mental health professionals have long been aware of the psychological effects of traumatizing experiences. And every partner of a sex addict has endured at least some of the long list of mental health ailments that trauma has been known to cause. The depression and brain fog alone can almost cripple a life with their symptoms.

Trauma specialist Daniel Sweeney, Ph.D., cautions that "It is important to realize that chronic exposure to traumatic stress affects the adaptation of these [neuro-] chemicals. In other words, it may permanently alter how people deal with their environment on a daily basis."[20]

Sweeney's strong words give us warning: to avoid such devastating damage we must take responsibility for dealing with our circumstances proactively, rather than letting traumatizing situations continue indefinitely.

Principle 10: It is up to you (with the help of the professionals who support you) to protect your health by courageously stepping out of traumatizing circumstances that can damage your body and mind.

Trauma's Supercharged Hormone Baths and Our Health

The supercharged hormone baths that are set off by the amygdala do extensive damage, especially when these baths become chronic, because fear and trauma continue in the circumstances of your life.

"Over time," says Christine Horner, M.D., "the continual stress reactions your body produces…become disastrous. This psycho-physiological response leaves us continually with chronic excess cortisol levels that cause high blood pressure, insomnia, anxiety, depression, frustration, anger, tension, depress the immune system and increase the risk of heart disease, diabetes and stomach ulcers."[21] Harvard neurologist Martin Samuels adds that "Norepinephrine is toxic to the tissues—probably all tissues, but in particular the heart."[22]

Clearly, prolonged stress, fear or trauma can take a major toll on your health, even without the onset of PTSD. It dampens the immune system, leaving us more susceptible to everything from colds to cancer. According to studies' data at the National Institutes of Health, approximately 90 percent of all illnesses— mental and physical—are caused or aggravated by stress. And certainly stress is present to the extreme when we experience the trauma of sexual betrayal.

Principle 11: As you seek to make decisions on your own behalf, you must take into account the massive toll that ongoing trauma may have on your and your children's health.

Cortisol: A Critical Culprit

When trauma continues over time, cortisol is a major culprit, producing disastrous effects on our bodies. Dr. Horner cautions what can happen under chronically stressful conditions:

...cortisol can be continually elevated in our body and can have damaging effects such as thinning of bones, diabetes, inflammation, cancer, fat deposition around the waistline and a weakened immune system. And cortisol can be extremely toxic to brain cells; high amounts for long periods of time can even cause brain cells to die. In addition, as we age our ability to turn off the cortisol response to stress slows down and this leads to elevated levels for longer periods of time...

Some of these chemical reactions also create oxygen free radicals, which are tiny molecules of unstable oxygen that can cause lots of destruction to cell membranes and DNA. The damage free radicals cause ignites and fuels most chronic degenerative diseases including heart disease, arthritis, Alzheimer's, aging, wrinkles and cancer.

...When cortisol goes up, blood sugar levels rise, inflammation levels go up. The blood becomes thick and sticky, and cancer cells spread more rapidly.

No wonder cortisol levels are correlated with increased cancer risk, particularly breast, as well as premature aging and diabetes, one of the fastest-growing diseases in the industrialized world today.[23]

Certified nutritional consultant Tarilee Cornish adds, "Our nervous system and endocrine systems communicate bi-directionally with our immune system in the 'language' of hormones and neuropeptides. This means that our emotions can induce health or illness and, in turn our state of health can induce emotions."[24]

This pattern—physical inducing emotional and emotional inducing physical—becomes circular and can complicate our attempts to break the self-perpetuating cycles it sets up in life.

Common Conditions that Trauma can Trigger
Trauma can foster a long list of common effects or conditions in emotional and physical health. Professionals who make trauma the focus of their work tell us: "Sometimes these responses can be delayed, for months or even years after the event. Often, people do not even initially associate their symptoms with the precipitating trauma."[25]

This resource goes on to reveal a long list of symptoms that can affect us physically, emotionally, cognitively or behaviorally, as well as affecting our ability to maintain healthy relationships. Complications from trauma are more likely to occur if there were earlier, overwhelming life experiences.

In our work with spouses, we've encountered other physical symptoms repeatedly. Fibromyalgia, chronic fatigue, hypothyroidism, adrenal exhaustion, inflammatory responses and susceptibility to infections appear often in partners' lives. As we can see, trauma— particularly when it continues over time—can spell disaster to our health.

Recognizing the impact that trauma has on our bodies provides help to understand why many of us have experienced devastating health changes since discovering our partners' addictions. In the face of all the evidence, can we, as partners, as mothers, as fathers, as daughters, as sons, afford to sink into powerless and "emotion-focused" thinking, rather than seeking help and taking positive, proactive steps that empower us to protect ourselves, even if our spouses refuse change or help?

Our desire is not to frighten partners of sex addicts with information about the danger their trauma imposes on their health. Rather, as members of this throng ourselves, we aim to empower partners to take charge of their lives and to find the necessary resources to get help, to move forward and to heal. In the next three chapters, we look closely at proactive steps you can take to protect your emotional and physical health from trauma's destructive impact and simultaneously advance your progress along the partner's healing journey.

On A Personal Note: Take some time and consider the effects of trauma you are experiencing. Do you have increased physical problems? A conversation with your medical professional can help to resolve these problems.

PART II

YOUR JOURNEY TOWARD WHOLENESS

Chapter 6

Healing from Trauma
and Post-Traumatic Stress

Katherine shares her need for support in order to regain a feeling of safety:

"I'm struggling with pornography," my husband calmly said. "This is not a new thing; it's been going on for years. I want to stop, but I need your help. I need you to hold me accountable." With that brief confession, my husband of three months shattered my dreams and my world.

Growing up, I was a goody-two-shoes and I stayed out of trouble. I was only eighteen when I married Neil, who, at twenty-six, was eight years older. Nothing in my short past had prepared me for the words that had just come out of his mouth. Suddenly, I felt so inadequate, so "second best."

His confession began our Friday night routine. At his request, every Friday evening I asked him one question: "How was your week?" Each week I heard a similar response. He told me how often he gave into sexual temptation, how many magazines he bought, what porn movies he watched on business trips. I tried to understand and be supportive of his attempts to overcome his addiction, but every few weeks I broke down and had a good cry. I could never measure up to those pictures. How could he say he loved me, yet continue to damage our marriage and our intimacy?

Nonetheless, my questions found no answers. Our Friday night ritual continued for fourteen years, through the birth of four beautiful children and the building of a full life. His addiction did not get any better for a long time.

Then one day Neil told me he was free from all temptation in regards to his pornography use. It was hard to believe what he was saying, but he was so convincing. To my knowledge he had never lied to me, so in the end I believed him. Yet I knew something was wrong because our physical intimacy completely stopped.

In every other way, I loved my life. We were very active in our church. I volunteered in another ministry and also at the school our youngest attended, where I eventually became the administrator. Though Neil traveled a lot for his employer, he was well respected in his field. Life was good! Everything but our sex life, that is. It remained non-existent for eight long years. I begged him to get help, but he always said he was getting help, and he always gave reasons for not wanting sex.

Then came that fateful day, April 1, which I described earlier in chapter 1, when the six police officers knocked on our door, came in and began their investigation. When they finally left late in the night, sleep eluded my exhausted mind and body. All I could do was curl up in bed, pray and weep.

Though I had tried to protect my twelve-year-old when the police had come to our house by taking him to his room and turning up his television set, he heard the police anyway. He later told me, "When the police came in our house I prayed, 'Please don't let my dad be dead; anything but that.'" Somehow the fact that the bad news wasn't death left him feeling partly responsible for the real reason the police were there.

The next morning my seventeen-year-old asked, "Mom, are you going to divorce Dad?" I hadn't even gone there in my mind! I just knew that my two older kids were on their way to the house to be told something that could devastate them. My children…they needed to know, but what was I going to say? How was I going to break the news that their father was in jail?

The kids had needs and so did I. I needed to feel safe in my house again. So many lies had been told; I felt like I was raped in my own home. Something in me made me need my parents to help me clean up so I could feel safe again. They came, because they love me, but they simply couldn't handle the situation. They left after a few days. However, I am blessed; my brother came in their place. He became a source of safety, strength and support; the rock I needed to get me through that difficult time.

Katherine's loss of safety and need for support when she learned the truth holds true for all partners of sex addicts to whom we've talked or we've studied. Betrayal trauma shakes the foundations of our beliefs about our safety in our marriages and it dissolves our assumptions about trusting our spouses.

"Trauma is a separation from safety," says Dr. Norman Wright.[1] Another expert, David Baldwin, adds that "Trauma creates overwhelming fear and leaves in its wake a feeling that the world is not a safe place. Many practitioners...thus believe that recovery begins with establishing a safe place, a situation within which the survivor can feel some sense of safety and predictability."[2] Daniel Sweeney, a professor at George Fox Unviersity's School of Education, says, "Safety may, in fact, be the crucial factor in treating traumatized clients. Trauma victims don't just feel psychologically unsafe, but also neurobiologically [unsafe]."[3]

Experts agree that a need for safety is universal among those who suffer trauma's pain and loss. We'll go into ways to regain safety a little later, but first let's take a look at healing from betrayal trauma as a whole.

Caveats in Healing from Betrayal Trauma

The journey toward healing can vary in length. Some partners heal in months; for others, it takes years. Like the routes you travel on any trip in life, detours may suddenly appear in your path, potholes may make the going rough and inclement weather—both in relationships and life circumstances—may make your journey more uncomfortable or even dangerous.

Perhaps the most important thing to remember is this: The trip is never linear.

Because the pain comes in cycles, often propelled by your triggers, very few partners can avoid traveling delays or double-backs. Just recently, one woman said through heartbreaking sobs, "As you write, be *sure* to tell them trauma cycles and recycles. I thought I was beyond this, but the pain is back and it's unbearable today!"

In spite of the meandering detours that healing often takes, here we can only accommodate a linear representation of the journey. For that reason, as well as to provide you with a guide, we've chosen to incorporate the healing process into a map. We do this because:

- It's helpful to see the big picture.
- We will become familiar with the steps that will eventually lead you from the wrenching initial discovery that your partner has betrayed your trust.
- We can then discover the final peace and joy found in integration and transformation of your loss and pain.

Refer back to our map when you lose sight of the pathway that leads to your healing.

Remember, you're not alone; we, and many millions of others, are your companions on this journey. Seek out and find these partners of sex addicts—in your town, online, on the phone, through a local counselor—and gain their support as you pursue your own healing.

Pathway to Healing, Empowerment and Transformation Following Sexual Betrayal Trauma

Stages of Healing	Resources and Techniques for Stages of Healing
• Initial Discovery and Crises	• Find initial support immediately • Re-establish safety • Consider controlled, supportive environments for disclosure; consider including polygraph testing • Get tested for sexually transmitted diseases • Practice good self-care
• Find/Build Good Support System • Re-establish Safety (continued)	• Family and/or friends if "safe" • Clergy if "safe" • Counselor (sex addiction and trauma specialist, if possible) • "Partners of Sex Addicts" support groups • Doctor's or psychiatrist's help if you're struggling with depression or anxiety • If you feel suicidal, seek help immediately
• Create the Boundaries You Need to Feel Safe in Your Home Again	• Do you need sexual boundaries with your partner? • Do you need a temporary separation from your partner: in-home or geographically? • What other boundaries do you need?
• Practice Good Self-Care in Each Area	• Mental/emotional self-care • Physical self-care • Spiritual self-care

Stages of Healing	Resources and Techniques for Stages of Healing
• Create Boundaries Between Yourself and the Trauma	• Use self-care to build a boundary from the pain • Learn and utilize self-soothing techniques • Eliminate cognitive distortions • Eliminate negative self-talk • Use healthy self-talk
• Counter Dissociation if it is a Problem	• Use grounding techniques to stay present • Use healthy self-talk to counter cognitive distortion that can lead to dissociation • Use your impersonal energy to access your strength and stay in the present
• Begin Emotional Processing and Grieving	• Recognize and process your feelings • Acknowledge and grieve your losses and the consequences they produced in your life • For some, face and adapt to separation or divorce • Alter your attachment to what you've lost by letting it go and saying goodbye • Develop resiliency
• Use Grieving and Processing Methods to Help Heal	• Externalize the problem by sharing your story • Renegotiate the trauma with a counselor's help • Consider nature-based healing or expressive therapy such as art or music therapy if talk therapy doesn't meet your needs

Stages of Healing	Resources and Techniques for Stages of Healing
• Use Grieving and Processing Methods to Help Heal (continued)	• Consider body therapies if talk therapy fails to bring healing and /or when trauma manifests in physical symptoms • Consider EMDR if talk therapy fails to bring healing and/or when trauma manifests in physical symptoms
• Continue Emotional Processing	• You will know when the pain has lost its power and you are free to let it go and move on
• Develop Personal Empowerment	• Continue and expand healthy boundaries • Develop solid grounding • Strengthen your self-awareness • Strengthen your impersonal energy/executive awareness • Develop healthy communication skills • Develop healthy conflict management skills • Reframe yourself as a survivor rather than a victim
• Integration and Transformation Resulting in Post-Traumatic Growth	• Integrate the trauma into your larger life story • Consider forgiveness • Find new hope by transforming the pain into a positive life purpose

The Starting Point: Find Support Immediately

Partners of sex addicts, like all "...wounded people heal in relationships....Growth, repair, maturity and faith development are all intimately tied to relationships. *People do need people* to achieve wholeness in a fractured world."[4] No one can deal with this particular heartache without the hope, comfort and support that only safe people can provide for our unique form of pain.

If you're blessed with healthy family members and friends, support can come from relationships that already exist in your life. In ideal cases, these people can provide the empathy, help and encouragement you need to deal with the immediate pain and disruption, as well as the ongoing rebuilding process that healing requires. However, in many cases, they cannot.

Certainly, many counselors are equipped to help you deal with this blow, though again, some aren't. We'll look at each potential source of support and discuss possible methods you can use to predetermine their abilities "to be there" for you. Before we do, we want to tell you about one additional resource that you might otherwise overlook, simply because awareness of this specialty may be outside of your life experience.

On A Personal Note: Think of possible support people. What friends or family members have demonstrated their abilities to love you and support you in the past?

If you can't think of anyone to call on, then consider what you want in a person on whom you could rely. What behaviors and traits would show you that a person can support you through this trauma?

Consider a Specialized Counselor Who Can Provide a Directed, Supportive Environment for the Addict's Disclosure

An important beginning step for your healing comes with hearing your partner's planned sexual disclosure. The disclosure is a set aside time during which the sex addict discloses his or her sexual activity outside of marriage or a committed relationship. Disclosure can be a painful event, particularly for the partner. *We*

encourage you to use a counselor trained in helping individuals and
couples impacted by sex addiction for this critical event.

Typically, in a planned disclosure the sex addict shares the
revelations of sexual acting out in its entirety. This disclosure can
shred your dreams and slice and dice your soul. Many partners
need a break from their normal routines following disclosure. On
the other hand, some partners feel relief, because they finally
know the truth.

In some cases, hearing about an addict's sexual behavior can
take hours. To help you process and manage the information you
may hear, we recommend you plan and prepare in advance for
your own self-care during and after the appointment. From
personal and professional experience, we know that preparation
and self-care will better equip you to face this critical and often
painful event.

- If you have children, pre-arrange for their care for the day and
  evening when the disclosure takes place so you can focus on
  yourself and your needs. Knowing they are well cared for
  allows you to focus on what you need.
- Consider pre-arranging additional time by yourself with the
  counselor after the disclosure. Most partners feel a need to
  process what is heard or read during the disclosure.
- Consider pre-arranging spending the night with a supportive
  friend, family member or at a hotel. This will give you time
  away from your partner to process and grieve.
- Predetermine—to the best of your ability—how much and
  what kind of details about the sex addict's sexual activities you
  want and need to hear. We encourage you to use your
  counselor's wisdom and experience to help you identify what
  you feel you need to hear in a disclosure. Does it need to
  include everything? Most partners begin by stating, "I need
  to know it all and I need it right now!" But they overlook the
  potential emotional consequences of such hazardous detailed
  information. Barbara often reminds clients that there is no
  cleanser for our minds. Once the information has entered, it
  is there to stay.

Your counselor can help you determine your need and motivation for the specifics in your desire to learn. Different people

have different needs. Give it deep thought and consideration, then know that whatever your need, its okay. Disclosure is in large part for your benefit, so do what you must to experience the good that finally hearing the truth can produce. One friend, a psychologist, knew herself well enough to know that without specific details she would ruminate about the possible secrets she hadn't heard and she wasn't sorry she asked for and got all the details she needed.

We believe partners need complete disclosure, but we find that most heal more easily without full details. Most of us want and need to know such details as when did the initial acting out begin? At what point did different behaviors enter into the acting out pattern? What behaviors did the addict participate in? Did the acting out include others? Did it involve children in any way? Did it include any same-sex pornography or interaction? If the addict divulges sex with others, we believe you would likely benefit from asking if you know any of these sexual partners personally. If you do, you'll probably want new boundaries to prevent contact with those people.

For most of us, little benefit comes from knowing details such as locations of acting out, positions used, descriptions of behavior, words used, etc. These little details tend to graphically and painfully stamp our memories with indelible X-rated pictures. They can poison our feelings about places we frequent, adding new complications to our lives, especially if moving to another place is not an option.

Once you determine the questions you need to ask during disclosure, your therapist can help you think your queries through and prepare to ask them in ways that will help you. Together, you can monitor how you might feel during the disclosure process and when to call for time-outs if you need them. Remember, the disclosure is in large part for you, so use good self-care and set the pace to meet your own needs.

Additionally, we suggest that because of the frequency with which sexual addicts lie and/or cover up the truth, if possible, you choose a therapist for disclosure who also incorporates a polygraph test in the process.

Consider Including a Polygraph Test in Disclosure

As we discussed in an earlier chapter, using polygraph tests in the treatment of sex addiction remains a controversial topic. Nonetheless, we've seen their use produce remarkable breakthroughs for the spouse, for the addict, for the marriage or for all three, depending on the factors in individual cases. We've turned to Dr. Milton Magness, one expert who uses polygraphs regularly in his work with sex addicts and asked him to share his perspective with us:

The idea of having a polygraph examination following a disclosure may bring hope to the spouses of sexual addicts, because they realize that with its use they can finally believe they have gotten the whole truth and not have to imagine and worry about what else in which their partners may be involved. Without a polygraph exam, the partner has no assurance that he or she is hearing the complete truth.

Another way to look at polygraph exams is to see them as the verification necessary to insure that true recovery is taking place. In drug treatment, a urinalysis (UA) is done at the beginning of treatment and then randomly throughout treatment and in aftercare. It is common knowledge that drug treatment programs would be completely ineffective without some way of verifying that the person being treated was free of drugs. Polygraph exams provide that necessary verification for persons in recovery from compulsive sexual behavior.

Sexual addicts lie to their partners, their therapists and themselves. In a research project I conducted a few years ago of sexual addicts and whether they were truthful about their acting-out behavior, I received a number of responses from sexual addicts who said they had not even been honest with their therapists about their acting-out behaviors.

After catching a sexual addict in a lie—especially repeated lies—the spouse or partner is left to wonder how to know if he or she is ever truthful. This doubt undermines every aspect of their relationship, creating such insecurity that wives or husbands may wonder, "Is s/he being honest with me?"

A disclosure that is less than 100 percent honest is not a disclosure but a deception. Partial disclosures only succeed in traumatizing the partner. Polygraphs help get to the truth. Without this procedure, I am convinced that many sexual addicts would never be able to tell the complete truth. And unless the hidden truth and accompanying shame are disclosed, the sexual addict may never be able to get free from his or her entrenched pattern of compulsive sexual behavior."[5]

Be Tested for STDs Even If You Don't Think It's Necessary

For many partners, one of the most difficult and humiliating aspects of discovering their spouses' addictions comes with trips to their doctors for sexually transmitted disease testing. Yet this test proves mandatory to protect yourself from one of the cruelest potential outcomes of a spouse's sexual addiction. A great many partners we hear from and work with end up with herpes, genital warts and other sexually transmitted diseases. Occasionally, a partner develops more complicated and risky sexually transmitted diseases because of a sex addict's lascivious behaviors.

Some partners confidently tell us in reference to them not needing STD tests, "My spouse swears he or she did not have sex with other people; it was limited to pornography." However, we know there are no guarantees when it comes to sexual addiction. Disclosure usually trickles out over time and those lost in the addiction lie rather than risk losing everything.

Protect yourself. Your partner has lied to you about his or her behavior by keeping it secret, and this pattern of lies leaves you at risk. Believing what you cannot prove about an addict can be dangerous at best and deadly in the extreme. We urge you to take this step of precaution and to ask your partner to do the same.

Re-Establish Your Safety

Trauma leaves in its wake a loss of safety on every level. In order to heal, we must find ways to re-establish our sense of safety, because without it we remain "on edge" and hypervigilant. Only safety can help us counteract that hypervigilance. "To move through the trauma," says trauma specialist Peter Levine, "we need quietness, safety and protection similar to that offered the bird in the gentle warmth of the child's hands."[6] Trauma of any kind "…may cause us to question strongly held beliefs—about our safety, how much control we have over our life and how predictable the world really is."[7]

Nowhere is your need for safety more profound than within the walls of your own home. And nowhere does safety present such complications; after all, you share your life and space with your spouse and your need to feel safe within that protective space is *essential.* So regaining your sense of safety at home must become one of your highest priorities.

We talk more about ways to build safety in your life later in this chapter and the next. Begin now to ask yourself, "What do I need to feel safe in my home again?"

On A Personal Note: Take a moment and think about your own experience of safety. In what areas of your life do you feel the need for an increased sense of safety right now? Write these down and as you read further, look for suggestions on ways to help you make safety changes for yourself.

Find or Build Good Support Systems
Dr. Levine explains, "With the support of friends and relatives, we gain a powerful resource for our healing."[8] For that reason, one of the first questions we ask partners of sex addicts is if they have someone in their lives who is walking with them in their pain. Sadly, far too often partners tell us there is no one who seems safe enough to trust with this secret.

Consider Family Members or Close Friends If They Are "Safe"
Unfortunately, even family members on whom we can count during other difficult times may be unable or unwilling to provide the support we now need, because the problems of sex addiction come wrapped in such explosive issues. Tessy's encounter with this painful truth is unforgettable.

Tessy comes from a large, loving, close-knit family that loved and accepted her successful husband. Then, several years into her marriage, she discovered her husband regularly had sexual encounters with random men and he had no plans to stop. That news alone shattered her world. Desperately needing empathy and support, she turned to her family members, trusting the qualities they had always held. Unfortunately, Tessy's already shattered world was further desecrated by their responses: The entire clan told her that neither she nor her children were welcome among them unless she chose the family over her husband.

Other stories we've heard reveal disappointment, a continued lack of comfort and care. Myra said, "I haven't told any family members. I have trusted a few close friends, though time and/or their insensitive remarks have weeded them all out. People are inpatient for me to 'get over it.'"

Still, some partners are blessed with family members or friends who have "grace in their guts": people who understand failure and pain from living out their own human experiences. People of this caliber can be counted on when you need them. But for most of us, determining our safety in sharing details of our trauma with those we love can require a process that includes time and great care. Here are some helpful guidelines and methods which can help you decide who, if anyone, in your world has what it takes to help you through this time:

- "Safe people" reflect a spirit free of judgment. Think back to conversations you've had with individuals you might consider as candidates for your emotional support. What have you heard them say about others who have "failed" in some way? Are they critical when people fall short?

- "Safe people" have "grace in their guts." This doesn't mean they have no values or morals. It simply means they understand that we all fail at times and in those times what we need most is an extended hand to help us up. Often, people with this kind of grace have known their own failures and found their ways back from it.

- "Safe people" honor your right and need to make your own decisions. Such people do not withdraw their support if they disagree with some of your decisions.

- Try "testing" the safety of your relationships by revealing a bit of personal information to people, one individual at a time, then wait for their responses. Safe people recognize that such shared information presents an invitation—a bridge—into another's inner life. Generally, safe people will not only honor what you share with acceptance and grace, but also they, too, will trust you with a bit of their inner realities. If you find that when you "test" the safety of your relationships in this way you end up doing all the sharing, you more than likely need to go outside your everyday relationships and build special connections elsewhere that will see you through this present trauma. Consider finding new support people who aren't presently invested in your life or marriage.

- Call counselors in your area and ask if they know of experts in dealing with this issue with whom you are able to connect.
- Research local counselors who specialize in sexual addiction and/or trauma, call them and ask if they will consider starting a support group for a few people dealing with this issue.
- Call local places of worship and ask if they have support groups to help people process their grief or loss.
- Call your local crisis line and ask what resources in your community might help meet your needs.
- Research online for telephone support groups for partners of sex addicts if you fail to find appropriate ways to have your needs met locally.

Consider Your Minister, Rabbi or Other Clergy if He or She is "Safe"

Sadly, not all pastors understand sex addiction, nor do all respond with gentleness and care when they encounter this issue in their parishioners. However, some do. As you consider the safety of seeking the help of your pastor, his or her history with moral failure in the lives of others provides the best gauge of how he or she might respond to your situation. Consider the following guidelines as you try to evaluate your pastor's ability to walk with you through your pain:

- How has your pastor handled other situations where couples have experienced problems or trouble?
- Ask religious leaders where parishioners seek counsel when they have a problem.

- How is this subject talked about in your church, synagogue or mosque? *Is* it talked about or is it a taboo subject?

Find a Counselor Who Specializes in Sex Addiction or Trauma if Possible

Sadly, even some counselors fail partners of sex addicts, because they lack specific knowledge and understanding of this problem. Even those who've received training in sex addiction sometimes fail to understand a partner's side of this issue. You need a counselor who is trained, experienced and knowledgeable about sexual addiction's impact on a partner.

Partners with whom we've communicated have reported a wide range of responses from counselors they've consulted. Some are even told that partners' sexual addiction presents an opportunity to spice up their marriages, so they should not only accept the extra sexual activities, but they should also join their spouses in them! For one who is experiencing post-traumatic stress, such advice gives little solace.

Here is a list of some guidelines you can employ to find a counselor who is the right fit for you:

- Do an Internet search using word combinations such as the name of your town or city plus "counselors dealing with sex addiction" or "partners of sex addicts support groups." If you live in a small town, you'll likely have to search using the name of the nearest larger town or city. Carefully read the Web sites of any mental health professional or counseling centers your searches produce.
- Call organizations or ministries that might deal with this issue—and get referrals and recommendations for counselors who might be equipped to help you. Again, do an Internet search using their names and the name of your city, then closely read their Web sites.

As you look at each site, look for facts and details that might indicate the counselors you're considering understand and have experience treating sex addiction and/or have skill in helping people heal from trauma and post-traumatic stress disorder. Then prepare to call the counselors whose sites bear evidence that they might be able to help you. Before you call, think through communicating a clear message stating as briefly as possible that you are dealing with your partner's sex addiction, you're experiencing trauma and you'd like to ask them a few questions about the possibility of working with you. You will more than likely have to leave this as a message and await their return call.

Prepare for the counselor's call in advance. We suggest that you formulate and then ask two or three questions over the phone when you have the opportunity to speak with the mental health professional directly. This set of questions can help you narrow your search to those who seem best equipped to help you heal. Questions to consider asking include:

- Have you had any training in the dynamics of sex addiction?
- What is your comfort level in working with the partner of a sex addict?
- What is your theory or framework in helping a spouse of a sex addict cope and heal?
- Have you worked with clients who have experienced significant betrayal trauma?
- Are you trained in dealing with trauma?

Take notes as counselors respond to your questions so that you will be able to refresh yourself later on each professional's experience and qualifications and determine which counselor might be a good fit for you.

The next step is to ask the one or ones who sound most promising if you can spend thirty minutes with them in a no-charge meeting to evaluate how working together would meet your needs. Good therapists will welcome an interview, because they know that no one counselor can possibly meet every potential client's needs.

Remember, this search needs to focus on finding the right counselor who will help you heal. Just as you would search for the right surgeon if you needed major surgery, you must also search for the right counselor to help your mind, heart and body heal from the toll trauma has taken on you. Know that you are worth it.

Next, prepare well for the evaluation interviews you will have to make your final decisions. As to working with a mental health professional, take with you a list of questions you want to ask the person. Some will likely be unique to you. Others you might want to ask include:

- Do you know and understand sex addiction well enough to realize the addict will probably lie to you, too?
- How do you handle an addict's disclosure?
- What therapeutic methods do you use to help a client heal from trauma?
- Can you help me heal from this experience?

Another important element you'll need to evaluate during these interviews encompasses the counselor's personality and ability to adapt to your needs. Years ago when Marsha finally dealt with the pain and confusion of childhood sexual abuse and its thirty-five year effect on her personality and life, she followed the steps just mentioned as she sought the right counselor for the work she needed to do.

Marsha says, "Of the three I finally interviewed, one stood out as perfect for me. Throughout our work together, her wonderful wisdom and skill helped me cross over a wide and deep gulch in the innermost recesses of my soul. The work we did together set me on the path that eventually led me to do the work I do today."

We hope that your experience will end as positively as Marsha's did. However, should your search fail to lead you to a helpful counselor, we suggest you take your search to the Internet once again. This time, sift through potential candidates who offer long-distance interaction via telephone. In our increasingly electronic and virtual world, counselors are employing such means to provide help for people in healing.

You May Need to Educate Your Support System about Trauma's Effects

As you evaluate a potential support system in your life or seek out a new one, keep in mind that most people do not have experience understanding trauma and its effect on you. Finding caring, supportive people presents a big enough challenge. Don't be discouraged if you need to educate them a bit about your trauma's impact so they can understand the feelings and symptoms with which you're dealing.

Join a "Partners of Sex Addicts" Support Group

History shows that during the Holocaust, some concentration camp survivors broke into tightly knit pairs and groups, instinctively creating the support that enabled them to survive. They knew that doing so would contribute greatly to their abilities to endure some of the most traumatizing conditions in history.[9] And so it did.

"Often, fellow victims provide the most effective short-term bond, because the shared history of trauma can form the nucleus for retrieving a sense of communality," says Levine, author and trauma specialist. "...In a group, patients can start re-experiencing themselves as being useful to other people. Ventilation and sharing of feelings and experiences promotes the experience of being both victim and helper. Even a trusting and secure relationship with a therapist who serves as a parental substitute does not necessarily enable the patient to assess his or her relationships with others accurately."[10]

Dr. van der Kolk states, "At first they use each other as mirrors to reflect traumatic memories and feelings, which allows a shared reliving of the trauma. Making the past public permits each...to find personal meaning in the traumatic event....By hearing others express their emotions verbally, and by learning how others manage to deal with the aftermath of trauma through reflection rather than action, many...become capable of using similar maneuvers to deal with their own helplessness and pain."[11]

We heartily agree. We *need* the opportunity to share and connect with others who understand our unique brand of pain, because they're experiencing similar hurts themselves. The bonds we forge with sisters and brothers on this journey lead to accelerated healing and renewed self-esteem by decreasing anxiety and restoring courage, hope and meaning in our lives; most of the partners we've worked with readily agree. Several with whom we've spoken share some from their experiences with groups.

After Myra's group ended she told Marsha:

The group set me free and put my feet on an educated path. Now I'm finally capable of experiencing joy again. It's been a long time. I no longer feel alone, nor do I still believe it's all about me. Discovering that other sex addicts play the same head games with their husbands and wives began to dissemble my false beliefs.

After her telephone support group one day, Kelly said:
　　　Marsha, today it seemed as if we were all sitting at a table sharing and caring for one another. Your leadership in guiding each of us to "check in" on ourselves is an impacting part of the group. I'm learning that it's hard to pull myself out of the hole long enough to view where I am, but so necessary. The group makes that possible.

Again and again we hear messages like this one Barbara received: "Thanks again for all of your help. Being in a group of women who have experienced the same painful situations is extremely helpful. It helps validate the many emotions I feel. I wouldn't be where I am today if I didn't have your help."

Qualities Found in Healthy Groups

Unfortunately, some groups lack the elements needed to make them healthy places to work through your pain. As you research potential support groups for your own healing, look for these group and facilitator qualities:

- A group facilitator who has experienced his or her own betrayal trauma because of a spouse's sex addiction can be very helpful. Personal experience with pain like yours enables a facilitator to respond as one who has been there personally and is able to fully understand your struggles.
- A group facilitator who gives the group meetings his or her highest priority by consistently showing up and being a caring and active leader. Of course, at times special arrangements must be made for illness or other life issues.
- Participants who actively engage in a shared process, whether it is working through a healing workbook, reading and discussing a book that everyone is reading or engaging in some other program that leads to your healing and empowerment.

- Participation and sharing on specific ground rules that keep the identity of participants and everything they share confidential from outsiders.
- Maintaining an environment of safety so everyone present engages in active listening and refrains from cross-talk. Cross-talk includes interrupting another person when he or she is speaking or giving advice.

In a healthy group where boundaries are encouraged, a bond develops over time and participants establish their own levels of comfortable interchange. However, the facilitator remains responsible for ensuring the safety of participants' boundaries and keeping the group safe.

On A Personal Note: As you read about support groups for partners, what thoughts or feelings occur to you? Does the idea of a group encourage you or frighten you? What steps can you take right now to find means of support for yourself like a good support group?

Seek a Doctor's Help if You're Struggling with Depression or Anxiety

Many partners find that their sadness and loss starts a deep slide into depression and/or their fears grow into anxieties, especially when marital solutions remain in the distant future beyond their reaches. For a few, depression plunges them deeper still until death offers the best solution for their lives.

If you find these side effects of trauma begin to interfere significantly with your ability to cope, turn to a psychiatrist or medical doctor for help. There's no weakness in needing antidepressants or anxiety medications when trauma has devastated your world. As we learned in chapter 5, such trauma can alter your brain chemistry; when that happens we're blessed to live in an era when the medical world can provide pharmaceutical help.

Nancy told us, "When I couldn't get out of bed and get my kids started on their days, because I was so depressed, I called my doctor. He prescribed an antidepressant and anti-anxiety meds. As my daughter said when she tried to encourage me:

'Giving birth is normal, but that doesn't mean you don't need some help to get past the pain.' She helped me realize that using medication to make it through this trauma wasn't a crime."

An Additional Word about Suicidal Thoughts or Feelings

If you have a history of suicidal thoughts or attempts in the past, know that your risk factor may be greater right now. Finding a caring professional who can help you navigate through this time becomes doubly important. If that isn't an option, call your local crisis hotline (usually a phone number may be found in the front of your local phone book) or call a national hotline such as the National Suicide Prevention Hotline at 1-800-273-TALK. One wise old saying is that suicide is a permanent solution to a temporary problem. From her own experience, Marsha can tell you that even though you may feel as she did, that you are entering in the darkest night of unbearable pain, life does get better in time.

Self-Check: Please take a moment and honestly answer these questions:

- *Do you find you have thoughts of wanting to escape, get away and/or disappear?*
- *Do you have times when you think you'd be better off dead?*
- *Do you have thoughts of wanting to take your own life?*
- *Have you had similar thoughts in the past?*
- *Have you ever acted on these thoughts?*

If you've answered "yes" to any of these queries, it is very important that you talk to someone immediately about your depression. Contact the National Suicide Prevention Hotline at the toll-free number we listed, your counselor or others you can confide in. Talking about your feelings can help you heal; hiding these thoughts can worsen your feelings of depression or hopelessness. **Talk to a mental health professional, clergy or other advisor right away.**

Create the Boundaries You Need to Feel Safe in Your Home Again

Earlier we suggested that you ask yourself, "What do I need to feel safe in my home again?" Though many of your answers to that question will likely bear similarities to other partners of sex addicts, others will be uniquely your own. Answering this important question requires going "inside" yourself and searching for what is needed for healing to begin. Understanding how safety, triggers and boundaries form three parts of a whole helps assess what is needed more clearly.

Triggers
Triggers are the situations, events, actions, behaviors or people that cause your sense of safety to suddenly evaporate when they enter your space. Triggers can vaporize feelings of safety and make healing from trauma extremely difficult or impossible. Learning what triggers you is an important step in re-establishing your sense of safety.

Boundaries
Boundaries are the imaginary lines we draw to keep certain things out of our space or our lives. Drawing boundaries can feel challenging and scary at first, but in time we recognize they provide the kindest, cleanest way to ask for what we need and to take responsibility for good self-care. Think of boundaries as a shield that is raised to block arrows flying at you, often quite unexpectedly. These arrows hold the potential to rip you apart unless you use your shield to successfully block them.

Safety
If triggers are the arrows and boundaries are your shield, safety is what you gain when you become skillful at using your shield to properly intercept the arrows. Let's take that metaphor one step further and examine how you can use the mental picture it creates to make your home feel safe again, because only in that safety can you hope to begin to heal.

A Shift in Focus from Making Your Partner Stop to Creating the Boundaries You Need to Feel Safe
Communicating Your Boundaries
Creating boundaries with the goal of making spouses "stop" certain behaviors places us in a sort of distasteful parent/army sergeant/police officer mode that embroils rebellion and is

destined for failure. On the other hand, when you kindly ask for what you need in order to once again feel safe, you place yourself in a position of vulnerability. For example, when a man loves his wife and his heart toward her is tender, her vulnerability softens him and he wants to help her feel safe in their home and in a relationship with him. Kindness and vulnerability are key.

What Do I Need?
However, before you can communicate your boundaries vulnerably, you must determine what boundaries you need. So let's begin with the simple question, "What do I need?" Those four little words launch an exercise that has empowered many to recognize their triggers by identifying what they need in order to feel safe and to vulnerably request that their needs be met as they seek to take responsibility for working toward their own safety.

Toni, whose story opened chapter 5, discovered newfound strength and a sense of empowerment after she did this exercise and shared it with her husband. He found it helpful as well, because then he knew exactly how to help his wife feel safe and loved as they worked toward rebuilding their marriage. We share three items that appeared on Toni's list to give you an idea how another partner worked through and expressed what her heart needed to begin to feel safe again.

Three of Toni's Needs
- I need complete honesty, the total truth, no lies, no deceit and no deception. I need this now instead of your telling me a little bit now and a little bit later, because "you think" I don't need to know because it's unimportant, or it will only upset me and it would be better to tell me later.
- I need a home free of all pornography and sexually addictive behaviors. I need peace in my home.
- I need you to create firm boundaries when you are around other women, to make good decisions, taking the "high road" and not having any personal or inappropriate conversations with other women. When you take risks with other women, I feel that you are taking risks with my heart and I don't feel safe.

Identify Your Triggers and Consider Boundaries to Block Them

Now it's your turn. Begin by making a list of the things that trigger your fears, pain and insecurities. Give it thought and do your best, knowing it will never be complete. Next, honestly ask yourself, "What do I need to feel safe in regard to each trigger?" We reveal several things that partners often find triggering, along with sample boundaries they have shared with us.

- Computer: "Knowing that certain boundaries are in place (i.e. computer lock or some other filter) gives me peace that these things aren't entering my home when I'm not there."
- Movies: "We don't go to movies anymore; we rent movies. Rather, my husband does. I don't go in video stores either, for the same reasons. My husband takes responsibility for staying sexually sober and looks away when he encounters sexual stimulation, but not going to movies is about me," one mental health professional shared with us. "Those scenes trigger my pain. Avoiding triggers that cause me to spiral downward is one way I take responsibility for my own needs. I take responsibility by creating the boundaries I need and then act on them. This practice is empowering and it allows for my healing, for his healing and for our healing and stability as a couple. It's worth it."
- His or Her Work-Related Travel: This can present one of the biggest challenges couples face, because frequently these business trips had been filled with a variety of instances of acting out sexually. Each couple needs to think through and determine what boundaries must be put in place to protect their marriage and the sexual addict's sobriety. More than any other area, this one may require help from your counselor or clergy.
- Video Stores: "I don't go there; that's just the way it is," one partner said. "It's been eleven years, but the stab of betrayal still hurts when it's triggered. I think it will *always* be there. Because of the betrayal, I see things I didn't see before. Things that were never triggers prior to discovering the addiction suddenly became triggering to me, and that has to be okay, because that's the way it is."

When one young couple faced the wife's triggers around television, movies and videos, her husband, who is now in recovery, told his wife, "I don't have eyes for that anymore." Yet in speaking with her, it was clear that *she* still does. That's simply a consequence and at least a temporary loss that resulted from his sexual choices. It's not about him anymore; she knows she needs this boundary in order to heal.

A client shared that their family now uses a special DVD player called ClearPlay for home viewing of movies. ClearPlay enables you to watch movies, but it removes sexual content, making the triggering problem much easier to deal with.

- Malls: Many partners of sex addicts find they don't enjoy shopping in malls anymore because of the seductive posters on store windows and the omnipresent lingerie stores. One woman shared that if she really needs to go to a mall, she goes directly to the necessary store and doesn't window shop, because doing so stirs up old pain as well as anger that our society uses sex and the female form to sell everything from soap to automobiles. "My peace and stability are worth too much to me to subject myself to that kind of stimulation," she said.

- Vacations: Vacations raise a host of issues for many couples, especially beach vacations and cruises. Many men openly report that summer in general presents the hardest time of year, because women's attire reveals more flesh. Like work-related travel, vacations must be dealt with by each couple one vacation at a time. If stability and healing remain the goals, consequences lose some of their sting. Beth said that when she encounters a beautiful young woman and the old discomfort of triggers begins to happen, she tells herself, "God, when I see this woman I feel afraid. But you created her and she's beautiful in your sight. She's not the enemy. She's someone's daughter, someone's sister, perhaps someone's mother. Please help me to see her as your creation and to not feel afraid."

Plan for Triggering Situations

What do you need to do to take care of yourself if you experience a trigger? What are you going to do if you see your partner's acting out? These sticky situations don't have to become ugly scenes if you've thought about them and discussed them in advance.

Abby's husband often went into a gregarious, flirtatious mode when they were out and he was around other women. His behavior hurt her deeply and she was angry about that. She thought through and began to plan for how to take care of herself the next time it happened. She made a decision. Before they left for a party one night, Abby calmly shared her decision with her husband: "If you begin your Don Juan routine tonight, I want you to know I am calling a taxi and leaving immediately. Consider yourself warned, because I will follow through."

Our grandmothers said, "An ounce of prevention is worth a pound of cure." Nowhere is that wise old saying truer than in life with a recovering sex addict. Even so, there's no guarantee that the follow-through won't become messy. But even if it does, it creates an opportunity to talk about and learn from the experience later when things settle down.

Some partners find they become so triggered in supermarkets that they now have trouble grocery shopping. There are some triggers you might be able to avoid while you heal. There are others that need to be removed from your life, because they are simply too damaging to you, at least at this point. Know that you are worth it and prioritize your healing.

On A Personal Note: Take a moment and write out the things or situations that are triggers for you. This will be an important list for you to work through with your therapist or other counselor.

Do You Need Sexual Boundaries With Your Partner?
Many partners find that even thinking about sex with their addict spouses carries a whole set of triggers, fears and discomfort. In group one evening, one woman said it would be as if every woman her husband ever fantasized about or had sex with was in the room watching them, were she to have sex with her husband. She decided there was no way she could have a sexual relationship with him under those conditions.

Others feel an immediate need to connect physically to re-establish the viability of their sexual bond after their partners have broken it. What do you do if you feel this way?

Although it's tempting to let down your guard and relax your boundaries, necessity demands realism about your physical and emotional safety. Can you *know for certain* that your partner has stopped acting out? If not, sexual boundaries are not only okay, they are also wise, at least until both of you are tested for STDs and receive clean bills of health. Some partners go one step further and wait until after polygraph testing to re-engage sexually.

We offer these guidelines to help you think through what you need regarding physical intimacy:

- Touch can be a trigger, so talk with your spouse about kinds of touch you find comfortable and uncomfortable, safe and unsafe.

- If you want or need physical intimacy, consider using other kinds of touch to make that connection until you're certain the acting out has stopped. Begin with loving, non-sexual touches like hugs or backrubs to help determine how safe or comfortable you feel with your partner's touch. If that feels okay, move slowly from there.

- A final caution: If you can't be certain your partner has stopped acting out with others but want to engage in sexual intimacy, do what many others choose to do: Practice safe sex. Use condoms to protect yourself against sexually transmitted diseases. Remember, there is no such thing as safe sex outside of a monogamous relationship.

Do You Need A Temporary Separation?
In-Home Separation

Many partners suddenly need more privacy following the discovery of their partners' sexual betrayal. Some need the person to move out, at least temporarily. Others prefer an in-home separation, so they set up boundaries that will help them minimize the triggers the sex addict's presence stimulates. By limiting exposure or interaction with that person for a time, a partner creates buffers that enable him or her to calm down so healing can begin.

If you find you need a similar arrangement, use your creativity to build your own buffers. Here are some ways to do this:

- Sleep in separate rooms.
- Schedule meetings to discuss finances and the children.
- Temporarily eat at different times and do laundry separately.
- Arrange for times when you each have the house to yourself.

Though arrangements such as these can be awkward and cumbersome, if you can't relax and begin to heal otherwise, take responsibility for your self-care and ask for what you need. Your healing depends on it.

Actual Temporary Separation
For those who find they need more physical separation, actual time spent apart can help in several ways. It can help the wounded partner begin to heal and to regain a sense of safety. It can allow time and space for the addict to begin rebuilding a sense of trust. It can also create an end to the old and a fresh start for the new.

Sophia found the time she spent apart from her sexually addicted husband important. She describes it this way:

It took separation before I could feel safe again in my home. Once I regained my safety, we began to see each other and slowly increased the frequency and length of our visits. I found that because he was working on his own problems simultaneously, he began to relate to me in healthy ways. As he consistently respected my boundaries, I became safe enough to let him back in, a little bit at a time. In that newfound safety, my trust began to grow. It's nothing short of a miracle that we've been able to establish a new, healthy marriage!

What Other Boundaries Do *You* Need?
Because some triggers are uniquely your own, they require unique boundaries that might not be the same for other partners of sex addicts. One woman felt triggered every time she got in her husband's truck, because that was where he acted out with other women. "Would you like him to sell the truck?" Barbara asked her. She asked incredulously: "Can I do that?" Together they worked out a way to communicate what she felt and what she needed. She arrived at her next session smiling broadly and announced: "The truck is gone!" From that day on, she reported increased confidence in asking for what she needs.

Lucy also struggled with a unique trigger that she asked us to share:

> As I prepared after much healing to make a recommitment to our relationship, I knew I couldn't make it in our home, because that's where he acted out. To me, it represented his addiction. So I told him how living in the house triggered me. We ended up selling our home and building a new one. For us, it has become a monument to our love, to my forgiveness and healing and to my renewed commitment. Taking responsibility for what I need opened a door for our brand new marriage and life.

Though we can't guarantee doing this hard work will heal your marriage, it *will* make space for your safety and eventual healing.

Practice Good Self-Care

Incorporating good self-care activities into each day helps us take responsibility for meeting our own needs so we can cope with the upheaval our spouses' sexual addictions have created in our lives. For many of us, however, finding the time and energy to prioritize ourselves may not come naturally or easily. Yet caring for ourselves proves mandatory to manage the burden of stress and to think through and make the decisions and choices we face.

The Three Components of Self-Care

Good self-care encompasses the three aspects of our beings: the mental/emotional, the physical and the spiritual.

Mental/Emotional

It's easy to overlook the importance of nurturing our mental and emotional well-being. Yet without good self-care in this area, it doesn't take much for us to spiral downward and fall apart. Prioritize caring for yourself mentally and emotionally:

- Give yourself time-outs from the stress.
- Say "no" when you need or want to.
- Continue a routine as much as you are able.

- Spend some time with people who love you.
- Talk about your feelings with safe people.
- Don't take responsibility for the other partner's behavior, no matter what that partner says.
- Don't make major life decisions in the midst of the emotional upheaval.
- Care for yourself the way you would care for a friend who had been deeply hurt.
- Read about sexual addiction so that you understand it enough to make wise decisions.
- Do things that season your life with "fun," even if they don't feel as good as they normally do.
- Cut yourself a break and don't expect as much from yourself as you normally do.

Physical
Here are ideas for caring for your physical being:
- Pamper yourself.
- Do soothing, relaxing activities regularly.
- Move your body in ways that feel good to you.
- Get enough sleep; nothing can deteriorate you faster than lack of sleep. Ask your physician for help if this becomes a problem.
- Undertake some exercise daily, both to care for yourself and as a release valve for the stress created by the trauma.
- Get a massage to calm and soothe yourself.
- Eat a healthy diet by avoiding junk food, alcohol and caffeine.

Spiritual
Paying attention to the spiritual part of your being provides a peace many say they can't find elsewhere. Here are some ways to care for your spiritual being:
- Develop meditation and other spiritual exercises that nurture your mind and soul.
- Read books or writings that provide wisdom and comfort to help guide you through the decisions ahead.
- Listen to music that comforts your mind and soul.

- Watch movies that show how others have faced difficult circumstances.
- Consider adding spiritual practices or activities with other people for the benefit that "fellowship" can build into your life.

Good Self-Care Can Help You Continue to Care for Your Children and Continue Your Job

When betrayal trauma depletes our energy and scrambles our focus, caring for others or going to work every morning can feel impossible. Prioritizing good self-care in all three areas not only protects our overall health and well-being, but also it can enable us to continue the other roles we play in life.

Self-Check: Take some time right now and write out a self-care plan for yourself. Be sure to include what you will do to care for yourself emotionally, physically and spiritually. Share this plan with your therapist or the person to whom you've turned for support. What things are you already doing for yourself? What things might be difficult but important for you to do for yourself? Remember, you are worth it!

Chapter 7

From Crisis to Stability

Marsha shares a journal entry she wrote as her marriage came to an end. It captures much of what partners feel and experience when betrayal shatters their lives:

My eyes are open and I'm instantly aware of the raw pain that has replaced the long-time joy in my marriage. I glance at the clock: 6:00 A.M. Somehow three hours slip by as I shower, dress and prepare for my day.

Finally ready to go, I reach into my coat pocket and...no keys. *Oh, no! Not again.* I am reminded that no matter how hard I try I can't keep order in my life with the increased stress, emotional pain and distractions that rule my nights and days. As I move from room to room, pulling out drawer after drawer, I begin to worry. *I don't want to waste another good day,* I mutter. *Could I possibly have left them in the keyhole on the outside of the front door again?*

I unlock and open the door. *No keys. Maybe the car door?* Out I trudge, beginning to become annoyed with my constantly slumbering memory. *Not there, either. What if someone took them from the front door so they can break in at night?* I analyze my thought and realize I sound like a paranoid woman.

The next three hours I spend looking for my keys. During those three hours, I discover that somehow my cell phone is missing, too. I dial it, hoping to follow its ring. But there's no ring to follow. Back out to the car, back in the house, back up the stairs. Just what I need: another bumper-car-in-the-fog-day.

I finally give up and call a friend who has a backup key. She's sweet and sympathetic and offers to come over as soon as she's ready. Moments after hanging up the phone, my eyes spot my terry cloth robe. I plunge my hand into a pocket. "My keys!" I shout, actually feeling joy for a moment. Hurriedly, I call my friend back.

Somewhere between opening my eyes this morning and losing time to my inability to stay organized, my enthusiasm for the day has vanished and I feel exhausted. But finally, around noon, I manage to get myself into a coat, gather my things and leave. Safely in the car, I head to town. There's still lots of sunshine and I'm hopeful that it will be good medicine.

Hungry and needing to be around people, I pull into a fast-food restaurant. Just as I join the end of the line to order, I accidentally dump the contents of my purse and a strange assortment of "stuff" splatters over a square yard of the floor. As I bend down to begin collecting my things, aware of many noontime eyes upon me, my sheaf of marriage separation papers drops from my other arm and scatters across the tile. The man in front of me—one of my "angels" for that particular day—turns and with a gentle smile says, "Let me help you."

"I'm going through a personal crisis, and it's beginning to show," I mumble awkwardly. He looks up and smiles softly, continuing to collect the oddities I've spread across the floor. He picks up my name tag and hands it to me. "That's my name," I blurt out, realizing after the fact how ridiculous it sounded. Again, he smiles. As we finish, I thank him and he turns to place his order.

After lunch I head to my favorite bakery, hoping they still have some apple cinnamon chip scones. Ah, they do. As I give the young cashier $1.75, a man dressed in a cyclist's gear comes in, holds up a prescription pill bottle and asks, "Do you know this person?" My eyes lock on the translucent brown bottle and my name highlighted in yellow jumps out at me. I reach up and almost snatch the bottle from his hand, once again saying, "Oh, thank you." *Lord,* I pray silently. *I'm a mess! Please help me and take care of me.*

I go next door to the drug store for a couple of things I need. Somehow, several minutes pass as I wander up and down every aisle in a daze. Again I'm shrouded in feelings that I know accompany shock; I realize I am dissociating. I feel cut off and disconnected from my body and from reality, as if I'm groping through a dense jungle in a white-out fog. I find myself in the greeting card aisle and suddenly the same emotions I felt following my father's death swamp me with heavy waves. As the tears flow down my cheeks unbidden and unchecked, I read cards with beautiful, heartrending expressions of farewell to someone you love. I pick them up, read them, put them back. And I wonder why I'm doing this to myself.

Finally, after another hour has passed, I pay and leave, carry my bags to the car, turn and walk into a coffee shop. Reaching in my purse for my wallet, I discover it's not there. I check my pockets. No wallet. *Oh, no, not again,* I think in disbelief. *I'm trying so hard to remain present and be extra careful, but I can't seem to control my brain that's bent on wandering through the years of my broken marriage.*

I hurry back into the drug store to ask the cashier, "Excuse me, did I leave my wallet here a minute ago?" "No," she says through a thick accent, "but I found one outside," and hands my wallet to me. Another one of my angels for the day! Emotionally spent and troubled by my condition, I give up, get in the car and drive home. I feel completely drained. I'm also aware that I'm blanketed in a deep, dark depression.

As I unlock the house door, heavy, heaving sobs begin to wring yet more emotion from my weary mind and body. I go into the bathroom; I can't stop wailing. The reflection in the mirror is almost pitiful and I'm grateful my soon-to-be former husband isn't privy to my pain. *He needs to know only that I'm strong and capable*, I remind myself, even as I hear the anguished moans gush out of my body.

The remainder of the day is spent heating a frozen dinner and eating at my computer.

Tomorrow I will go back to the Y and exercise, I tell myself, hoping to get some kind of order back in my life.

Finally, this pain-filled day is over and I'm grateful I survived it. And grateful, too, for the grieving process at work within me. I know it has to happen if I am to heal. As I reach into the closet for tomorrow's clothes, I am pulled toward my husband's jacket. I take it from the hanger and press the collar to my face, breathing in the scent of him. *Oh, God, I love that man.*

Please deliver me from these feelings and this anguish, I pray.

I'm sure you know the feelings Marsha expresses in her journal entry only too well. How then, do we get from here to hope and healing?

On her "Stages of Surviving and Recovering From Trauma" chart, Tana Slay, Ph.D., describes the second stage of trauma as surviving.[1] Dr. Slay says that in the surviving stage, which follows the crisis stage on her chart, we consistently feel safe, we're doing no self-harm, we're clean and sober, we demonstrate good coping skills and self-care.

That's a lot to ask on the heels of a crisis. For most of us, the surviving stage doesn't come quickly or painlessly. Yet even in the pain, experience has produced valuable tools that will help any of us if we learn to use them for our benefits. We can create boundaries between ourselves and the trauma by using self-soothing techniques, changing cognitive distortions and negative self-talk to healthy self-talk, learning to ground ourselves if we begin to dissociate and using self-care activities to take responsibility for meeting our own needs.

The Paralyzing Power of Fear and Grief

As we discussed in the last chapter, we need to create boundaries to block the triggers related to our spouses and their addictions in order to heal. In addition, we must learn to give ourselves breaks from our triggering fears and the grieving process going on inside of us. Without breaks, both our fears and our grief have the power to paralyze us and make life unmanageable.

Because our minds spin in endless circles with our seemingly unsolvable problems—sort of like merry-go-rounds piled high with the baggage of broken lives and pain—we must find ways to interrupt that negative process. This takes on greater importance when we understand why: It's because that mental circular motion, called rumination, *reinforces its grip on us with each revolution.* Unless we challenge ourselves to "take a recess" as needed, we'll find it harder and harder to interrupt the spiraling cycle.

The Power of Fear
Marsha says:

> I ache when I listen to women share from their mental merry-go-rounds, because I so clearly remember my pain and fear as my marriage fell apart. Sleep became nearly impossible during the weeks I spent on circular thinking's endless revolutions. One day after I had healed, life presented me the perfect picture of how futile it is for us to get stuck in those cycles. It happened when, somehow, a large squirrel got trapped in my living room in the Pacific Northwest.
>
> The poor little guy raced around the large room in a frenzied panic, leaping from one piece of furniture to another. He ended up focused on a small, circular table covered with a floor-length tablecloth that sat in front of a large, plate-glass window. He set up a perpetual pattern of running at the table, flying through the air, touching down on the table then leaping against the window in a frantic effort to get outside. He hit the window with such a thud that it threw him back to the floor, where he lay stunned momentarily, then he got up and began his routine all over again, repeating his own version of circular thinking.
>
> In his frenzied fury, the squirrel failed to recognize that we had opened the French doors creating an escape to his freedom. After more than an hour of wild-eyed hysterical antics that were painful to observe—his little heart beating fast and hard against his chest—he finally allowed me to direct him through the doors. But even then, he didn't find his way

outdoors. Rather, he bounded up the steep stairs that led to the third floor of the old home I lived in. He leaped two steps at a time as he blindly tried to save himself.

In my opinion, that squirrel's activities gave a perfect picture of the futility of fear's panic and our repetitious circular thinking. We need every tool and technique that is available to us to avoid our own wild-eyed merry-go-rounds. Hopefully, you'll find those we present here helpful.

The Power of Grief

Sharon, the mother of six, found herself in a dangerous position when grief's power left her crumpled in a heap. Sharon and her husband both wanted many children and together they planned for six and built what appeared to be a solid life filled with love, many friends and community activities. She seemed to have it all, just as she'd dreamed.

Then one day Sharon's husband made a careless mistake: He forgot to cover his tracks. From that one error his house of cards came toppling down and with it, Sharon's world. She learned a truth she couldn't fathom: the wonderful father of her children, the man she loved and adored, made frequent visits to prostitutes, strip parlors and much more. Suddenly, everything was gone, including the financial stability she thought was theirs.

Having six children ages one to fourteen, Sharon and her husband separated and her husband moved out of the house. Sharon couldn't force herself out of bed; she couldn't care for her family and she couldn't stop crying. She was blessed with loving, supportive friends who took turns getting her up and into the shower every morning and helped care for her family, but it was a long time before hope dawned in her life again. In the interim, Sharon needed to learn how to take breaks from her intense feelings by creating boundaries between herself and her trauma.

Creating Boundaries Between Yourself and Trauma's Fear and Grief

Bearing the full impact of our pain twenty-four hours a day, seven days a week, takes a terrible toll on our minds and bodies, as we have learned in chapter 5. Not only do we *need* breaks, but we also *must* take them if we have to work at a job, care for family members or protect our health.

Learning to Self-Soothe and Renew for Greater Self-Control and Peace

Bessel van der Kolk explains what happens to our ability to self-soothe when we experience trauma:

> As they mature, human beings continue to rely on feedback from their bodies to signal whether a particular stimulus is dangerous or agreeable. Even as we vastly expand our repertoire of soothing activities, we rely on being able to establish physical (sensate) homeostasis to give us our sense of flow or of being grounded. For traumatized people who develop PTSD, however, this capacity to sooth oneself is compromised. Instead, they tend to rely on actions such as fight or flight or pathological self-soothing (for example, mutilation, binging, starving or turning to alcohol and drugs) to regulate their internal balance.[2]

Most of us recognize that our ability to self-soothe has been compromised by the trauma, but what can we do about it? We can learn to take breaks by using self-soothing techniques to calm and comfort ourselves in the face of our pain and difficulties.

Self-soothing can serve many purposes in our lives, whether or not we're dealing with trauma. Under ordinary life circumstances, the practice of self-soothing helps us cope when things don't go our way, helps us relax when we feel fried and frazzled from daily stress, helps us relax our way to sleep at night and produces better health in the long run because our bodies and minds receive mini-breaks in the form of soothing, focusing time outs.

For those of us who face the pain and trauma that sexual betrayal produces, learning to practice self-soothing techniques proves essential. By using them, you will quickly gain access to a long list of benefits if you make this technique a part of your days—and your nights, if need be. By learning to use self-soothing techniques, we create a space between our trauma and ourselves: a buffer of sorts, a protective layer of calm between our inner world and the grinding friction of our fear, anxiety and pain.

Self-soothing techniques give you ways to:
- calm anxiety,
- handle fear,
- take time out from anger,
- comfort yourself,
- find compassion for yourself in the midst of what you're feeling,
- create a buffer between you and the trauma,
- care for yourself the way you care for others,
- stay present when you face emotions that cause dissociation,
- replenish and restore yourself emotionally so you can give to others,
- gain the ability to connect with yourself to understand what you're feeling.

By learning and using self-soothing techniques, we intentionally "let go" for a little while. Letting go is an antidote to the tensing, tightening constriction that trauma places on our minds and our bodies. According to mindfulness teacher Shinzen Young, resistance amplifies and expands suffering. "Loosening" the tightness, however, can help difficult emotions (or other sensations) pass through us more easily. So think of self-soothing techniques as a way you can let go and allow your muscles to lengthen and relax while allowing some of trauma's toxins to melt away.

Mental and Physical "Loosening Techniques"
One powerful, truly wonderful self-soothing resource for "loosening" and dealing with stress, if you have access to a computer, is available twenty-four hours a day without cost from the Mayo Clinic Web site. We encourage you to check it out at http://mayoclinic.com/health/meditation/MM00623. With a beautiful, single lit candle, soothing piano music and a calming woman's voice, it guides you through a short, breath-focused relaxation break. As you use this video, you will feel your body and mind letting go of the anxiety and the tension you're carrying. Best of all, you can use this resource as many times a day as you need to in order to manage negative emotions that threaten to keep you feeling powerless over your fear and pain.

There are many other ways to relieve your tensions, calm and soothe yourself:

- Bubble baths
- Getting a massage
- Taking a nap
- Practicing Yoga, Tai chi, Qi Gong or meditation
- Playing calming music while visualizing a peaceful nature scene

Distraction

Distraction provides a relaxing interruption when we intentionally utilize activities that distract our minds from our pain, knowing the business at hand will still be there when we get back to it. Like self-soothing, distraction gives us a break, but it's more like a relaxing recess for adults. "Relaxation," the Mayo Clinic Web site tells us, "is a process that decreases the wear and tear of life's challenges on your mind and body." As we learned in chapter 5, dealing with sexual betrayal can take a terrible toll on both our minds and our bodies, so we have good reason to use distraction as often as possible.

To gain the most benefit from distraction, choose activities that you enjoy or that you'll find absorbing enough to take your focus off your pain. The following list provides some examples.

- Reading
- Watching a movie
- Enjoying a comedy
- Attending a play
- Dancing
- Exercising
- Taking a walk
- Participating in a group sport
- Biking
- Doing an activity with friends
- Being around people/children/animals
- Spending time in nature
- Playing a musical instrument
- Attending a church service
- Visiting a nursing home or a shut-in
- Swimming

- Hiking
- Cleaning
- Cooking or baking
- Organizing your closets, kitchen, photos, etc.

Use these and add other forms of distraction that work for you to help you reconnect with life and to remind yourself that a better future will be waiting for you when this season of pain is behind you, which we promise *will* come one day.

Processing
Another way to let go, though we don't pretend it to be "fun," is to process what's happening in your life and how you feel in response to it. We think of processing as a way to "empty" ourselves of all the emotion of the day, whether we write in a journal, call a friend, attend a partners' group or go online and empty our feelings in a forum for partners.

- Journaling: If we use journaling as a "processing" method, as we might use a counselor, writing or typing what's happening in our lives and what we feel and think in response to it, this practice can become a powerful resource. During the darkest year of her life, Marsha journaled 160 single-spaced typed pages to cope with and process the events, the pain, the losses and her reaction to it all. "I really don't know how I could have survived without that no-cost, instantly-available therapeutic resource," she says looking back on that time in her life.
- Talking: When we can talk out our feelings with someone we trust who listens without giving unwanted advice or share our feelings in the safety of a partners' group, we feel understood; we relieve the inner pressure produced when our thoughts race round and round in circles without resolution. As we talk it all out, we often discover the next step we need to take, simply because we were able to process our pent-up emotions. Fortunately, even if we don't have a person to share with face-to-face, we have other options that can provide a similar effect.
- Partners of Sex Addicts Online Forums: Many partners have discovered a way to "vent" their pressured feelings and access support by joining online forums where partners can write and respond to one another's "posts." This free or low-cost

way to combine talking and journaling remains available day or night; something most friends and counselors are not.

There's one additional detail to remember as you consider using distraction to your benefit: Distractions that involve exercise offer physical ways to vent the mental pressure that ties knots in your stomach and neck and back muscles. It will also make it easier to sleep at night. Lastly, exercise elevates your mood by temporarily increasing the circulation of endorphins. We've talked to many partners who swear by their favorite physical activities.

Build the Quality of Resiliency in Your Personality

Each of these methods for countering overwhelming fear and grief produces a bonus gift you can draw on for the remainder of your life. When practiced regularly, *they build into your character something called resiliency.*

Resiliency, according to Edward Creagan, M.D. of the Mayo Clinic, is a "bounce back factor" or "emotional buoyancy." People with resiliency have a rich resource to draw upon anytime life throws them into painful circumstances. But how did they get that "bounce back factor" in the first place?

Most resilient people gained this trait by utilizing forms of self-soothing and renewal to navigate challenging rapids earlier in their lives. And they know they can do it again if and when they need to. That self-knowledge produces strength and provides an insurance policy of confidence that covers the future in their minds. By learning to face our pain with these same resources, we too can develop a resiliency that will give us that durable edge.

Understand and Conquer Dissociation
Dissociation

Learning to self-soothe and renew ourselves produces multiple benefits for partners, none of them more important than the ability to keep from slipping into a dissociative state.

Those who've struggled to stay present when dissociation's trance casts an isolating veil over their senses of time, space and reality know only too well how dissociation feels. Others may not know exactly what we mean by this term. Author Katherine Hannigan describes the feeling well in her children's book *Ida B. and Her Plans to Maximize*

Fun, Avoid Disaster, and (Possibly) Save the World:

>And then everything went dark. My body was still
sitting there, and my eyes were wide open, but the real me
that feels things and talks and makes plans and knows some
things for absolute one hundred percent sure had instanta-
neously shrunken and shriveled up and gone and hid way
deep down inside me. I couldn't see anything except
blackness, or hear anything except a kind of ringing, and all I
felt was emptiness everywhere around me.

>I don't know how long I sat there like that, but it felt
like years and years of being alone, huddled up and hiding in
the darkness.[3]

Perhaps many of you who previously felt unfamiliar with the
term dissociation can identify with the character Ida B. as you
read her words. For some, dissociation may be slight, leaving you
able to function on one level. For others, it can be so all-encompassing that your world grinds to a halt and functioning normally
becomes impossible. In the extreme, it produces amnesia about
the traumatic event. Why does it happen in the first place?

What Causes Dissociation?

Trauma specialist Peter Levine explains what causes dissociation:

>When neither fight nor flight will ensure…safety, there is
another line of defense: immobility (freezing), which is just as
universal and basic to survival. For inexplicable reasons, this
defense strategy is rarely given equal billing in texts on biology
and psychology. Yet, it is an equally viable survival strategy in
threatening situations. In many situations, it is the best choice.
On a biological level, success doesn't mean winning, it means
surviving, and it doesn't really matter how you get there. The
object is to stay alive until the danger is past and deal with the
consequences later. Nature places no value judgment about
which is the superior strategy….Animals do not view freezing as
a sign of inadequacy or weakness, nor should we.[4]

Dr. Levine is telling us several things about dissociation. First,
it is an instinctual defense (protective) response to threatening
situations when we can't run and we are unable to fight back.

Second, it's a way to "freeze-frame" what's happening, knowing we can't respond to it any other way at the moment because we're overwhelmed. Third, this response is universal—meaning we all have the instinct within us if we find ourselves in a situation where we believe no other choice is available to us. Last, it's not a sign of weakness or inadequacy. Staci Haines, another specialist, echoes Levine by saying that "Dissociation is a normal response to trauma, and allows the mind to distance itself from experiences that are too much for the psyche to process at that time."[5]

Most of you have probably dissociated, either knowingly or unknowingly, at times. Jessi shared a dissociative experience after a counseling session with her sex addict husband:

> We had a very difficult session tonight. The counselor said to take inventory and share what we are willing to do. I sat and I guess dissociated—basically stared at the flower on the counselor's tissue box for ten or fifteen minutes. The pain around my lack of hope that I will ever be desired or sought by Bob was all-consuming. It was a challenge to keep a lid on the pain.
>
> I think I methodically stuff—freeze my pain—then put a cap on it to keep it from swamping me, engulfing me. Even my vision became very focused and narrowed, kind of like when you're in labor. The words that kept swirling through me were *I don't have any hope that I will ever be desired or sought by him.*

Dissociation can be unsettling, embarrassing, frightening or even dangerous, depending on when the unanticipated fugue settles over you. Learning how to counter a dissociative state before it happens is not only empowering, but it can also prevent you n from getting lost behind the wheel or embarrassing yourself in public.

Countering Dissociation with Grounding and Impersonal Energy

When we begin to dissociate, our awareness grows fuzzy, as if everything slides out of focus and our attachment to the earth weakens or disappears. We lose our "grounding" and our sense of solidity. Yet in nearly every situation, we can learn to recognize that fuzzy sense of reality before it sucks us away and break its pull by re-grounding ourselves immediately. Getting in touch with the "concrete" world is one quick and easy way to do that. Think of getting grounded as "breaking a spell." Perhaps an example will add clarity to our explanation.

Several years ago Marsha was taking domestic violence counseling training which included a dramatic movie. As she sat in the darkened room with a small group of peers, one character in the movie began to verbally, emotionally and finally physically dominate another, and as he did, Marsha felt herself begin to slip into overwhelming old feelings:

It was sort of like being anesthetized. I could feel myself "going under." I was losing touch with my trained, strong self and sliding into an old pattern. I knew I had to act fast to avoid getting lost in it and getting grounded was the fastest, easiest way. I jumped up and left the room, walked around in the hall, put my hands against the wall and got in touch with my concrete world. I also "switched emotional gears": I mentally moved into the stronger aspects of my personality—much like switching into overdrive to drive up a steep mountain highway—and began to operate from a place of strength in me, rather than that old, well-worn place of weakness.

When I went back into the room I was careful to not allow myself to get emotionally drawn into the remainder of the movie. Instead, I chose to watch it from the safety of a professional distance, which enabled me to remain grounded for the rest of the day.

In this example, Marsha uses both grounding and impersonal energy to "stay present," rather than allow herself to dissociate. While dissociation provides one instinctual survival skill *in the moment of trauma,* it can become a pattern that takes over when it's no longer needed. And when it does, it interferes with our ability to cope by using the stronger aspects of our personalities. Grounding and impersonal energy provide tools you can use to stay anchored in the present.

Impersonal Energy
"Trauma survivors have a monocular view of themselves," Trauma specialist Tana Slay, Ph.D., informs us. Dr. Slay

communicates that our pain and loss become so all-consuming that we begin to see ourselves as one-dimensional: We hurt like crazy and it feels impossible to survive and cope. We can get so lost in our painful emotions and feelings that we forget our many strengths. But in truth, we all have strong, empowered parts of ourselves we've drawn upon during earlier difficult times. While it's true that for most of us this experience exceeds any pain we've known before, we do still possess those strengths. And those strengths *are* transferable to our present dilemma if we draw on them by learning to "switch gears emotionally."

To make that switch, we must recognize and affirm those stronger aspects of our personalities, which Dr. Slay labels as our impersonal energy.

"Impersonal energy means to come from an aspect of one's personality which is not bound to one's emotions and feelings," Dr. Slay says. "The client is able to step outside of his emotions and feelings and view himself and his experience from another perspective. This allows the client freedom in choosing his response to an experience instead of being driven by his unresolved trauma pain and cognitive distortions."[6]

If we can grasp this concept, it becomes a powerful resource to help us deal with our current traumatic situations, because it offers us another emotional "gear" to switch into. Julia was able to identify her impersonal energy by "locating" the place inside her that she used to deal with her daughter's epilepsy.

> When I first read about impersonal energy, I didn't understand what the term meant. But the more I listened, the more I began to realize all I had to do was to think about how I dealt with the challenges my little girl's epilepsy brought with it. Back then, I had to square off with park and recreation districts, with school teachers and with other parents who didn't understand the disorder. I had to try to not make her a prisoner of my fears in that if I let her do things other kids do she might die if she had a seizure. I was able to do that by thinking and acting out of a common sense, logical part of me that refused to operate out of raw emotion. Realizing that place still exists inside of me was half the battle. The other half was learning to switch into that mindset as I dealt with my husband's sex addiction.

Eliminate Cognitive Distortions

Do you ever hear yourself thinking "If he/she really loved me he/she wouldn't do this?" While such an assumption might sound logical when we're hurting, in reality it falls into the category of cognitive distortions, because nearly every sex addict will tell you the addiction has nothing to do with his or her spouse. Though few of us realize it, our feelings about ourselves, other women and men, sex addiction and our spouses become skewed, because our thinking on those topics is distorted.

Cognitive distortions are inaccurate thoughts or ideas that maintain negative thinking, which helps to maintain negative emotions. This self-perpetuating cycle of inaccurate thoughts —>negative thinking—>negative emotions, holds the power to defeat us, or at least suck all of the joy from our lives. Challenging and changing these distorted patterns of thought can take us a long way toward our own healing. The most common cognitive distortions:

- All-or-nothing thinking: "If he looks at porn/other women, etc., it means he doesn't love me."
- Overgeneralization: "Men are all a bunch of animals."
- Mental filter: "My husband is in recovery but I saw him check out the waitress, so his recovery is all a sham."
- Discounting the positive: "I know I'm feeling better, but it's just a matter of time before I am triggered again."
- Jumping to conclusions: "She's irritable today...she must be acting out again."
- Magnification: "This is the worst, most horrible day."
- Minimization: "It's not that bad; others have it worse so I shouldn't feel this way."
- Emotional reasoning: "I feel frightened; therefore he must be acting out again."
- Making *should* statements: "I should be over this by now."
- Labeling: "I married a pervert" or "She's a whore."
- Personalization: "If he doesn't stay in recovery, it's because I am not a good enough spouse."

Learning how to steer our thought patterns can take us a long way toward a happier outlook on life, no matter what our spouses choose to do about their addictions. Cognitive therapy specialist

Arthur Freeman tells us, "Many clients find it useful to label the particular cognitive distortions that they notice among their automatic thoughts and find that simply doing this weakens the emotional impact of the thoughts....Once the client understands what each distortion is, he or she can watch for examples of 'personalizing,' 'mind reading' and so on, among his or her automatic thoughts."[7] Psychologist Edmund Bourne says:

> Learning to identify and counter these unhelpful modes of thinking with more realistic and constructive self-talk can go a long way toward helping you handle everyday stresses in a more balanced, objective fashion. This, in turn, will significantly reduce the amount of anxiety, depression and other unpleasant emotional states you experience. Remember that your immediate experience of the outside world is largely shaped and colored by your own personal thoughts about it. Change your thoughts and you'll change the way your world appears.[8]

Eliminate Negative Self-Talk

When we face the pain of our partners' sex addictions and all the damage they bring, negative self-talk can slip in the back door of our minds and we aren't even aware of its presence. You know, those nasty little voices in your head that nag at you and devour your peace?

It's easy to understand why this happens when you realize that negative self-talk flows from a brew of distorted reality (cognitive distortions), over-focusing on the problem, half-truths and poor logic. It's hard *not* to over-focus on the problem when it is destroying our lives!

Yet even if it occurs automatically, if the calm and peace required to survive and heal remain our ultimate goal, we need to work to replace negative self-talk with positive internal dialogue. If we don't, negative self-talk keeps fear, anxiety, pessimism, unrealistic guilt and even shame percolating deep within our minds.

Some people find they can change this pattern on their own; others might need to work with a counselor. In either case, there are four steps required to catch and break this damaging habit:

- <u>Step 1</u>: Become aware of it. Know that recognizing it on your own can present a challenge. If you can't afford a counselor, consider a support group or a trusted friend to help point out negative self-talk.

- <u>Step 2:</u> Find out where the negative self-talk originated. You may have learned to deal with life in this manner from your childhood.
- <u>Step 3:</u> Acknowledge the pay-offs. What do you get out of the steady stream of counter-productive monologue in your head?
- <u>Step 4:</u> Take conscious steps to stop the negative self-talk. Begin to listen to your inner voices, challenge the distortions you hear and replace them with positive self-talk.

Learn and Use Positive Self-Talk

- <u>Step 1</u>: Notice your patterns. We can't change anything until we realize we have a problem. So the first step requires that we pay attention to our self-talk patterns. As we do, we'll begin to realize how often negativity appears in our personal monologue.
- <u>Step 2</u>: Recall thought stopping. As you begin to catch that inner roar of negative self-talk, use the words "Stop it!" to interrupt yourself. Actually saying it out loud helps reinforce the message. Some people also choose to wear rubber bands on their wrists and snap them when they notice negative self-talk. Breaking old habits makes way for positive new ones.
- <u>Step 3</u>: Turn self-limiting statements into opportunity producing questions. Statements like, "If I give my partner time to try recovery, I'll never have a chance to be happy!" increase our fears and stress and interfere with our abilities to contemplate which choices we really want to make. When such fears well up in you, try rephrasing them into opportunity producing questions: "If I give my partner a chance to try recovery, what can I do to take care of myself until I see the outcome of my partner's efforts?" opens the way for planning and determining how to meet our own needs. This approach produces hope rather than destroying possibilities.

Begin Emotional Processing and Grieving
Just as the journey of 1000 miles begins with one step, so, too, does the journey that leads to healing from sexual addiction's betrayal

trauma. Though a partner's healing journey is never linear, the hard work of healing generally begins with facing reality—with accepting what we have lost—and beginning the process of grieving.

Get the Help of a Counselor if Possible
As we said previously, a counselor can help you do the processing and grieving work you need to do. Even if you can't afford professional counseling, you can heal. Use the resources included here and try to join a short-term partners of sex addicts group so you can experience the numerous benefits a group of this nature provides.

The Steps that Lead to Healing
Different models and methods for emotional healing exist, especially for healing from trauma. Opinions and experiences about what works best can vary among professionals as well as partners of sex addicts. What works for one may not work for another. While our needs bear a kaleidoscope of similarities, they bear differences as well. In this section, we seek to present both the general steps we all must move through as we seek to heal from our losses, as well as a variety of methods available to you as you press on toward hope and healing.

In this chapter and the next, we lay out the steps of healing. Remember, in your life the process will never be linear. You will find yourself repeating some steps again and again until they finally become a part of you and your journey to healing and healthy living. Also, remember that the overall process will likely take months or perhaps years, depending on your circumstances and the quality of your support system. If you persist in working towards your own healing and growth, your pain will subside and finally leave. Your joy will increase many times over and life will take on new meaning and hold surprising new things and new people. We promise you that the effort will be more than worth it!

Possible Methods for Processing Your Pain
- Externalize the problem by sharing your story
- Use nature-based healing therapies
- Use expressive therapies such as art or music
- Eye Movement Desensitization and Reprocessing (EMDR)

- Renegotiate you trauma with a counselor's therapeutic interventions
- Use body therapies

A Closer Look at the Healing Methods Listed
Externalize the Problem by Sharing Your Story:
The Power of Story as Medicine

This method of beginning our healing is available to any of us, even if we don't have a counselor or a support group. The addition of these supports will certainly increase the healing effect of sharing our story. However, until we find the support we need, a multitude of online forums for partners of sex addicts are available on the Internet, providing you the opportunity to connect with other hurting partners and share your story and your pain as they share theirs with you. Here your pain is understood, recognized and validated; you're no longer alone.

You may ask yourself why talk about the pain and what's going on in our lives? Does it really do any good?

"The best way to escape horror is to create your way out," says Clarissa Pinkola Estes, Ph.D, a therapist who used the power of story as therapy with the children at the Columbine school in Littleton, Colorado, following the 1999 school shootings. She says:

> Talk to people—talk is the most healing thing you can do. Talk it out. You may have to tell your story over and over before it loses much of its pain.
>
> And so, in groups and individually in class, but also in hallways, at the drinking fountain, in the parking lot, kids and teachers would tell what was the best, the worst of the stories for themselves. In this way, the ground of their souls was kept soft—not allowed to harden, as it may when one has experienced a great blow and has no one to talk to who can respond with useful insights, words, gestures or looks....Each time you tell your story and receive someone's caring, you will be healing yourself.[9]

Externalizing your story by telling it, by sharing it, is powerful medicine in and of itself.

Nature Based Healing

Though most of us will find our healing path through more commonly practiced methods, other modalities exist for those who fail to find adequate words to access their pain and release its pent up power. Nature's beauty and wisdom can provide the powerful presence of the natural world and offers endless possibilities for learning, growth and change.

During one particularly difficult period in Marsha's life, the outdoors became a healing sanctuary for her, enabling her to continue to meet life's demands in spite of her pain: "I found that if I could spend one day each week interacting with nature via hiking, biking, cross-country skiing or boating, I could endure just about anything. I could feel God there and my body, mind and spirit fell into the rhythms of the earth and the natural world."

Expressive Therapy

The "expressive therapies" open several creative healing realms as well. "While talk is still the traditional method of exchange in therapy and counseling," says Cathy Malchiodi, author and expert in the field of art therapy, "practitioners of expressive therapies know that people also have different expressive styles—one individual may be more visual, another more tactile and so forth." The use of expressive therapy "...can more fully enhance each person's abilities to communicate effectively and authentically."[10]

Expressive therapies include a variety of modalities for healing:
- Art
- Dance
- Music
- Writing
- Theater
- Puppetry
- Psychodrama
- Play

Eye Movement Desensitization and Reprocessing

Eye Movement Desensitization and Reprocessing (EMDR) is an "information processing therapy" that approaches healing trauma from yet another angle. Proponents of EMDR believe wholeheartedly in its ability to access and integrate traumatic life experiences, usually in a relatively short amount of time.

The EMDR institute explains:

> During treatment, various procedures and protocols are used to address the entire clinical picture. One of the procedural elements is "dual stimulation" using either bilateral eye movements, tones or taps. During the reprocessing phases the client attends momentarily to past memories, present triggers, or anticipated future experiences while simultaneously focusing on a set of external stimulus. During that time, clients generally experience the emergence of insight, changes in memories or new associations.[11]

Renegotiating Your Trauma with a Counselor's Therapeutic Interventions

Peter Levine, the developer of an approach to trauma treatment called Somatic Experiencing, says:

> The human immobility response does not easily resolve itself, because the supercharged energy locked in the nervous system is imprisoned by the emotions of fear and terror. The result is that a vicious cycle of fear and immobility takes over, preventing the response from completing naturally. When not allowed to complete, these responses form the symptoms of trauma....
>
> It is essential that the unresolved activation locked in the nervous system be discharged. It has to do with the process of completing our survival instincts. [12]

Levine's "renegotiation of the trauma" offers a revolutionary way for a client to metaphorically return to that place within where his or her survival instincts were frozen at the moment of trauma's impact. Here, with the help of a trained therapist, the partner can complete the frozen action and, in so doing, set him or her self free.

"The drive to complete the freezing response remains active no matter how long it has been in place," Levine explains. "When we learn how to harness it, the power of this drive becomes our greatest ally in working through the symptoms of trauma."[13]

He continues, "...you need a strong desire to become whole again. This desire will serve as an anchor through which your soul can reconnect to your body. Healing will take place as formerly frozen elements of your experience (in the form of symptoms) are released from their trauma-serving tasks, enabling you to gradually thaw."[14]

For those who would like to learn more about Levine's approach, we suggest you read *Waking the Tiger: Healing Trauma* by Peter A. Levine.

Body Therapies

Body therapy can open an alternate avenue for release for those who find their trauma has taken up residence in their bodies and now expresses itself in physical symptoms.

"Trauma is 'locked' in the body," says Levine, "and it's in the body that it must be accessed and healed."[15] Gaylie Cashman, a friend whose accumulated trauma from life experiences left her with PTSD, discovered that it took the addition of body therapy for her to heal. She shares her story of finding hope through this method:

> I thought that when I married Dan, his loving, supportive understanding would enable me to begin to heal, but instead I fell apart. Shortly after we were married over seventeen years ago, my body almost completely shut down for about four months. I was deeply concerned that I slept for about twenty hours of every day. There were days I slept through the night right into the next evening. To stand up from kneeling down to get a pan in the kitchen, I had to pull myself up by hanging onto the counter. I fell asleep while I was with my favorite guests or watching a movie at the theatre. Doctors suggested I could be suddenly allergic to our pets or I was depressed, but no clear diagnosis was made and no one could help me.
>
> Once I got through the worst of it, I learned to avoid loud gatherings and I paced any physical work, because any excesses meant I spent the next day in bed. In retrospect, it seems that my body was just taking a much-needed rest from years of dumping fight-or-flight hormones into my system. It

was now functioning without that stress response. I was weak and wrung out, yet determined to heal.

I eventually hit a sort of dead end with my therapy. I felt I had talked about it thoroughly, yet I knew there was more.

"Is there any kind of therapy that can get at what is *in my body*?" I asked my therapist one day. "I know my stuff is somehow trapped in here but I don't know how to get it out."

"No," my therapist said. "I don't know of any." I was passionate to find healing for myself, yet I still wasn't making the progress I wanted and needed to make. I was addressing every perspective I knew, but still hadn't connected enough parts of myself to find hope of wholeness. It was at this point in my process that I enrolled in seminary to heal my damaged image of God, a product from my past. Yet I still needed to find a way to include my body in my healing.

After years of therapy while attending seminary, I remembered the benefits of yoga classes I took years ago. I felt drawn to try it again and found a nearby class. That class changed my course in life. During a session, I was propped up in a supported, opened-chest pose for an extended period of stillness. My usual rounded or closed down shoulders mirrored a self-protective posture I had carried a long, long time. This new pose offered me a physical openness, one with less defensive protection of my frequently guarded heart. In that open pose, an impromptu flow of tears was released from deep within. My deeply felt grief came from a part of me that talk therapy had not yet accessed.

I felt a surge of hope that my body was actually connected to my story and my healing process. I needed to find out more, though the instructor didn't know how to help me go further. Within months, I found Phoenix Rising Yoga Therapy (PRYT) and it perfectly nourished me where I was in my healing journey. A PRYT practitioner supports the client in movement and/or poses along with non-directive dialogue, assisting the client as she experiences the connection between her physical and emotional selves.

I took an intense ten-day course, and from this experience, I found I am the type of person who needs *to engage my body* to access, process and release emotions trapped in me. Getting back in my body helped me taste the empowerment I desperately needed to heal. I was sold. I decided to enroll in the eight-month intense Phoenix Rising Yoga Therapy training program so I could continue to heal and become certified to do this work with others. I also appreciated that PRYT was a *spiritually neutral* therapeutic yoga practice, because it gave me an experiential way to invite my new healing images of God on my wholeness journey.

"I learned how faithfully my body carries my story at the cellular level as I revisited and sifted through the layers of trauma in this process that helped me give it new meaning. I was empowered to integrate these old wounds with a new perspective, often with compassion toward others and myself. I was surprised to find compassion on myself as I revisited old anger I had shamefully stuffed inside. Now I could view it from my body's perspective. Though stuffing my anger had enabled me to survive at the time, I was now free and empowered to choose how I would live with my past in a healthy, safe way. I was overjoyed.

"Soon I completed my Master of Arts in Spiritual Formation, which prepared me to become a certified spiritual director, adding to my Phoenix Rising Yoga Therapy certification. My life experiences have led me to find two practices characterized by deep listening on all layers of being, for which I am indebted. I understood that my body, thoughts and emotions were in need of healing. But just as much, my spirituality was reconnecting with my life as I experienced a love *within my own body* that is greater than the trauma and feelings that were trapped inside of me.

"While I am deeply grateful for the medication-free health I currently enjoy, I am always aware that my body is a little bit broken. If tough situations in life set me back, I honor how my body acts as a reliable resource."

Gaylie's experiences offer hope to all, even those who've become stuck in their healing processes. Her life story embodies the completion of grieving and healing, the development of personal empowerment, the integration of trauma into a larger life story and the transformation of past pain into a positive life purpose. We desire those four components of a healthy and happy future life for you as well. We'll discuss each component in the next chapter.

Chapter 8

From Integration to Triumph

Katherine continues to tell us about her harrowing and unforgettable story:

It's been five years now since that fateful day. Neil and I are still married, but the healing process has been painful. However, there is now light at the end of the tunnel.

My husband was, as we discussed earlier, charged with possession of child pornography and released from prison after one week. He was immediately fired from his job with no severance pay. He had spent twenty-five years in the company. The media publicized the story heavily and I felt my life spinning totally out of control. I worked in an elementary school as an office administrator and loved my job, but it became difficult. All the parents heard the news and when I walked by, many who came to the school for one reason or another stopped talking and stared at me. I was the talk of the town.

It was so hard to do anything in town; I felt like everyone was looking at me, talking about me. I glanced around me like a hunted animal. When I saw someone I knew, my first thought was *I've got to get out of here!*

I kept asking myself painful questions. Would I keep my job? How would our church react? Neil was the lay pastor at our church and was scheduled to speak in a couple of days. What was going to happen with that? I had a meeting with the principal of the school where I worked; I needed to explain what was going on and asked for two days off of work to sort out my life.

You would think that I could find comfort in my church. But no, the pastor asked us not to come back. That was truly one of the most difficult things I had to face: The church I grew up in didn't, or couldn't, support me. Because of what my husband did, I was asked to stop coming to services. I had no support; I was to face this alone with God. Any self-esteem I may have had was now gone.

After my husband was released from jail, he went to live at a Catholic retreat center a few hours away. The director was his legal surety. The center was in the country where no one knew us and I visited him on weekends. I still did not know for certain the whole truth of what he had been involved in, so I remained in our hometown with our children who still lived at home.

A few months later, Neil was placed on two years' probation and the kids and I had to move, because we couldn't afford our home anymore. I quit my job and we moved into an old trailer at the retreat center, which was all we could afford. Neither one of us could get a job for over a year. We ended up with $49.00 in the bank before my husband got a job as a salesperson. We had made over $100,000 a year prior to all of this; now we make less then 25 percent of that. Finances were a huge adjustment; just trying to pay our basic bills was a struggle. My family was falling apart. It was especially hard on two of our children.

I had to get checked for HIV and any other possible STDs, which was a humiliating experience. Fortunately, I was disease free. However, my doctor was worried about me, because I had lost a lot of weight; I was unable to eat and sleep, which became a problem following my husband's arrest. Even now, four years later, I am only able to sleep four to five hours a night.

On weekends during the time before I moved to the retreat center, I visited Neil and it was there he told me about his other life. His first affair lasted almost two years and he fell in love with the woman. That devastated me and left me feeling sick. Due to the hurt of losing his affair partner, my husband said he began to have non-emotional affairs. He had eight of them. Some were one-night stands; others he met with often. He also told me about some homosexual affairs.

One day when we were on our way to Neil's counseling session, he attempted to drive the car into a power pole. I saw the pole coming closer and closer and thought of my children without their parents. I especially thought of my youngest son, now the only one still living at home. How would he cope? At the last moment—with me screaming "please stop"—he pulled the car back into our lane. I was out of my mind with fear. I sat there, sobbing, trying to catch my breath and I couldn't step trembling.

The losses were great. I lost my ministry, which I mourned for almost three years. This loss was so deep. I felt like God could never use me again because of what had happened. But after a time, I realized I had to stop looking back to what I formerly had and did so that I could move on and believe in God's redemption.

And miraculously, God is redeeming my life, and healing is beginning to happen in our family and children's lives. I now regularly help other wives married to sex addicts who live in our community, and I facilitate a partners' support group. And Neil is now helping other men who struggle with sex addiction. He gives them hope and help as they work to overcome their addictions, just as he has worked hard in the last four years to gain freedom from his. The miracle of new life can happen, even after the most devastating pain. We're living proof. God is giving us new life!

Somewhere during a partner's healing process he or she begins to integrate the past and its losses into his or her present life. In that integration the loss takes on new meaning, and the partner may recognize it has produced valuable growth and new purpose in his or her life, as it has in Katherine's.

This growth, first called "posttraumatic growth" in 1996, can lead to "...improved relationships, new possibilities for one's life,

a greater sense of personal strength and spiritual development...
they also may find themselves becoming more comfortable with
intimacy and having a greater sense of compassion for others who
experience life's difficulties."[1]

That is the paradox of trauma: Miraculously, from life's most
painful losses we can gain life's most valuable gifts. For most partners of sex addicts, arriving at this place requires time.

In this chapter, we continue to plot the trail through trauma,
which leads us to our ultimate destination: integration and
triumph. To one day arrive at triumph we must continue the
grieving process, which began in the last chapter. Then, as pain
begins to subside and time and space become available to focus on
growth, we can move through the remaining stages to complete
our grieving, arriving long last at transformation's door. Here, we
can find joy, because we realize that what has hurt us and cost us
the most has also led to new hope, new passion and new purpose.
And, ultimately, to new life!

Let's look again at the stages of grieving we discussed in the
last chapter, while also referring back to the "Pathway to Healing,
Empowerment and Transformation Following Sexual Betrayal
Trauma" chart.

As you look at the stages of healing, remember only you—
with perhaps the aid of your counselor if you have one—can
determine where you are in your healing process. Wherever you
now are in your journey to healing, we encourage you to continue
your emotional processing and grieving, remembering that you
will know when the pain has lost its power and you are free to
move on.

- Acknowledge and process your feelings
- Acknowledge and grieve your losses and the consequences
  they produced in your life
- For some, face and adapt to separation or divorce
- Alter your attachment to what you've lost, let it go and say
  goodbye
- Develop resiliency

Such lofty goals, which include altering our attachment to
what we've lost and letting it go, integrating our losses into our

larger life story and finding new hope by transforming our pain into a new purpose, may seem impossible from the place in which you find yourself right now. However, please trust that every step along the way moves you one step closer to healing.

Mary shared her grieving process several months after learning about her husband's addiction:

> We were sitting in bed reading together and I got up, went to the shelf outside our bedroom door where I kept a display of wedding memorabilia—our wedding photo, cake knife, guest book, sentimental pieces that I've loved—and I took them all down. I felt tempted to throw them out, but feared I'd later regret it, so I packed them away, storing them until perhaps the time comes that they don't represent loss to me. And then we cried...sobbed hard together for several long minutes. So hard that I kept choking and thought I was going to throw up. I spent part of the time over the toilet, sobbing and choking and gagging. But even as I did, I thought, *This is grief! This is good!* I knew it was important work. And when I finished I felt better; I felt *different!*

Mary's experience of catharsis in grieving about her husband's addiction makes ever more meaningful Peter Levine's insight about healing from trauma: "There may be dramatic and poignant moments as well as gradual and often mundane stretches on the road to recovery....For each of us, the mastery of trauma is a heroic journey that will have moments of creative brilliance, profound learning and periods of hard tedious work."[2]

Healing requires time. It also requires that we continue to pursue personal empowerment so that we can face the losses in our lives and proactively participate in creating the new reality that our healing will bring.

Cultivate Personal Empowerment

Because traumatization strips us of our personal power—of our abilities to protect ourselves and our children from the pain and disruption that sex addiction thrusts into our lives—the re-establishment (or perhaps the first-time cultivation) of this personal empowerment/self-empowerment quality proves vital for our healing. This quality enables us to manage and direct our own lives; to take responsibility for ourselves and to act effectively on our own behalves and the behalves of others who seek or need our help.

What *is* personal empowerment? Let's begin to answer that question by first citing what personal empowerment *is not*.

What Empowerment *Isn't*
- Empowerment is not trying to control others
- Empowerment is not about getting our own way
- Empowerment is not selfish or self-centered

What Empowerment *Is*
"Self-empowerment is about becoming powerful," says Marcia Chellis, author of *Ordinary Women, Extraordinary Lives.* "It is a process to use for overcoming any barrier. It is a way to achieve personal success, a way to handle challenging circumstances, a way to make your life work."[3]

"Can one quality really encompass all that? And if the answer is yes, how do I get it?" we might ask. The first answer is yes; the second is, "With lots of practice and hard work!" But we can attest to the fact that empowerment is well worth the work it takes. Let's look at six ingredients of empowerment.

Six Ingredients of Empowerment
1. Healthy boundaries
2. Maintaining solid grounding
3. Self-awareness, impersonal energy and executive awareness
4. Healthy communication skills
5. Healthy conflict management skills
6. Reframing ourselves as survivors rather than as victims

Next we will touch briefly on each of the areas of growth that make up personal empowerment. Afterward, we will quickly outline and explain the qualities and skills that will help you continue to heal as well as contribute greatly to your development. Work, if possible, with a counselor or group and read more on each topic where you need additional growth.

1. Healthy Boundaries

Here we will only address boundaries as they relate to dealing with our triggers when we are in a relationship with a sex addict. Identifying, then sharing those boundaries with your spouse is one way you can take responsibility for your healing and growth:

- Identify your triggers.
- Determine the boundaries you need in order to deal with your triggers proactively.
- Communicate your boundaries in a healthy way, remembering the other person can say "No."
- Find alternative solutions if the other person says "No."

Of all the ingredients of empowerment, boundaries prove to be the most mysterious and challenging. Boundaries require *both our powerlessness and our empowerment.*

Not only is empowerment taking responsibility for ourselves by drawing boundaries and asking for what we need, it is also accepting our powerlessness over others, including our spouses. We can't *make* anyone honor our position or do what we'd like them to do. Part of being empowered is to be okay with letting others say "No." Honoring a person's right to say "No," then honoring yourself—even if the other refuses to honor your boundary—needs to be okay. When that happens, we must then take responsibility for finding other ways to meet our own needs.

At what point, then, does it become impossible to share a life with the one you love, because he or she isn't interested in honoring what you need to feel safe or does not want to give up the addictive behavior? Many among us must face this question and must find the answer for ourselves. Therein lies much of the mystery and challenge of establishing boundaries.

2. Maintaining Solid Grounding

In the last chapter, we discussed the importance of solid grounding as a way to avoid habitual dissociation. However, gaining and maintaining this ability also contributes greatly to our personal empowerment. Because our ability to stay grounded and remain present adds to our ability to cope with whatever life experiences we have, make sure you develop and build this ability into your empowerment arsenal. Additional help in the area of boundaries may be found in the book *Boundaries* by Henry Cloud and John Townsend. This insightful book has helped millions of others grow in this important area.

3. Self-Awareness, Impersonal Energy and Executive Awareness

Self-awareness is the ability to observe ourselves "from a distance." Executive awareness is the objective, rational part of our personalities—the impersonal energy part—we discussed in chapter 6 in our discussion about triggers and boundaries. Both of these qualities play important roles in building our personal empowerments, that ability to manage and direct our own lives, no matter what our partners do with their addictions.

Self-awareness enables us to understand what we're feeling, why we feel and why we act the way we do. Self-awareness is equivalent to "getting in touch with ourselves." Finding ways to talk about or write about what's going on inside your mind and heart are the keys to gaining self-awareness. Use a counselor, a support group, journaling or people who love and care about you to help you gain the understanding you need to truly know yourself. Only by gaining self-awareness can we get in touch with what we feel and need so we can act in our own interests.

Once we gain that awareness, we can use our impersonal energy/executive awareness to make empowered decisions and changes in our lives. These abilities are desperately needed when life has been turned upside down by our partners' addictive behaviors and we have no idea what to do next.

4. Healthy Communication Skills

Interpersonal communication can make or break a relationship in the best of times. In the aftermath of sexual betrayal, however, knowing how to communicate in a healthy way, then remembering to express yourself in a period of heartbreak, can help you survive the upheaval in your relationship.

Healthy communication includes really listening with your heart; it is direct, respectful, clear and clean, meaning there are no hidden messages, no insults or digs. If you find that communicating in a healthy way seems impossible right now, reach out for help from a counselor, clergy or someone else who can help you communicate during this difficult time.

Here we list tips to employ as you work to grow in your skill as a healthy communicator:

- **Listen without countering.** Actively try to hear the other person's point of view. Stop planning what you are going to do or say next and just tune in. Don't be defensive.
- **Make eye contact.** Look at the person as you listen and speak.
- **Speak for yourself.** Make "I" statements about what you feel and need. Make sure you really understand your partner.
- **Seek clarification.** State and reiterate what you have heard.
- **Stick to the subject.** Make your point without throwing around accusations. Provide examples or details to support your point.
- **Look inside yourself.** What is the motive behind the words you choose to say? Are they used to defend, provoke, distract or to really communicate?
- **Ask for behavioral change.** Bring the conversation back to your everyday life. What will be different after this discussion? What can be expected?
- **Remember your partner's trigger points.** Resist the temptation to use them.
- **Remember your own trigger points.** Resist the temptation to react.
- **Agree to disagree sometimes.** Practice respectful acceptance of difference.
- **Remember the power of apology.** If you know you have been hurtful or wrong, apologize.

5. Healthy Conflict Management Skills

The shock, the hurt and the anger generated by sexual betrayal trauma pollutes both our marriages and our minds with toxic conflict. While counseling, support groups and journaling can help us resolve our *inner* conflict, we must rely on healthy conflict management to navigate the relational conflict between our partners and ourselves. But such interpersonal conflict requires

..a skills if we want to do it in a healthy way.

..recommend a truly helpful book titled *Speaking Your
..nd Without Stepping on Toes* by Henry A. Virkler. Dr. Virkler
does a wonderful job of simplifying healthy conflict management skills and helps readers learn to use them in their everyday
lives.

He helps us understand that assertiveness and respect are key
to managing conflict in a healthy way. "Assertiveness," he says, "is
the ability to express your thoughts, feelings, beliefs, and desires
in direct, honest, appropriate ways that do not violate the rights,
needs, and self-esteem of another person."[4] That is the goal we
must strive for.

6. Reframing Ourselves As Survivors Rather Than As Victims

All of us who have sexual addicts as partners are, in essence,
victims of sexual addiction and the toll it takes on our lives. But
for some, the victimization experience locks their psyche in a state
referred to as learned helplessness. Bessel van der Kolk explains it
this way:

> People in whom the effects of the trauma become
> ingrained often develop a chronic sense of helplessness and
> victimization. The [trauma] experience is so unexpected and
> overwhelming that the very foundations of a person's
> coping mechanisms are challenged. If the victims already
> have tenuous personal control, or if the stress persists, they
> may lose the feeling that they can actively influence their
> destinies.[5]

Through no fault of their own, partners who become
stranded in this state of helplessness generally need a counselor's
help to find their way out. If you recognize yourself in Dr. van
der Kolk's words, find a way to get the professional help you
need to gain access to your empowered self who remains
dormant within.

The "F" Word: Consider Forgiveness

Barbara will never forget one particular group session for partners
where she brought up the idea of forgiveness as part of a

partner's healing process and immediately a woman across the circle from her nearly shouted, "How can I *ever* forgive this?!" As the woman spoke about her own experience, it became clear to Barbara that for this woman the word forgiveness held the dark burden of misuse. She had been taught that forgiveness encompasses reconciliation.

Barbara and I believe the act of forgiveness does not necessarily include reconciliation. Forgiveness requires only the action of the offended, while reconciliation requires action from both the offended *and* the offender. Though reconciliation, if it is possible, often renders a joyous outcome, in reality, many times it simply cannot happen.

Nor does forgiveness mean "It's okay," "It doesn't matter," "I must forget" or "I must act as if this never happened." Rather, forgiveness acknowledges great pain and offense, then releases resentment, bitterness and revenge. Forgiveness recognizes that release allows us to move closer to our own healing.

Robert Enright, a researcher on the subject of forgiveness, says that when we forgive "we are no longer *controlled* by angry feelings toward this person [italics added]."[6] In essence, forgiveness can set *us* free when we are finally able to offer it. Forgiveness is a process as well as an event; it requires an act of will and often, much time.

Integration and Transformation

Each of us, when we are ready, must do the work required to integrate the losses we've experienced into our larger life story if we truly want to heal and move on. If we fail to do the work integration requires, we risk remaining fixated on, not to mention controlled by, the trauma, as specialist Peter Levine explains:

Through transformation, the nervous system regains its capacity for self-regulation. Our emotions begin to lift us up rather than bring us down...We are able to learn from our life experiences...We will no long view our world through fearful eyes.

Though our planet can be a dangerous place, we will no longer suffer from the constant fear that creates hyper-vigilance—a feeling that danger always lurks and the worst often happens. We begin to face life with a developing sense

of courage and trust...Every trauma provides an opportunity
for authentic transformation.[7]

We know that integration and the process of turning old
wounds into transformational experiences that build character
presents a daunting challenge to those still early in their healing
and perhaps for those who aren't. We hope Levine's beautiful
picture of integration in nature will enable you to grasp the goal:

> When a young tree is injured it grows around that
> injury. As the tree continues to develop, the wound becomes
> relatively small in proportion to the size of the tree. Gnarly
> burls and misshapen limbs speak of injuries and obstacles
> encountered through time and overcome. The way a tree
> grows around its past contributes to its exquisite individuality,
> character, and beauty. I certainly don't advocate traumatiza-
> tion to build character, but...the image of the tree can be a
> valuable mirror.[8]

Finding New Hope by Transforming Past Pain Into a Positive Purpose

In talking about her work with students, parents and teachers
following the Columbine School tragedy in Littleton, Colorado,
Clarissa Pinkola Estes said that those who had lived through the
horror asked again and again how they could escape the terrible
memories and the ongoing pain that the trauma left in their lives.
Her response was to tell them to "Create your way out, I say.
Love your way out. It is the same. Through prayer, through the
story *you* have lived; through dance, through invention, through
loving and serving others, create your way out."[9]

We wholeheartedly agree. We know of no other way out of
the deep anguish and loss sexual betrayal trauma produces in partners' lives than to create your way out, to love your way out and
to serve others. Estes' perspective holds true in each of our lives,
even though our betrayal stories ended very differently. Barbara's
marriage not only survived, today it thrives; while in Marsha's life,
nearly every element she once held dear vanished with the
changes wrought as the consequences of the addiction played out
over time. Yet in each of our lives, new hope, new beginnings,

new passions and new purpose *did* come. To illustrate that reality in her life, Marsha shares a final entry from her journaling:

> The long winter of my healing is finally over. Though as I reread an old entry that was written early in the darkest nights of my loss, I find it hard to believe that the sun has come out again. In the midst of my deepest pain I wrote these words: "It's as if someone has torn open my chest with their bare hands, yanked out my heart, ripped it in half and stuffed only half of it back in while muttering these words: 'There now! Just see if you can go on beating!'"

> Oh, there remains that dull ache from time to time, the awareness of the loss of one-time dreams forever gone. Finally, spring bursts forth. New hope and new beginnings are unfolding in my life like the season's fresh green leaves.

And we know springtime will come once again in your life, too, as you move forward, one day at a time. Clarissa Estes captures well the truth that we must participate in our forward motion by actively pursuing the healing when she describes a student who lost his best friend in the shootings. This young man had not been able to escape the mental torture the trauma and loss left on him. But in one of the parables Estes told how he was able to finally grasp his release, let go of the past and move on.

> I remember one particularly haunted young man who had lost his best friend in the shootings ..."I have been tortured out of my mind for days now. Today during the story I was free for the first time in a long time. That story about the mouse who could hear the roaring in his ears, who went to live in a new place where he could see and hear his soul? Since I heard that story, I feel I am free to go; to not stay in the old story any longer."

> In creative life, his words are considered holy: free to not stay in the old story any longer. To not stay where sorrow always looks backward, where worry always looks around to see what else might go awry, but instead to look up, to take the leap, so see a fresh new world, lifting up one's eyes to new life now and ahead...[10]

This is our hope for you: There will be a moment when you, too, are free to not stay in the old story any longer, but to look up and take the leap to new life. Press on in your healing until your life is your own.

PART III

STORIES FROM
THE OTHER SIDE

Life After Trauma's Impact

The process of healing is a long journey. It is difficult, life-changing and oftentimes gut-wrenching work. However, the difficult journey is worth the price. Our colleague Milton Magness shares with you these words of encouragement:

> When will you get over the hurt? When will you be ready to move on with life? It is important to note that ignoring the trauma or determining you will not think about the past or talk about it only results in creating an incubator that allows the wound to fester to the point of becoming debilitating. Be patient. Though the journey is not quick, it is well worth the effort. Take a courageous stand today and look through the trauma lens; find healing on the other side.

In the following pages, we present stories from both men and women. Some are from those who have struggled with sexual addiction, then watched as their partners experienced the devastating pain of their sexual betrayals. Others are from the betrayed themselves.

In their own words, these men and women describe their thoughts, feelings, experiences and journeys. Many share the things that did not help them, and all share things that brought hem hope and healing. It is our hope that these letters and the stories contained within validate your experiences, give you encouragement and let you know that healing is possible.

Chapter 9

From the Hearts of Sex Addicts Who "Get It" and Care

Story One

The pain I have caused my wife cannot be explained in a short letter. It would probably take an entire book. In any case, I will try to give you a little insight from my perspective as to how I hurt her. To get a true sense of the immensity of her pain, I must first give you a short history of our relationship and how I hurt her through the years:

- Abandonment: I abandoned her after we returned from our honeymoon to focus on my other passion: architecture. I effectively put her on the shelf. While she and I were dating and engaged, we talked at length about all kinds of things. She told me about the pain she felt all her life from being abandoned. I don't think she used that word but that was the subject matter. I knew she was adopted as a baby. I knew of her adoptive mother's death when she was still a baby. I knew of the troubled relationship she had with her stepmother and of the rejection she felt from that. In hindsight, I think I, more than anyone else in her life, should have understood the impact of my putting her on the shelf. Unfortunately I didn't. I hurt her over and over and over again.

    My wife didn't have a choice with the others who abandoned her, but with me she did. She chose to love me and I let her down. When we were engaged, I gave her all my free time. Once we were married, I ignored her needs. She trusted me to love her and protect her. I didn't deserve her trust. Instead of protecting her, I turned my affections over to another passion. I effectively rejected her night after night as I studied for the professional licensing exam. I should have balanced my study time so I could give my wife what she needed and deserved, but I didn't. Out of a false sense of self-sacrifice, I stole my time from her and gave it to architecture. It would have been okay if I had sacrificed my personal time to invest in my studies. Unfortunately, I took the time she deserved. There are so many things in my married life that I wish I could undo. This is one of the big ones. The domino effect of this one choice, made over and over again, has rippled down throughout our marriage and caused immense pain to both of us.

- <u>Using her</u>: Many times after we had sex, my wife cried. She could never say why she cried. I thought it had to do with other men who had hurt her in her past. I couldn't believe her tears were because of me. I believe I finally understand. I was the one hurting her. I was effectively rejecting her daily by my ignoring her need to spend time with me. She felt used by me for sex. It was the feeling of being used that caused her tears. All those times she cried it was entirely my fault. I was hurting her. I will never totally get over the idea that I was hurting her like this. I thought I was a good person. I thought I loved her. It is obvious from my actions that this was not the case. I failed her miserably!

- <u>Blame</u>: I blamed my wife for our sexual problems. I thought that if she could just touch me and let me hold her, everything would be fine. We would naturally have sex more often and I would be more attentive to her. If only. If only. What a joke! The real issue was my selfishness! I was deceiving myself. By blaming her, I didn't have to search myself to find the problem. Because of this, I couldn't address the real issue and seek help to solve it. This meant we both had to suffer for twenty-eight years of marriage until I could come to grips with this pattern and honestly seek help.

- <u>Lust</u>: When we lived in a different city, I lusted after any good-looking woman I saw. This included most of my wife's friends. At some point while we still lived there, I told her about this in a moment of guilt. She was extremely hurt. She told me that if I did this again she would leave.
- <u>Deceit</u>: I was often not truthful with her. I was a coward. I often said whatever I had to in order to avoid conflict. I would not tell her what I honestly thought when I anticipated it would result in angering her. When we moved, there were many days I planned on working a little late, but then lost track of time. I often hoped for traffic congestion so I could blame my late arrival on traffic. I know she didn't believe me when I gave my "reason" for being late, but that didn't stop me from lying anyway.
- <u>Rejection</u>: I didn't effectively support my wife in raising our boys. I assumed she felt I was not just rejecting her, but our boys, too. I was almost never home and when I was there, I was too tired to do much of anything with my family. This must have been very painful for my wife. When I was unwilling to spend money on either her or the boys, she probably felt I was rejecting all of them again and again and again.

  We always fought over how to discipline the boys. I was afraid we were raising kids who could not obey since we were not effectively disciplining them. Since we could not agree on how to discipline them, I just withdrew and let her carry the entire burden. I knew she was exhausted but I didn't help out.

This list is not all-inclusive of the injuries I caused. They are just the ones that come to mind today as I write you this letter.

Recently, my wife found instructions for how to clean the history off of the Internet browser. I had printed them out so I could cover up a search I had done on the word "sex". She asked me if I had been looking at things on the web that I shouldn't have. My first response was to lie to her. I basically said no. She then walked out of my office and started folding towels in the family room. I realized my answer was not only untruthful, but also simply ridiculous. I then went to her

and told her I had lied to her. I became more truthful, but
not totally honest. I told her I had viewed some pornography
advertisements, but that I had not gone into the advertised Web
sites. This was not the truth. Even though she begged me to
be completely honest, I just couldn't do it. I believed that if
I were completely honest, she would leave me. In addition to
that, I was not willing to take full responsibility for my actions.
In my heart, I believed my actions were caused by how she
treated me. Today I categorically know this is not the case. My
unwillingness to take full responsibility lasted for quite some
time. This resulted in me sporadically spewing out a little more
truth. This hurt her deeply. Each time I gave a little more truth,
I was re-injuring her. She was traumatized all over again. Not
only did this cause more pain, it also gave her tangible evidence
that I cannot be trusted. It got to the point that she told me the
lies were worse than the truth. Here are a few examples of the
trauma I caused my wife:

- After we had gone through about eight weeks of my
  revelations, I felt I had confessed everything. She and I had
  been doing much better for several days and perhaps even a
  week. By that I mean she could see I was actually taking
  responsibility for my actions and was actively working on
  recovery. I had finally come to understand that I was 100
  percent responsible for my sinful behavior. (If you're
  interested in how I came to that understanding, read Edward
  T. Welch's *Addictions: A Banquet in the Grave*.) I was actually
  showing by my actions that I cared for her and had empathy
  for the pain I had caused her.

     We were lying in bed talking. She was crying. She was
  afraid—afraid to trust me, afraid to trust my recovery. She
  knew of men who had been sexually sober for several years
  and had eventually fallen back into sexual addiction. She
  spoke from deep in her heart as she tried to express her fear.
  She knew she could not handle going through the pain
  again. While she wouldn't say it, I believe she was having
  feelings for me and that was what was generating her fear.
  She didn't want to feel again, because it would open her up

to being hurt again in the future. Looking into my wife's eyes, it was not hard to see the emotional pain she was in. It is hard to admit I am the cause of that pain. Sometimes I wonder if she isn't right. Would it be more compassionate of me to let her go? I don't think I can do that. I don't ever want to hurt her again! I pray that God will take me home in a car accident before I ever hurt her by acting out in my addiction again.

• I hope I never forget the Saturday morning when she asked me what I regretted most about my sexual addiction and what we were going through. I was in my home office at the time. I thought about it a bit and said what I regretted the most was how I used her cousin to fantasize about. I don't remember her direct response to my comment. However, she came back into my office about a half hour later with another question. When she came back, I was working on my computer so my back was to her. She asked something to the effect, "So was she the only one you have been fanaticizing about for the last several years?"

   While still facing the computer I said something like, "For the most part, yes." At this response, I heard the most blood curdling scream I ever heard in my life. It scared me to death. I turned to see my wife with her hands to her mouth continuing to scream. The object of my fantasies is not just a cousin. In all of my wife's family, both direct and distant relatives, this one young woman is dearest to her. This has so traumatized my wife that she cannot fathom me ever seeing her dear cousin again. When she comes to visit, I will find an excuse to be out of town, even if that means I find a hotel for the weekend. This issue caused my wife great emotional pain that transferred into physical pain. She has been on strong pain medication for back pain and sciatic nerve pain for the last three months. I believe this pain was solely caused by my revealing this truth to her.

• One evening recently we were watching TV. All of a sudden she was angry with me. She didn't have a reason for her anger that she could describe. Her body language just exhibited disgust for me. She was upset all weekend long. It wasn't until the middle of the following week that she was able to understand the cause of the anger. Something on the TV rekindled the pain of my sin on her. I was thankful for the advice I received from a woman whose husband has dealt with sexual addiction effectively for years. She told me my wife will have bad days for seemingly no apparent reason. She told me I cannot fix it. I need to be with her to comfort her. This has turned out to be great advice. My being with her through these times has shown her I care. Even when she doesn't want me there, she knows I am there for her.

My wife's traumatic pain has been unbelievable. The fact that the pain is not easily overcome is very difficult for me. I hate seeing her hurt. I pray that God will take the pain I have caused her off of her shoulders and put it on me. I should be the one to carry the hurt. This is enough about me.

Story Two

I don't really know when it began. Or even why.

I was brought up in a wonderful home with two parents who fully imparted God's love to me and nurtured me in faith...

I didn't struggle with most of the temptations urban teenagers encounter: drugs, alcohol, cheating at school, fighting, stealing. I had a superego the size of a department store. Yet, sexual fantasy was a challenge for me, a source of incredible guilt and torment. Fortunately, through high school, I had limited exposure to explicit material.

But in college, that changed. I was living with non-Christian roommates and in the kind of environment where pornography was pervasive. I found myself drawn to it, at first when no one was looking so as not to ruin my witness. By senior year, I gave up pretending and convinced myself that looking at porn was not *wrong*. This wasn't by some theological revelation; it was because I got tired of having to constantly confess when I *gave in*.

I got married two years after I graduated. By now, I'd renounced my attempts to make pornography use morally acceptable. I was sure that marriage would solve this problem (by now, it was a full-fledged addiction). It didn't. No problem like an addiction gets solved by marriage. It made things worse.

Things deteriorated over the years. As technology changed and my resistance diminished, I found that behaviors I'd previously deemed unthinkable became quite normalized. All this while being deeply conflicted, ashamed and terrified of being discovered.

Many days, I woke up not wondering if I'd yield to temptation, but wondering how bad it would be. For several months at a time, I stopped taking communion when I went to church, knowing that the next day I'd probably be back at my addiction again.

Even though, at times, I shared aspects of my struggle (including going to counseling), no one, including myself, understood and realized the extent to which this sin-sickness was consuming my soul. But soon I became desperate; I saw clearly that I was being destroyed and was no longer able to hide my secret life. I disclosed all to my wife, parents, selected friends. For the next few months, I tried to change my life through counseling and accountability relationships.

However, I did not really understand how deeply embedded the addiction was in my soul, nor did I or those around me have a clue about the recovery process. And, in retrospect, I never really stopped addictive behavior. While I cut off the worst forms of acting out, there were many "minor" concessions I was continuing to make to lust. Soon, I was in full relapse and too frightened, proud and self-deceived to admit it.

One summer morning, my wife confronted me after I'd stayed up all night surfing online for pornography. In many ways, that morning, my life ended. In an instant, I went from being a superstar in my community, the ideal husband and father, an admired leader in the church, even the model recovering addict, to being a moral failure, a visual adulterer, a liar, a porno junkie.

As I confessed and came to realize how low I'd gone, as I saw the unspeakable pain these admissions caused my wife, as I bore the humiliation of church discipline (I was a leader and employee of my church), as I tallied the amount of money I'd spent and the time I'd wasted, as I was confronted with my moral bankruptcy, I began to question the ability of God's love to extend to me. I understood grace, unconditional compassion, mercy beyond understanding, but I started to wonder if I was the exception clause, the one that God had abandoned. I wondered if my family and my community would be better off without me and even considered suicide, though for the sake of my children, I did not dwell on this for long.

Fortunately, my story doesn't end here.

In the darkest night of my soul, I began a new life. And for the past eleven years, I've been involved in a journey of recovery, transformation and restoration. And I can say that today I walk in freedom and victory.

God has used many tools to accomplish this, including deep friendships that involve much more than just reporting my failures, periods of counseling with a therapist who really understands addiction, intense involvement with a 12-step group, the discipline of routine self-reflection and helping others who have struggled like me.

Without question, the most miraculous gift has been in the ongoing restoration of my relationship with my wife. I will never fully grasp the depth of pain I caused her, the degree to which I betrayed her trust and shredded her self-esteem. Our former pastor described the impact of my addiction on my wife as like that of a truck driving though a beautiful stained-glass window.

My actions ruined our marriage beyond repair. God has given my wife the amazing grace, the inexplicable capacity to forgive, so that we could work together to build a new marriage. I can never again question God's love, for each morning I wake up next to a wonderful, beautiful woman whose love I don't deserve.

So, where am I now? I am free and I am being freed.

Free in that I no longer worry about how bad it will be. Situations, environments, opportunities, emotions that would have led me to my addiction no longer do. I really can say "no." Free, because I have developed a lifestyle of rigorous honesty, routine accountability and behavioral safeguards, knowing that I am still vulnerable to temptation and self-deception.

Story Three

At eighteen I went off to college to get an education. Today, at forty-three, I look back on those years and realize that what I learned was far from the intended subject matter. I majored in drinking beer, lifting weights and picking up girls. I began a pattern that lasted for the next twenty-five years. It caused tremendous pain and suffering to my (soon-to-be-ex) wife, my two children, my family, my close friends and, ultimately, myself.

I began having sex as soon as I arrived at school. Each day presented a new opportunity to bed a different girl. I developed flawed views of what love is and what value a woman holds. In the nineteen years that I have been married, I have had numerous affairs, most of which my wife never became aware of. The first time I was unfaithful (three years into the marriage) I felt a bit guilty, but not too awful. For the next sixteen years of our time together as man and wife, I behaved like a sailor: a woman in every port. To me it was a game—a notch in the bedpost. *What my wife doesn't know won't hurt her*, I told myself. I was oblivious to the consequences of my behavior, and I justified it as something men do.

Twelve years ago my wife became aware of an affair I was having. Her immediate reaction was horror: tears, screaming, denial. "Why Me?" she said, rolling around on the floor in a ball crying uncontrollably. She cursed me and hit me; the days following this were awful. But after a few months things were back to normal. She let it go, or so I thought, and I returned to the same pattern and behavior. No harm, no foul.

Then two years ago she became aware of another affair I was having. Again there were tears, screaming, disbelief, anger, cursing, rolling around crying uncontrollably. "How could you do this to me?" she cried. "How could you do this to my family?"

What I'm about to say makes me ashamed of myself, but this is the truth: When I was caught twelve years ago, when I was caught two years ago and when my wife was in the middle of her turmoil, I did not care. As she rolled around on the floor in tears, I didn't think of her. I didn't really care about her feelings. I just wanted her to stop crying. I actually wondered if there was a ball game on television. Or was there any leftover fried chicken from last night?

The woman I had been married to for nineteen years—the woman I had two children with and shared thousands of hours with—she was laying there in pain and agony, and all I could think about was me. Did I apologize? Sure, but I didn't really mean the words. They were just words. My thoughts hadn't changed on the subject, so why would the behavior change? I thought I was justified. My friends tried to tell me to clean up my act, but I didn't want to hear it. I was the master of my domain.

Six months ago my wife decided that she didn't want me anymore. She had been betrayed one too many times and didn't want any more of my kicks in the stomach. Soon after our separation, she began divorce proceedings. It was about that same time that she also began to date. Bingo! Light on! At that very moment, something changed. Not a total change, but something in me was brewing, and I didn't like the lack of control.

I went to my wife and told her I wanted her back, I would change, I was sorry. Yadda, yadda, yadda. She rejected me. I couldn't believe it! I tried harder, yet again she rejected me. She continued dating. Something began to change. My heart was ripped out. I couldn't eat. I couldn't sleep. I couldn't work. I didn't want to live. I began taking an antidepressant to help me cope. What was happening to me? The guy who has his cake and eats it too was not getting his way! I couldn't survive. Each moment—especially the nights—became a horrifying experience. I hated my life. I hated myself. I was in a bad place. I didn't know it at the time, but I had been broken. Now it was me lying on the floor crying.

God was knocking on my door. He took me to a place He needed me to go. He was aware that my life was out of control, that I needed help and that I wouldn't listen until I was broken. I lost my wife. I lost my kids. I lost my house. I lost my friends. I lost basically everything. In those weeks and months following my brokenness, God spoke to me and educated me. He explained to me that it is He who sits on the throne—not I. It is God who gave His life for me, and the life He wants me to have does not involve going outside of my marriage.

I needed help and it is through the help I received that today I can honestly say that I finally get it. I finally care about that beautiful woman lying on the floor crying. I wish I had been man enough to pick her up and hug her. Better yet, I wish I had been man enough to not go outside our marriage in the first place. I cannot say that I know how she felt, or how she feels even now, but I can honestly say that I have spent long hours reflecting on her pain and what it must have been like. I began to look deep inside myself and to realize that I broke the ultimate vow. I didn't play fair: I treated the one who loved me the most as if she didn't matter.

I finally "get it," because I was broken. I had to be broken to get it. I had to lose something: For me, it was my family. As a result of my loss, I've begun mentoring my friends and fellow church members on the sanctity of marriage, on the virtues of monogamy to your mate, on the joy of honoring your marriage.

My divorce will be final soon. God is on my throne, not me. My pride is gone. I am broken. I have repented. I have not only apologized to my wife, I also meant the words I spoke to her. Today I suffer the consequences of my actions and I have no one to blame but me. The lessons I needed to learn have been painful. But in the end my pain does not compare to the pain I put my wife through.

Today my future is cloudy. I love my wife and want another chance, but she may never be able to give me one. Yet I'm hopeful that in time she will see my heart change and she will give me a chance to cherish her the way I should have all of those nineteen years. And I hope that she can realize that when I went outside the marriage it had *nothing* to do with her. She's beautiful; she's young; she's wonderful. The reason I went outside of the marriage was me. I learned that behavior prior to our wedding, and I continued it throughout our marriage. My wish for all the women out there who read this is for you to understand that what he's done is not your fault.

If my wife is not willing to remarry me, I will move on. With God's help, I must do this. I will continue my recovery, recognizing that like an alcoholic, I'm never fixed. But I have changed my thought processes, and through this change in thinking I have been able to change the behavior to this point. Some day—hopefully with my wife—I will finally be able to treat a woman the way she deserves to be treated.

Story Four

I consider myself truly blessed to be married to Katherine. I consider the fact that she is still married to me an unbelievable example of mercy and forgiveness on her part. My wife married at the very young age of eighteen, a naïve young lady whose immaturity was only balanced by her devotion to God and her marriage. I had told her about my "problem" with masturbation when we first met but she had no idea of how deep the issue was inside of me.

This is not about me so I will summarize my journey briefly so you can understand the hurt I inflicted on her for twenty-five years. My obsession with sex began at a very early age. I recall having a fascination for the female body even before I was ten. Like so many developing addicts, my deviate behavior grew slowly over the decades—"playing doctor" with male and female friends, chancing upon a neighbor's cache of pornography, discovering pornographic novels, fantasy and masturbation. As time went by, I discovered the Internet, chat rooms, sex talk, online porn, all this leading to affairs and one-night stands. As my downward slide continued, I began to view and download even more depraved images, which eventually led to my arrest for possession of child pornography.

The entire journey lasted for almost fifty years. With few exceptions, nothing interrupted the advance of my sexual addiction—not accepting Christ, not marriage, not becoming a deacon and then a lay pastor.

For the final twenty-five years, I had a fantastic job for an international company. I travelled the world and used every opportunity to indulge in my sin. Through it all, Katherine suffered. At first she kept me accountable with weekly check-in sessions but eventually I began to lie and spiritual darkness overtook my life and marriage. Eventually, the end came. I was arrested and spent six days in jail. Released on bail, my slow recovery began.

At this point, I need to purposefully change my focus from me to Katherine.

In her earlier comments, my wife spoke about the trauma she suffered the evening the police descended on our home, a home I should have been protecting. I hadn't been protecting my wife for years. I was always "away somewhere else" in my sin. Now, the consequences of my sin had landed me in jail. Yet I was again not there for her. She was blindsided and I was nowhere to be found.

Not only was Katherine traumatized by this invasion of our home, my arrest was widely publicized in the local and regional press and TV. It is only recently that I have begun to understand the impact this has had on my wife.

Through it all, I have been so selfish, self-focused and prideful that I was not able to see Katherine for who she was—a loving, faithful, committed wife who was willing to give up everything to stand by my side. Worse still, my selfishness went from an obsession on sex to an obsession on my healing. My life over the past four years has been about my recovery from habitual sin and from shame. It became focused on denying and ridding me of the consequences of my sin. All this, to the further hurt of the wife of my youth. My shame and denial led me to reject my wife sexually. She was trying to speak the truth to me but I could not accept it.

Over the years, God has spoken to me several times, mainly through other people. He has been trying to get me to understand something but I have not been listening. In retrospect, I can hear Him—"Neil, look at your wife. You have and are hurting her. She has suffered tremendously. Don't abuse her Christian commitment to the marriage. Her commitment doesn't mean she isn't deeply hurt."

About a month ago, God tried again. The director of a ministries program spoke at the church we have been attending for two years. He was speaking about the woman with the issue of blood who snuck up and touched Jesus' robe. She was healed immediately but that was not good enough for Jesus. He needed to know who had touched Him. He needed to say something to her.

The speaker asked if we understood how a woman like that would be treated in those days. According to Old Testament law, she would be ceremonially unclean, all the time! For twelve years she was unclean. She would have to go around saying "Unclean! Unclean!" She could not touch anyone, not her husband, not her children. What does that do to a woman? What does that do to her spirit? Continual rejection!

I was sitting there listening to this and something happened. Something broke inside of me, but I wasn't sure what it was. All of a sudden the tears started to flow. Then I knew. I had been treating Katherine like that woman. Because of my shame, my pride, my selfishness, I have been holding so much from her, treating her like an unclean woman. This manifested itself not only in the lack of affection and intimacy but also in many other ways. I have rejected much of her counsel and expressions of hurt. I have judged and accused her. I have blamed her for my sins. I have hidden myself in my "cave", running from her as from a leper.

I realize now that I have been sinning. Yes, free from sexual addiction but sinning nevertheless. To make things worse, I have been ignoring a huge truth. Katherine is a traumatized wife. The Christian in her, her faith in God, has helped her stay the course, but the wife in her is deeply traumatized. My sexual addiction through our entire marriage, my infidelity, my arrest and my selfish recovery, all these things have added to the hurt.

My wife and I have now been given the opportunity to work in the lives of sex addicts and their spouses. I, like so many sex addicts, was totally selfish. I believed that my addiction was caused by something outside of me. Addicts will blame abuse, society, their jobs, their marriages, their wives—anything but themselves. I was no different. I was so busy focusing on enjoying my acting out and then my recovery that I forgot about the deep trauma I inflicted on Katherine. May God forgive me.

Story Five
When my secret was discovered, my wife's response was immediate. I think I was at my desk at work when I got the phone call. She asked my directly if I had been visiting pornographic Web sites on our computer. Maybe I could have tried to make up some

story, but I think her direct questions helped me feel like I couldn't hide it any more. Her initial outward response was quite direct, wanting direct answers from me.

The following weeks were the most painful of our lives. There was fear on both of our parts, not knowing what was going to happen. I saw in my wife pain that I had never seen before. I had turned our life upside down. I think I was like a stranger to her. Everything about me that she was sure she knew was now a question mark. She asked me some questions that I never thought I would be asked: Was I having an affair? Had I been with prostitutes? Did she need to get tested for STDs? Virtually everything came into question. It was very clear that this was the most significant life-altering thing she, that we, had ever experienced.

There were days and nights when there were nothing but tears and mostly quiet between us. I remember with deep sorrow how much I hurt her, how I was the cause for her tears. Just seeing her cry was a very sobering experience. But somehow she was also able to be vulnerable with me in expressing the level of pain that I was causing. She could have chosen to minimize, to turn inward as a way to protect herself from further pain. Or she could have said it was my issue that I should go and get tested. But she was able to express the depth of her pain in a way that wasn't shaming or condemning. What she said held up a mirror to help me see the depth of my betrayal, but still concerned me. She was able to be honest, acknowledging the truth of my betrayal.

All of these early responses helped me see that I was responsible. Her hurt was all because of me; it was *my* fault and my failure. There was nothing that she had done that was any excuse for my decisions. I couldn't place any blame anywhere else but on myself. So then I needed to verbalize to my wife that I was at fault. I'm sure that wasn't any consolation to her in the beginning. Big deal, so I didn't blame her. I don't think she really cared that much at the time that I blamed myself. It didn't change anything that I had already done, didn't lessen the pain.

However, for me, for sex addicts, it is the first, maybe most important truth to understand: that this mess is *my* fault. I couldn't lay blame anywhere else. And then since it's my fault, I'm the one who should start to take responsibility. And once I could see that, there was something I could do; something I had to do. I'm the one to look at ways to change the situation. I wanted to do whatever I could to save our relationship. That was an important idea for me to grasp.

Another aspect of owning the problem was that I couldn't really demand much from my wife. I couldn't say, "You should be patient with me" or "You should try to understand" or "I need you to help me fix my behavior." I was the problem, not her. I made the bad choices, not her. I was the source of her pain. So my wife wasn't the one who needed to do anything to change me. I was the one who needed to go to work.

To the wives who are partners of sex addicts:
- You didn't do anything to cause this. It isn't your fault.
- Be as truthful as you can about your anger and pain.
- Hold him responsible, but you can't fix him.
- It's okay to grieve the loss.

To the husbands who are sex addicts:
- Suck it up and take responsibility for your behaviors.
- Quit lying to yourself that no one is being hurt. Even in the secret, there is a barrier, a lie between you and your wife.
- Become truthful, to an excess.
- Open up your life, be accountable.
- After you work on the behaviors, start working on the underlying problems.

Story Six
As a man in recovery who is also a therapist specializing in helping those with sexual addictions, I always tell clients I like to help them both from a professional and personal standpoint. I'm happy to offer my own story around that with my own wife.

First, let me just acknowledge and validate the pain that wives go through when hearing of their husbands' infidelities whether that's actual adultery or a figurative form such as pornography, compulsive masturbation, habitual, willful fantasy or any other kind of compromise to the sacred and holy marital covenant. It's been my experience in treating hundreds of men and marriages for such sexual and relational problems that there are few things that are more painful for a woman than sexual unfaithfulness.

Sadly, this pain is often compounded by dishonesty and lack of forthrightness. In fact, more than once a wife has told me after learning of her husband's mistakes that she felt confident she could handle the trespass but devastated by the lack of truthfulness about it. It's as if the lying far overshadowed the sin itself. Conversely, when men have been honest with what's happened to the degree that a wife requires, more often than not, I've seen wives able to not only handle the truth but also be extraordinarily gracious and forgiving. On behalf of all men who have sinned against you, I say to you wives, "I hope you can come to a place of forgiveness for how you've been harmed."

I think we as men, less skilled in relationships, tend to project our own condemnation, fear and shame onto our spouses, which makes sense why we would be hesitant or less likely to come forward with the truth and more likely to isolate and hide. This is no excuse but rather a challenge: we as men have our relational and character work cut out for us!

I have seen these same dynamics to one degree or another in my own marriage and recovery story. In fact, my wife is the main reason I finally chose true recovery and why I remain open, honest and accountable today as I work out my integrity and healing from pornography and compulsive masturbation. Not that she forced me, but she was real with me in showing me her pain.

I'll never forget the first time my wife ever asked me, "When was the last time you acted out?" Now, up until then she had always just prayed for me and tried to hear me out whenever I came to her with my slip, choosing to believe that "This is between him and God." After going to a seminar for wives and getting empowered to be more responsible for the marriage and the integrity therein (not that that made me any less responsible on my end), she decided to ask for the first time.

Well, to that date, I had always just brought things to her when I failed and did so within a day. This was largely out of a sense of wanting to be honest and open but also out of shame and a desire for her to "fix" me by forgiving me and praying for me. This time was different: I had a slip a couple days before and hadn't gotten around to telling her yet, because I was getting more and more desensitized. So, when she asked me for the very first time, unfortunately, I had bad news!

After telling her what had happened, my wife had a simple yet profound, calm yet pained response: "The Bible says that when you commit the sin of lust it's like committing adultery in your heart." Wow. There it was. It was like getting hit in the face with a skillet. I was instantly grieved for my wife's heart— I never wanted to see that look on her face or hear her have to say those words again. So, I immediately got online that day and found some resources and made a call to get myself into a group that week. While I have been in recovery ever since (five years now), I am not perfect. While I have come a long way, I still make mistakes. Besides not making those mistakes as often or to the degree I used to, the main difference now is that I am accountable and this gives my wife comfort and a sense of safety. When I make a mistake, I still need to confess it to her and to my accountability group brothers. But I also need to tend to her heart. She needs someone to talk to about this so we've arranged for counseling for her when she needs it. She sometimes needs space or to express understandable anger in a healthy way before she can forgive and before we can be reconciled. And I can't shame or condemn her for that.

I'm still honest but I want more for my wife than just honesty—I want success in honoring her with my sexuality. I want her to know that she is the only one for whom that special part of me is reserved. And in that, we not only honor each other, we also honor God, our creator.

Chapter 10

From the Lives of Partners and Former Partners of Sex Addicts

Story Seven

It was early May. I was going online to prepare for the coming worship service. My husband and I were worship leaders and it was our Sunday to lead. I found the perfect song for my husband to sing. I thought, *He will do it well and with real integrity. What a special Mother's Day this is going to be!*

I went to my computer and got online to look at a Web site. I was going back to a site I had visited previously, so I clicked on the history button on the Web browser and the drop-down box held lists of all the sites I'd visited in the past two weeks...only there were sites that I didn't recognize. Not only did I not recognize them, also the names of these sites were of a sexual nature. My heart began to race and a tingling sensation spread throughout my body as I selected one and clicked. Then I sat there breathless as a Web page filled my computer screen. The page was a full-size photograph of a naked woman. My hands began to shake and my heart rate increased even more as I went back to the history list and clicked again, only to have yet another pornography Web site load onto my computer screen. I don't remember how many I looked at, but it was enough for me to see that the sites were many and filled the week's history. This was no accidental download; this was evidence of intentional seeking out and viewing pornographic materials on my computer in my home—the place where I felt safest.

I no longer felt safe at all.

I shook uncontrollably and cried. I called my husband at work. He answered the phone and I said something like, "Someone's been viewing pornography on the computer", which was met with silence. The silence answered the question. I told him we'd talk about it when he got home from work. I was filled with rage, with incredible fear and shock. I'm a therapist. I knew about compulsive sexual behavior, and I knew that's what I was seeing on the computer. Things started to make sense: the times I had nightmares about him having an affair, the times I found him early in the morning in front of the television, quickly changing channels, the times I had walked into our office when he was on the computer and he quickly minimized the webpage. "What are you doing?" I asked, and he always said, "Just shopping" or "Sorry, I didn't change the channel quick enough... looking for the news" or something like that. Of course, I believed him. He's my husband and he would never involve himself in something so degrading to women or to marriage. He'd never do something he knew would devastate me or shatter my trust.

But reality set in and it was clear that he would and did. Again, being a therapist, I knew that compulsive sexual behavior was less about sex and more about pain management or escape. Knowing this in my head didn't have nearly enough effect on my heart, which was broken and terrified. If he could hide this, lie to me this way, what other things might he be doing? Is he having affairs? Does the pornography include child content? Am I at risk of an STD or AIDS? Is my marriage at risk? What about my girls? Our daughters...are they at risk? As much as I wanted to slow my thoughts down, they did not stop. They were racing, along with my heart.

Over the next few weeks, we had many conversations and sought out help and accountability. These were life-saving actions. But the racing thoughts, racing heart, anxiety, fear, dread, irritability, flashbacks...all of that continued for a very, very long time. I could not allow him to touch me some days and others I needed his touch. Yet his touch felt very unsafe. I paced the room sometimes, got lost when driving or when in strange places. I couldn't focus, couldn't control the timing of my tears and I felt a seething anger that I could not let out. It left my chest feeling so tight, so sore, I thought (and wished) I was having a heart attack. This was real, physical heartache.

I noticed things that didn't stand out to me before. I couldn't walk through the mall without seeing sexual material, all of which felt like horrible reminders and current threats. Even standing in line in the grocery store with the glossy-covered magazines triggered fear, anger and dread. Watching television could initiate waves of sadness or fear. Walking past my computer or going into my office brought pangs of sadness and grief. Anything and everything seemed to rip open the wounds; there was no healing. I felt raw.

An acquaintance who ran groups for men gave me a box of books. I read and read, trying to understand. How did this happen in my marriage? What could I expect in the future? As I read, I found very little that helped me. It all explained about my husband's behaviors and recovery or gave a little information that validated that I was in crisis. I knew that. Then I started reading materials with the term "co-addict." I read what were described as the characteristics of a co-addict. Then I found the definition or criteria for being this "co-addicted" person. All you needed was to be in a relationship with the addicted person. Well, again, I'm a therapist, and I know you just don't diagnose or label a person based on with whom they are in a relationship. Yet the materials written by sex addiction professionals all called me a co-addict. They assumed I was codependent. They assumed things about my personal history that, of course, "set me up" for marrying a man who would have a sex addiction. So on one hand, the books said there was nothing I can do about *his* addiction and I did not cause it. Then, the books said that my co-addiction helped fuel and maintain his addiction. I was a co-conspirator! So my pain and trauma and incredible fear, according to these books, was destined to occur—I was just as sick as my sexually addicted husband. If I didn't believe this truth about myself, it was evidence of my state of denial. Everything within me knew that, although I do have my issues, in no way am I or could I ever be responsible for how my husband chooses to act out his pain. I am not and will not accept that I am responsible for his actions. I bear no complicity. Any denial I may have entertained was shattered when I discovered my husband's dark secret of sexual betrayal through compulsive sexual behavior.

My husband allowed this crisis of discovery to propel him into health. He did anything and everything he could to demonstrate to me his intention to change and to become a man after God's heart. And he has consistently done so. He never blamed me, and he worked to discover where and how his emotional wounds led him to this place. He tried with all his might to help rebuild what was shattered in our relationship.

Early on, we both realized there was no rebuilding...we were building anew. Our relationship had to be a new work because the old relationship had been shattered. It no longer existed. And although he was doing well and feeling stronger every day, my sadness, anger and fear became almost constant companions for a long while. And now, some twelve years later, I still have scars and even soreness in places. I'm not sure these scars will ever heal. I still cannot stand naked in front of my husband. I will not allow him to see me dress or undress. The innocence is gone. I do not want to share that part of myself, because I cannot be totally open to him. I trust his heart towards health and towards me, but I also know deep in my bones that he has the capacity to act out again and I would again be left to pick up the shattered pieces. I don't know when or if that fear will ever go away.

And through my own healing of this traumatic betrayal, I have found safety in other places: in God, in myself, in friends and in my abilities to seek out what I need. I feel safer now with my husband than I did, say, ten years ago. But totally safe? Not yet. Will I ever? I know I will be safe at last when I am finally home with Jesus. There is no other totally safe place.

Story Eight

I am entering my sixteenth year of a relationship with a sex addict. That part of the story includes porn, incest and multiple affairs. I know firsthand the depth and breadth of the emotional challenges, the financial consequences and multifaceted damage a family incurs when such a challenge enters a woman's life...a family's life.

In the beginning, I had a false sense that somehow I could fix the damage or that somehow, if I worked hard enough, it would all get better. So I focused all of my energies into making sure that my husband and my family got all the counseling and support they needed. I mistakenly thought that if my family was okay then I would be okay. The biggest mistake I made early on in this journey was not making sure that I got the support I needed to allow healing to occur in *my* heart and mind. It wasn't that I didn't look for help; I looked, but discovered that at that time in my recovery, no one—either Christian or secular—knew how to give me the help that I needed. After a while, I just stopped looking.

But the bigger story in all of this is what God has done and is doing in my life. One of the first challenges I had to resolve was figuring out whether or not God really loved me. Were the promises in the Bible for me or were they just meant for people and families who lived better lives than I had, people who were somehow part of God's "inner circle"? Our pastor gently explained that either I would have to accept everything the Bible had to say or I would have to reject it in its entirety. I couldn't pick and choose and decide for myself what God meant for me and what he intended for other people. Knowing I couldn't throw out the whole Bible, I decided to believe it all.

Through these sixteen years the hardest thing has been realizing that my husband has not yet—and he may never—understand the depth of the damage his actions have caused. I used to believe that I could not be in a relationship with him unless he came to that realization. And I used to believe that I could not heal until he was willing to enter my pain, to know my loss and to walk with me from that place of understanding.

Perhaps the greatest thing God has shown me is that my well-being can exist totally apart from my husband's behavior and totally within God's sphere of care. It has taken a great deal of time to come to this realization, time that included a lot of personal growth and self-care. I have learned that my responses to situations have to do with me and my choices. I have learned that I get to be who I choose to be in spite of others' actions or the circumstances that life presents. I can choose to find healthy people who are able to support what I believe God has called me to do. I can choose to enter deeper into the mysteries of forgiveness and reconciliation and in so doing, come to know my Abba Father in a way I had not known Him before.

Your journey will be unique, your story sacred. I cannot tell you how your story will progress or how it will end. But I can tell you that God will be faithful to you, even when it doesn't look like He is anywhere to be found. The desert places will be dry and oftentimes lonely. But each step on your path will have purpose, whether it leads you through a desert place or to a mountain top.

Work towards surrounding yourself with a support team. This step holds such importance that you must make it a priority, both with your time and with your finances. Wherever you are right now, you can heal *only* if you decide *not* to stay where you presently find yourself. Know that you have many brothers and sisters who know this place well. Pray that God will help you find them or bring them into your life.

Remember always that God is a big God. He is the God of the impossible and He is not bound by our human perspective. Nor does he bother conforming to man's solutions or his statistics. He holds the power and the healing creativity to write unlimited redemptive endings to your story. He can take you from pain and barely surviving to a place of wholeness and thriving.

Story Nine

My husband and I have been married for almost fifteen years and have been in recovery for about nine. When he first started his recovery process, things got extremely difficult—more difficult than they had been before, even with his addiction going unchecked. For the first several months, he went to his group weekly, while I sat at home trying to cope with having no one to talk to. He came home from group meetings lighter, happier, having gotten love and acceptance from the other men. I quickly became resentful. It was his addiction that was tearing my world apart, and I seemed to be the only one suffering from it. I had no one to talk to—no one who understood.

When a group became available for me, it was such a godsend to finally find other women who understood what I was going through—who didn't say it was a "normal guy thing" or that I was doing something wrong. Still, things continued to be difficult as I finally was able to process my feelings, hear the stories of others and learn what was necessary to start stepping forward into a healthier place where I could make decisions. I had to learn to accept that there was nothing I could do, not do, become or change that would make my husband change. I had to let go and leave my marriage in the hands of God, knowing that there was the possibility that it would not be restored to me.

My husband's program helped him learn to see things more from my point of view—and to accept that he had hurt me deeply, which was something he could never make up for. He couldn't change the past, and he could not control my timeline of getting through the pain—or even *if* I could get through it. He learned how to develop transparency by remaining accountable to someone who was willing to hold his feet to the fire and call him on it when he started talking like an addict again. Thanks to his hard work, a Christian 12-step program and especially the grace of God, he has developed a solid pattern of sobriety that has lasted about five years so far.

Over time, as he developed a more honest pattern and longer stretches of sobriety, I was able to start trusting him again. It wasn't easy. It was terribly frightening. As in the past, if someone broke my trust, they never got the chance to do it again. I had to learn how to trust a person who had hurt me. He had to learn that trust was not a given—he had to earn it, and it was not going to be easy. We had to develop strong boundaries with each other—some temporary, some permanent. These boundaries outline, for instance, what I can and cannot live with. One such boundary is that if he does ever choose to go back to the addiction, he will have to leave. Another is that he must continue to attend his group at least once a week and talk with his accountability partner at least once a day. These boundaries have helped me develop a sense of safety in our relationship. Are they always easy? Absolutely not. There are some weeks when I would much rather he stay home with me than go to his group. It seems like over half of our children's school activities conflict with it, meaning that I often have to go on my own to a parent-teacher conference. But whenever I allow myself to start nursing the frustration that threatens to grow into resentment, I remind myself that his group is a vital part of his recovery, and I would rather have him gone one night a week and be able to maintain his sexual sobriety than skip it and have one missed group turn into two, two turn into a month and so on.

That doesn't mean our marriage is perfect. Far from it. There are speed bumps and difficulties along the way. Like any marriage, we argue, don't talk, get tired of each other. Those issues common to every marriage do have an added element to them. Sometimes things happen that trigger horrible memories from the past when my husband was active in his addiction. Sometimes the panic has been so intense that I feel as though the events of the past have just happened and it can be difficult to pull myself out of it and focus on the reality of now. I still go to a weekly group and stay in touch with other women throughout the week who help keep me grounded and focused on what I can control. For his part, my husband faces temptations pretty much every day. He has a well-developed plan to deal with those temptations so that he can avoid the slippery slope toward acting on them. He talks with his accountability partner on a daily basis, as well as other men from his group throughout the week between group meetings. They ask him the tough questions and don't let up until they have the answers.

One of the biggest struggles we face, though, is focusing so much on our own recovery process—which is an essential part of being able to put our marriage back together—that we sometimes forget to do our work together. We forget how to communicate with each other—even though he has a master's degree in communication and I am a life coach! We easily get back into the habit of assuming each other's motivations rather than asking. It sounds like such a trivial thing, but it does a lot of damage in our relationship.

While I have come to the point where I no longer dwell on it, I am aware somewhere in the back of my mind that someday my husband could choose to give up his recovery and go back to his addiction. This knowledge does not rule my life any longer. It is just part of the facts I have learned about sex addiction—the high probability of relapse. Yet because I have spent time focusing on my own recovery and releasing myself from trying to control his, I know that should he ultimately make that choice, I will survive. I have regained who I am—the person I'd lost to obsession and fear. This does not mean I am not committed to my marriage or that I am just waiting around for him to go back to his addiction. Quite the contrary. We are building our marriage to be stronger and more fulfilled than it ever was before the addiction nearly destroyed us. Looking back, there have been many times, both before and since getting into recovery, when it would have been very easy to leave.

So why am I still here? I've been asked that question a lot and have asked it myself, too. What it boils down to, for me, is that I am willing to be here and continue to work through the problems in our marriage—both related to his addiction and those common to every marriage—as long as my husband is doing his part. If he gives up his recovery, that would change. I am not willing to go back to living with an active addiction. Each woman has to make her own decision in that regard. The one piece of advice I would give women who find themselves trying to decide whether to stick with it with a recovering spouse or not is to manage their expectations. There will be times when it is like being on a second honeymoon and the love is so strong and potent that it feels like nothing will ever come between you again. But that's not the way life is all the time. We have our mountaintop experiences along with the valleys. It is how we choose to approach them that matters. I believe whole-heartedly that God has been the source of all that has kept us together, and He will be the source of life for you regardless of which path He directs you to choose.

Story Ten
Some thirty-six years ago, I decided to marry a dear friend. We were friends in elementary and high school. There were many things we had in common. We never really dated as "boyfriend" and "girlfriend." The relationship looked more like brother and sister. Over time we were "in love." Little did I know the journey that this marriage would take. It was a route that I personally would have not taken.

Two years ago, I accidently discovered some things that my husband was working on for the men's group at our church. When I found this I really didn't know what to think. Did my husband have a sexual addiction problem? What did it mean? I knew I had to confront my husband regarding this information that I had found, but I was scared. Scared to find out the truth and what the truth would mean for our life together.

In the weeks before I confronted him, I went on a "witch hunt." I searched the Internet for information, looking for signs of an affair or sexual acting out, trying to make sense of all my feelings. I read a number of books dealing with husbands' secret wars and battles and how to respond with tough love. It took me about a month to get up the strength and courage to confront my husband. I was in prayer and seeking God's direction in regarding what was the right thing to do. But I knew I had to confront this problem. Little did I know the journey I was about to take.

What was really interesting was a number of years before this discovery our marriage was spiraling down. I felt that something was not quite right. I couldn't put my finger on it. I kept encouraging my husband that we should seek counseling. I begged for many years then finally he decided that he would stop all outside commitments and work on our marriage. This was his personal quest to discover himself. It had nothing to do with working on our marriage. We never went for counseling until the disclosure.

I finally confronted him. My heart grieves and tears well up in my eyes as I remember that night. That night I discovered that my friend, my lover, my companion and the father of our children was a horribly wounded spirit. It was revealed to me that during his early life he had been sexual abused by an uncle, an incident that threw him into same-sex attraction and masturbation throughout junior high and high school. His home life consisted of a very domineering and controlling mother with a passive-aggressive father who was not the mentor a young boy needed. Marriage did not solve his problem.

My husband revealed to me that over our thirty-six years of marriage he had been having sex with numerous men. These men included a former brother-in-law, a couple of our good friends and a former pastor. There had been about seven to eight years of that time where he wasn't involved with other men, but during that time he was addicted to masturbation. It was evident that he was seeking approval from men and dealing with his emotions in unhealthy ways. I remained silent just listening to a man whom I loved so very much pour out all the guilt and shame that had been bottled up for years. He was so sorry and broken.

Immediately I was thrown into a whirlwind of emotions. I felt like someone had just shot a hole in my heart. A part of me just wanted to curl up and die. Where was I when all of this was happening? Am I that dense that I didn't see all this happening in our life? What is wrong with me? Our marriage is one big fat lie! What am I to my husband: the mother to his daughters, the housekeeper, the nurse, the chef, the laundry lady, but not good enough to be his lover? He preferred other men and himself over me! How can I compete with that? In my heart I was crying out to God to help me understand what the purpose was for all this, because I had grown up with a father who was just like my husband. I am like a magnet to same-sex attracted men.

Right away I wanted to know who, what, when, where and why. I wanted to know details and time frames. The pieces of the puzzle were being put together. I learned we had nothing special as a couple. Our master bedroom had even been shared. I learned things that I wanted to know but really didn't want to know. Did he think of these other men when we were making love or was I just an object for sex like these other men? One thing that was really revealed to me was that we lacked emotional, spiritual and sexual intimacy. Was my husband even capable of loving a woman like a man should love a woman? Oh God, help our marriage!

That night the hidden sins that were disclosed involved individuals who were "upstanding" in our small community and church. I had to be silent about this nightmare, except to a counselor we were seeing from out of town. If my husband was serious about wanting forgiveness and willing to repent from his sins, I had a big decision to make. I realized that I had come to a big fork in the road. I had a big choice to make. Do I allow the magnitude of my hurt, anger and rejections to take the path of vindication? Do I leave all the memories and years we had together? What is true love all about anyway? Would I leave him if he broke his leg? Or do I choose the path of forgiveness, healing and restoration that only comes through the redemption of the Lord Jesus Christ?

When I looked at the road of vindication, I saw more harm being accomplished than good. More hopes and dreams would have been destroyed than just mine. What would it have accomplished if I allowed my bitterness to flow from my heart like radioactive waste contaminating other innocent people? That was not my goal. There was too much at stake for me to open my mouth.

I chose the hard path of forgiveness, healing and, most of all, hope. The hope lies in the Lord Jesus Christ and the blood He shed when He went to the cross for all sin. At the foot of the cross the ground is level; no sin is greater than another sin. I have to be able to forgive just like Christ has forgiven my sins. My husband is changing and is being redeemed through the blood of our Lord Jesus Christ. He has no desire to go back to his former lifestyle. He is enjoying the hope. Without faith there is no hope and without hope what is left? The hope is that with time and healing our marriage will someday be a sweet fragrance to the Lord.

The dreams I had for our marriage are different than what the Lord had planned for our marriage. Maybe I am the wife God planned for my husband: to be the helpmate to walk this trail with him, to be the encourager, the forgiver, the unconditional lover, to be Jesus in flesh to him. I have asked God to give me his dream for my life and marriage and the strength to walk through that dream. My desire is for my husband to become the man God wants him to be, not the person I want him to be. I pray daily, "God help me not to get in the way of your work in my husband's life and help me to be the special wife he needs to heal."

I have come to the place in this journey where I know who God says I am. I am loved and cherished by my Heavenly Father like no other man can love me. My earthly father and my husband are not capable of loving me like Him. I know that my husband's same-sex attraction has nothing to do with me. He is a wounded spirit. I know my mind has to be renewed daily by reading the Bible or it goes places where I don't want to go. I keep reliving the nightmare. I have become stronger and wiser. I have been created special for this time. But I have daily choices to make: Is my cup half full or half empty? Am I going to allow this to make me bitter or better? I can be reactive or proactive and responsive, that is a choice. I have chosen the positive for my life no matter what my husband does. I am not a victim! My purpose in life is to glorify my Heavenly Father. My journey is up and down. It is rocky. It is smooth. But I am in God's care, which makes the scenery so beautiful and I am thankful.

Conclusion

The Rest of the Journey

In this book we've shared a pathway to healing that has worked for many partners of sex addicts, yet in the end, healing is a *choice*. It is a choice all of us must make, because we want it—we *need* it—so much we will passionately pursue it, work for it and never give up until we can call the choice our own. We hope we have helped ignite that passion in you, because *we believe you are worth it.*

You *can* heal. You can grow stronger in spite of (or as a result of) this most difficult time in your life. We also believe that you need others in your life to help you navigate this journey. Allow others into your life. Let them encourage you and help you. Locate and work with a trained counselor or psychologist who understands trauma and sexual betrayal. Whatever you do, make your healing a priority in your life!

We've talked a lot about your recovery and what it is composed of and put little focus on what a sex addict's recovery requires or what measures are needed for couples to heal. We know from experience that many of you have more questions about those areas and others. We'll now try to answer some of the questions we're frequently asked about sexual addiction and your concerns about this debilitating behavioral problem.

Frequently Asked Questions about Your Sexually Addicted
Spouse and How You Can Cope

What is sexual addiction?

Let's look briefly at the signs and symptoms of sex addiction. First, there are commonly accepted labels. Some call it sex addiction; others label it sexual compulsivity or dependence. Still others add the diagnosis of sex and love addiction to people who act out for the additional need of love and connection. Whatever you choose to call it, the effects on the person engaged in the behavior are both dangerous and devastating. You may know all too well the devastation experienced by the loved ones and families of sexual addicts. When someone is involved in this out of control sexual behavior, it takes over the addict's life and leaves destruction in its wake. [1]

Addiction in general is widely understood as a pathological relationship with a mood altering substance or behavior. A person who is addicted uses a drug or behavior to numb out, escape or otherwise change his or her mood. Some people act out with drugs, alcohol or sex to get a "high" or a sense of excitement. Others use these behaviors to calm down. The important thing to understand is that addicts have formed relationships with their drugs or behaviors; they orient or organize their lives around the activities. It becomes so important to them that it takes over their focus. They increase the amount of time, energy and resources they devote to use of the drug or to their search for an opportunity to engage in the addictive behavior. Addicts compulsively act out their addictions and spend a great deal of time obsessing or thinking about their next "high".

<u>Four Elements of Addiction</u>
- Progression in the intensity of use (may move to different drugs or different behaviors)
- Increased tolerance (it takes more of whatever the drug is to achieve the desired effect)
- Repeated attempts to quit the use, only to return
- Continued use despite potential or real negative consequences

Many kinds of activities can be viewed as addictive when we measure them by their mood-altering roles in the users' lives. Behaviors become addictive on an emotional level as ways of coping with life; behaviors can also be physically addictive due to the natural chemical reactions within the brain when the person acts out.

Sex addiction or compulsivity can take many forms. It can involve fantasy, masturbation, pornography use, anonymous sex, use of prostitutes or involvement in multiple affairs. Some addicts engage in several behaviors, while others act out with only one or two of these behaviors. Any sexual behavior used to alter mood in a driven or compulsive way is destructive to the person and to the ability to be engaged in life and relationships.

Sex addicts do what they can to make their lives appear normal, marrying and maintaining committed relationships. The Mayo Clinic's Web site offers some important information about sex addiction and those it affects:

> [Sex addicts] often have trouble establishing and maintaining emotional intimacy. They seek gratification through sexual behavior, but are unlikely to achieve emotional fulfillment and their lives may feel empty. Compulsive sexual behavior can affect anyone regardless of sexual preferences, including heterosexual, homosexual and bisexual preferences.[2]

People with sexual addictions often have addictions to other substances or behaviors. Marsha, on her Web site *A Woman's Healing Journey*, responded to a question about multiple addictions:

> Addicts of any kind generally have what is called an addictive personality. Therefore, multiple addictions and/or addiction swapping are not uncommon. Overspending and overeating or bingeing on food seem particularly frequent in sex addicts.

> The key to understanding can be found in recognizing what usually drives addictive behavior: the addict is trying to soothe emotional pain with a substance or activity. Only by working with a counselor can the sexually compulsive person get to the root of the pain, which is often from childhood and do the work required to heal.

> But it is equally important to understand that addiction has a physiological component as well. Whether the "drug" of

choice is heroin or sex, science has proven that neuro-
chemicals are released in the person's brain, giving him a
chemical "hit" that provides some soothing and satisfaction
for the inner pain he carries. Over time, more of the chemical
is required to achieve the same hit, which causes the addict to
use more and more of his drug. With sex addiction, this
reality generally drives the addict to move on to riskier sexual
behaviors in his quest for satisfaction.[3]

So, people with sexual addictions or compulsions are in pain
and have learned to use sexual activity to cope with this pain. They
may not even remember when they started or understand right
away why they are involved in this kind of acting out. But addictive
behaviors are there for purposes: they soothe, lift a mood or help us
escape from things in life that are difficult or uncomfortable.

When your loved one started acting out sexually, he or she had
no idea the behavior would reach the level it did by the time he
or she was found out or confessed to you. This addiction happens
over time. It only makes sense, then, that healing and recovery will
take time.

Certainly, the idea that a person might be addicted to something,
especially to something like sex, is a difficult admission. The label "sex
addict" carries a weighty stigma, creating confusion and assumption
about illegal acts. If your spouse exhibits sexually addictive behaviors,
yet resists the idea that he or she might be a sex addict, here is an
excerpt from Marsha's Web site that can prove helpful:

Although your concern about your husband's feelings is
seemingly kind and caring, in order to "get well" your husband
must face how deeply he has hurt you and compromised
himself and his marriage. Yet we understand your desire to not
use words or labels that would cause him to tune you out or to
get angry and direct attention away from his own behavior. The
term "sexually compulsive behavior" is a little easier for a man
to wear, and if it seems important to you, it might provide the
verbal bridge you are searching for.

However, be careful not to work so hard to protect
your husband from pain that you make it easy for him to
avoid reality. As partners of sexually compulsive men, we

often err on the side of over-protecting our partners' feelings, and by doing so, become a part of their problems. Let him feel his failure, and pray that it causes him to realize where he is going and to reach out and ask for help before he sinks any deeper.[4]

No matter what we call the problem, compulsive or driven sexual behavior is out of control, destructive, progressive and has destructive consequences. Out-of-control people damage not only themselves, but in the end, all those around them suffer as well.

For more information, we recommend you go to the Web site offered by the Society for the Advancement of Sexual Health (www.sash.org). You'll find other resources throughout this book.

How was I so stupid or why didn't I know?

This question ranks high on the list of frequently asked questions we hear from women and some men who find out about their loved ones' sexual betrayals. Partners who have been duped, deceived and lied to feel stupid. "How did I miss this?" they cry.

Please hear our simple answer: you didn't know, because they didn't tell you. They didn't want you to know! They are masters at hiding; they have to be great at covering up for the behaviors to continue. Sexual addicts go to incredible lengths to prevent their secrets' exposure. They compartmentalize their minds and their lives by creating separate "worlds" where their compulsive behaviors are planned, entertained and protected. They believe that their separate lives or other worlds do not need to touch the rest of their lives. They delude themselves (as part of the addiction) into believing that what you (the partners) don't know won't hurt you. The worlds don't need to touch. But of course, they do.

Most likely you had some idea something was wrong. Perhaps the sex addict's behaviors bled over into the life you shared in the form of increased irritability, unaccounted for time or expenses, disinterest in sex with you or your involvement in the compulsive behaviors.

Most of us sense that something is out of kilter; we just can't understand what it is. Perhaps you even asked your spouse if he or she was having an affair, only to hear a response like, "I'm just tired" or "Of course not! How could you think such a thing?" Such answers leave us doubting our own intuition and perceptions and we feel shamed or blamed for lack of trust. Some partners report experiencing relief after finding out about their spouses' infidelities; at least now they know they're not crazy after all! Perceptions are finally validated, but at a terrible cost.

Truth, even when it comes late, arms you with new knowledge. And this knowledge teaches us to "trust our gut." Learn to honor and trust your perceptions again. Act to protect yourself until honesty and trust return to your relationship.

How will I know he or she is in recovery?

A true recovery process at work in an addict's life bears significant hallmarks. First, you'll see that recovery is a priority. Whereas before pursuing recovery the sex addict arranged his or her time around acting out, he or she now organizes time and effort around healing and health. The partner goes to counseling. Most utilize a group recovery process and accountability of people of the same sex—people who understand the addiction, because they've battled it, too. A recovering sex addict sets boundaries in his or her life to help avoid temptations. A person in recovery takes personal responsibility for his or her actions and the resulting consequences. The person reduces the amount of blame placed on others and owns up to his or her own decisions.

People in recovery soften. They "thaw out" or show emotion in different and healthier ways. Their ability to empathize with others—including you—increases. They allow others to really *know* them; they allow others to help hold them accountable. They take risks in trying on new ways of relating. *Real* change becomes visible.

This change does not and cannot happen overnight. It takes hard work and time. Here, we measure time in months, not days. Consistent change over time provides the best indication that a sex addict embraces the work and life of recovery. Realistically, ups and downs will continue. Failures and successes may happen, at least for a time. However, as the recovery process takes place, and true growth and freedom begin to blossom in the addict's life, you will begin to see the evidence that the addict desires true change and is putting all his or her effort into achieving that goal.

When can I trust again? How can I trust again?
Trust is shattered when sexual betrayal and relational trauma occurs. Looking at the shards and fragments of your former life, you may think, *There is no way these pieces will ever go back together.*

Trust is something that must be earned, yet trust is something we give. The hard truth about trust is that it must be earned before it can be given, especially after a sexual violation. Such a violation shatters the foundation of a relationship.

Trust can be viewed as a gift that is ours to give or to withhold. Trust is a choice. You can choose to trust; you can rescind it as well. Think of trust as a drawbridge over a river. It's your bridge and you control how much or how little you lower it to let someone cross over into your world. You control how vulnerable you choose to be and with whom you are vulnerable.

After betrayal, experience and wisdom advise that we raise our vulnerability bridges: that we withhold trust until we see evidence that enables us to believe we can safely allow those who misused our trust back into the innermost recesses of our lives.

A trustworthy person bears certain markers: they are consistent (predictable), they take responsibility for their own actions and they admit when they make mistakes rather than blae others. They do what they say they are going to do and their behaviors match their words. Trust is something that takes only seconds to shatter but takes what feels like an eternity to rebuild.

How long will it take for me to heal?
This is a difficult question and the answer may be uniquely your own, because healing doesn't come in one-size-fits-all sizing. Some suggest that it takes three to five years before we feel "normal" again following the devastation and relational trauma that sex addiction produces in our lives. Unfortunately, there is no timetable for healing.

We've described those things which help the healing process in the previous chapters of this book. Some things hinder the healing process: things like continued exposure to traumatic stress and betrayal. Like wounds to the flesh, wounds to the heart, mind and soul cannot heal if they are continually re-injured.

However, *you* can heal and grow, no matter what your spouse does. And your relationship to the addict does not have to be restored for you to heal. Nor does the sexual addict have to remain in recovery for you to heal. Your healing can be separate from the addict's choices and behaviors.

You heal because you take good care of yourself, you process your pain, you find ways to incorporate it into the whole of your life and you find meaning and purpose for yourself. Though there will most likely always be a scar in your memory, it will grow less tender over time.

The process is really up to you: Will you allow this dark and difficult time in your life to define and defeat you or will you allow it to serve as an opportunity for you to become a stronger person? That choice will help determine how long it takes and to what degree you heal.

As we discussed earlier, there are some essentials that need to be in place for you to heal. There needs to be other people in your life who know you, know what you are going through and who are available to you. These should be people who won't judge you or tell you what to do and will support you. No matter what.

Another important element needed to heal is safety. Find ways to provide that for yourself. Make decisions for yourself based on that need. If you are in physical danger or if you cannot control your own responses to your betrayer, you may need some space and some degree of separation so that you can begin to allow your heart and body to heal from the traumatic stress.

You need to take care of yourself physically, emotionally and spiritually. Do what you can to eat healthy foods and get adequate rest and sleep. Say "no" to additional responsibilities until you are on the path of healing. Discover what encourages you and feeds you spiritually and do them regularly.

Get care from people who are trained and equipped to help you. Counselors, spiritual leaders and support groups are all wonderful resources if and when they understand what helps a partner heal following sexual betrayal and trauma. Do your homework and find someone with whom you can work comfortably as you cope and heal.

Be patient with yourself. As Barbara tells her clients, "This is the hardest work you will ever do!" It can be exhausting and discouraging. It can, and most likely will, require more effort on your own behalf than you've previously expended on yourself. But you are worth the effort; healing is worth the effort.

I've been told that "detachment" can help me cope while my partner works on his or her addiction. What exactly *is* detachment and how do I do it?
Detachment can prove extremely helpful when emotional turmoil and relational conflicts create struggle in your relationship with the sex addict, particularly when the addict is early in the recovery process or if he or she has no interest in recovery and growth. In such situations, detachment can buy us time and space to see if our partners decide to work for change.

Because our view of ourselves can be so tied up in our partners' inappropriate sexual activities, we may face great difficulty in controlling our reactions to what our partners have done or are doing sexually. We may withdraw emotionally, attack, become verbally abusive or react in other unhealthy ways. None of these actions or reactions will help. They only create ugly scenes and demean us in our partners' eyes. Detaching is a skill that helps us step out of that reactionary pattern and remain focused on that which we have the power to change and help heal: ourselves.

Detaching is *not* withdrawal or isolating or punishing. It *is* putting a buffer space between you and your partner. Detaching is like installing a storm window over a single pane of glass. A barrier is created between the two panes. You are on one side of the double glass window and your partner is on the other.

Another metaphor for detachment can be found in picturing a tornado. When we see a tornado, we need to keep a safe distance to stay out of harm's way. We watch to see where it is going to remain informed, but we are careful not to get caught up in its swirling vortex, because we've learned how destructive tornados can be when we get too close.

In our relationships with addicts who have not yet embraced true change, we often feel hypervigilant, anxious or afraid, the results of our trauma. These painful feelings cause us to instinctually long for closeness so we can try to change the situation by calming the sex addict and directing him or her toward recovery and healing. Many want their life partners back! However, such behavior rarely works and it places our own healing and the marital relationship in further jeopardy.

Detachment can help. Think of yourself as an interested observer. From a distance, watch and observe your spouse's action. His or her behaviors and patterns may hurt and upset you, but use detachment to hold back emotional attacks and attempts to fix the person. Detachment can enable you to remain in the relationship if you choose to; it enables you to watch carefully and to assess and monitor the necessary distance required to remain safe. It enables you to honor your own health and healing. Distance, or detachment, is a tool to help you remain emotionally safe. And safety, as we learned earlier in this book, is the cornerstone of eventual healing.

<u>What Detachment *Isn't*</u>
- Abandoning another
- Ignoring another
- Refusing to talk
- Putting up icy walls
- Withholding friendship
- Feeling angry or resentful

<u>What Detachment *Isn't Necessarily*</u>
- Living separately
- Withholding affection
- Withholding physical intimacy
- Sleeping in separate bedrooms
- Withholding *all* emotional intimacy
- Living totally separate lives

<u>What Detachment *Is*</u>
- Fully accepting and embracing your own powerlessness to change your partner.
- No longer watching your partner out of the corner of your eye, snooping, etc.
- Letting go of controlling your partner and what he or she does.
- Refusing to get "hooked" into reacting in old, counterproductive ways.
- Taking three steps back from the situation, breathing a deep breath and relaxing; then refocusing your time, energy and

attention on your own life and growth. You may need to repeat this process many times each day.

- Remaining kind, non-defensive and undemanding while expecting responsible behavior, kindness and mutual commitment for the household, finances, child care, etc.

- Creating a space between you and your partner that serves as a cushion of grace, while, if you have a religious faith, you give God, your partner and the process time to bring about change.

- Knowing what you need in order to remain in the relationship—detachment *does not* mean being blind to sexual acting out or making yourself a doormat.

- Realizing and remembering that, in the end, your marriage may not make it.

- *Never forgetting that you are a precious creation, endowed with your own unique qualities, gifts and traits.*

Detaching is not negative or reactive—it is a positive, *proactive* step that adds to your empowerment arsenal. It enables you to gain objectivity, face reality, deal with your emotions and determine the best course of action for your life. It isn't something you do once and never need to do again. You will find you need to do it again and again and again. The poem "Let Go" defines the essence of what it means to practice detachment:

Let Go

To let go does not mean to stop caring;
It means I can't do it for someone else.

To let go is not to cut myself off;
It's the realization that I can't control another.

To let go is not to enable,
But to allow learning from natural consequences.

To let go is not to try to change or blame another;
It's to make the most of myself.

To let go is not to care for,
But to care about.

To let go is not to judge,
But to allow another to be a human being.

To let go is to not be in the middle, arranging all the outcomes,
But to allow others to affect their own destinies.

To let go is not to be protective;
It's to permit another to face reality.

To let go is not to deny,
But to accept.

To let go is not to nag, scold or argue,
But instead to search out my own shortcomings and correct
them.

To let go is not to adjust everything to my desires,
But to take each day as it comes, and cherish myself in it.

To let go is not to criticize and regulate anybody,
But to try to become what I dream I can be.

To let go is to not regret the past,
But to grow and live for the future.

To let go is to fear less and love more.[5]

Detachment, and the work and growth it allows, helps eliminate
old patterns and unhealthy cycles of reaction in a relationship with a
sex addict. These patterns sometimes develop in our marriages as a
result of the instability, confusion and pain trauma brought to our
lives. Detachment helps us replace those painful dynamics and feelings with peace, balance and eventually joy in our own recovery and
healing, no matter what choices the addict makes.

What about reconciliation? How does that happen?

"Reconciliation," writes Virginia Todd Holeman in her book, *Reconcilable Differences,* "is the active commitment to the restoration of love and trustworthiness by both injured party and transgressor so that their relationship may be transformed."[6] Reconciliation takes action and commitment. It is based on a *decision to seek* reconciliation, followed by behaviors and attitudes that enable restoration.

Holeman's definition holds yet another key: reconciliation requires something from both parties. One person cannot reconcile; both are needed for its accomplishment. However, after both parties choose reconciliation as their goal and commit to its efforts, the betrayer or offender must take the critical first steps: he or she must seek forgiveness, demonstrate change and practice trustworthiness. Clearly, such honorable efforts require a true change of heart and behavior.

These heart-level changes include true remorse for the wrong that has been done and empathy for the wounded party. Empathy requires the offender to see his or her actions—and their consequences—through the eyes and experiences of the wounded party. The offender demonstrates that he or she "gets it"; the offender comprehends at some level the sorrow the sexual betrayal caused in his or her partner. Without these elements, reconciliation remains impossible.

Reconciliation does not end with a change of heart. A changed heart remains invisible until evidenced by changed actions. Behavioral changes that build toward reconciliation include consistent and predictable actions, actions that match words spoken and minimize surprises by announcing change in advance. These changes build trust when they are consistent over time.

We discussed rebuilding trust earlier. It is impossible to fully reconcile a broken vow without rebuilding shattered trust. While total trust may never be restored in the relationship, there must be the ability to trust the motivation and heart of the offender. For this to occur, the wounded party must see heart-level change over time. As we say in most counseling sessions, "Believe behaviors, not words."

So how much time does the re-establishment of trust require? As long as it takes. Months, rather than days or weeks. Perhaps a year. And often longer. Ideally, after the offender begins repair attempts by taking responsibility for his/her actions and then demonstrating that change, the offended party responds with compassion and empathy for the offender and begins the work forgiveness requires.

Most couples benefit from the help of a professional counselor as they work toward reconciliation. A counselor can help the couple communicate about the very emotional topics and experiences connected to the betrayal wounds, while providing a safe place for these conversations to occur. Counseling also provides a level of accountability for the couple. Most people work harder when someone witnesses and tracks their actions and when they must pay someone to help them. Counseling is an important and valuable investment as you seek reconciliation.

Along with counseling, couples heal and progress better when surrounded by a supportive community, whether that be family, friends or perhaps members of a recovery fellowship. Healthy community promotes healthy relationships.

But even with good support, reconciliation is difficult work; work that takes the commitment and diligence of both parties. Neither party can accomplish this task alone.

What role does the addict's childhood play in his or her addiction?

Different counseling and addiction professionals may offer different answers to this important question. But we believe that nearly all addicts have experienced at least some area of hurt or wounding in childhood that contribute to their addictive behaviors.

Certainly, childhood neglect or abuse can contribute to the development of sex addiction. Neglect is the withholding of something that a child needs to develop or to remain emotionally and physically safe. Abuse is doing something to a child that interferes with safety and development. Think of neglect as a lack of something and abuse as too much of something.

Interestingly, one doesn't have to be the direct recipient of abuse or neglect to experience its damaging impact. Just growing up in a home where these elements are present can severely impact a child's normal development.

Some children receive all the food, shelter and other physical things they need (they are physically cared for) but do not receive the nurture and affirmation children need to develop into emotionally healthy adults. This kind of neglect is emotional abandonment. Children who are emotionally abandoned have parents who do not bond well with them or caregivers who are inconsistent in how they emotionally interact with these children. A caregiver can be physically present, but not emotionally available to the child.

Some kids grow up in situations where they are expected to take on adult roles and, in some situations, to even parent their parents, which add burdens of responsibility they're not yet ready to bear.

Emotional neglect and abandonment can leave children feeling empty inside or unable to form healthy relationships as adults since they have little experience with honest, open relationships while growing up.

Abuse can take several forms: physical, emotional or sexual, but any kind of abuse can negatively affect a child's development. Physical abuse is commonly seen as doing things to the child's body that can cause injury. Emotional abuse involves doing things that attack the child's emotional well-being and sense of self. Sexual abuse is any sexual activity on or with a child. This can include direct contact or indirect activities like exposure to pornography or other graphic sexual materials or activities. Some children are sexually abused through coarse sexual talk and the actions of those around them.

Any form of abuse can increase a child's vulnerability to the development of addictions, including sexual addiction, but sexual abuse in particular can increase a child's later tendency to move toward sexual addiction. Children who are sexually abused learn while still young that attention and affirmation comes from sexual activity, even though their sexual abuse most likely felt bad or painful and left them feeling great shame.

Sexual abuse creates extreme confusion in children. Their perpetrators may be people they know and trust. This can leave a child thinking thoughts such as, *This can't be a bad thing if this*

person (friend, family member, neighbor, church leader, etc) acts
friendly most of the time; therefore, this must be okay.

Or children may feel responsible for the behavior and respond
with thoughts like, *There must be a reason they are treating me this*
way. Sexual abuse can also feel good as children's bodies respond
physically to sexual stimulation. If the abuse creates sensations of
physical or emotional pleasure, children can experience a great
deal of confusion and shame. Sexual abuse encumbers children
with powerful traumatic experiences.

Such early trauma injures children's development and may
lead to post-traumatic stress. Out of this trauma, PTSD symptoms
may develop. As children develop, they seek activities that help
them cope with their trauma and shame. For many sexual abuse
victims, sexual activity becomes the activity of choice, even while
still quite young.

Sexual fantasy is powerful. At this vulnerable time in their
lives, abused children who didn't receive what they needed to
learn to bond or relate in healthy ways now discover that sexual
activities work to remove their pain and to take their minds off of
their loneliness. As they soothe and stimulate themselves, new
sexual addicts are born and sexual activity ultimately takes the
place of healthy interactions and intimacy with others who can
meet their deepest emotional needs.

Abuse and neglect are not the only conditions that can contribute to later addiction. Other childhood situations that can
affect development include anything that brings about inconsistent caregiving. Such situations can result from a caregiver's
intentional acts or they can result from situations and conditions
beyond the caregiver's control.

Divorce, a family member's addiction, mental or physical
illness in a family member, extended separations from caregivers
or parents who are too overly involved in their own lives to
adequately provide for the child's nurture can all contribute to
pain and confusion. Situations such as these fall outside a child's
ability to effectively cope and leave holes in the foundation of love
and nurture a child needs to grow up with a fully developed self.

Healing and completing these developmental tasks requires
the help of a trained therapist, especially when sexual addiction or

compulsion is present. We have found that addressing these deep wounds is key to effective recovery.

Does 12-step sexual addiction recovery help deal with the addiction?

We believe that 12-step recovery can play an important part in dealing with sexual addiction, along with the other necessary work required to address and heal early childhood wounds. The structure and fellowship involved in 12-step groups can provide a place for addicts to feel heard, understood and safe as they learn about themselves and try out new behaviors. These groups provide education about addiction and what it takes to gain freedom, while providing support for new coping behaviors. 12-step groups reduce the isolation sex addicts feel and provide a level of accountability as sex addicts seek to discontinue the addictive behaviors.

Not all sex addicts attend 12-step groups. Some addicts find similar support through other kinds of groups or fellowships. Safe fellowship with other members stands out as the most important element a group of any kind can offer a sex addict. If a group fails to function in a safe way, as we discussed when we described safe groups for you, such a group offers no value for the hard work an addict must do.

In our experience, a group alone cannot offer the level of support and treatment most sex addicts need to heal. We see individual therapy as the primary means of discovering and addressing the underlying wounds that led to the addiction in the first place. Groups, whether 12-step or others, can then support the addict's growth and the character change needed for sex addiction recovery.

What about the childhood issues of the partner of a sex addict?

Most people grow up with some form of hurt or wounding from their childhoods and most accumulate fresh wounds along the trail of life. For some of us, those wounds are minimal, for others, profound. In either case, when we learn about our partners' addictions, our earlier histories of hurt or harm are suddenly tapped into. For those of us who have not yet done the work required to resolve old issues, the discovery of our partners' sexual addictions can increase old pain as we take in the new.

Not only do you feel the anger, rage, hurt, confusion and betrayal from what your spouse did, you may also re-experience a measure of pain from previous betrayals, abuses or assaults. This re-experiencing dynamic can make it difficult to determine exactly what you're responding to at any one moment.

As we said earlier in this book, fresh trauma nearly always taps into old trauma. Even if we've formerly dealt with old wounds in therapy, they can resurface now like an ankle formerly weakened by a serious break. We find that most partners we work with will need to talk about such past wounds as they heal from their current trauma and betrayal.

Past abuse, especially sexual abuse or assault of any kind, can become particularly tender when we experience sexual betrayal at the hands of our partners. Any pain or negative energy around former wounds simply mean we need to pay attention, process it and drain any residual ancient pain. If you find this happening to you, we encourage you to find a therapist or other helping professional to help you deal with both your current betrayal and the residual pain and loss from prior wounds.

Also, we want to note that those with prior trauma are at increased risk for developing PTSD—another reason why partners can benefit enormously from individual counseling.

I'm a person of faith but now I feel like God doesn't care or he wouldn't have let this happen. What can you tell me that might help me make sense of all this pain in my life?
For people of faith, this may be one of life's most difficult questions. How do you make sense of something that hurts so much, especially when it makes no sense at all to you? Devoid of reality, sex addiction makes no *rational* sense, either. Nor does it make sense *relationally*. So surely it can't make sense spiritually!

Yet we believe it does. From our perspective, the sex addict attempts to fill spiritual needs with physical pleasure. Some say addiction is mankind's attempt to meet God-sized needs outside of

God's provision for their fulfillment. To us, that part makes sense.

But why does God who is supposed to be loving and able to protect allow this kind of pain to enter your life? Why didn't He protect you or intervene? Why did He allow you to marry this person who promised so much commitment but inflicted so much pain? Surely He knew this was going to happen! These questions bear striking resemblance to others that all people from the beginning of time have asked as they've journeyed through life: Why does a supposedly loving God allow pain and suffering in the world? Why do children die? Why doesn't He protect us?

We know nothing we say here can bring an end to your questioning and that isn't our purpose. Rather, we encourage you to keep on asking God your toughest questions! Converse with him as you struggle to find the answers you need. Barbara encourages her clients of faith to write letters or "Psalms" to God and to pour out their pain and questions as they do. This provides another way to "externalize" our pain and to get those strong feelings out of our heads and onto paper. Do this exercise on a regular basis and down the road, you will have a written history of your journey and of God's presence in it.

Talk to pastors or priests. Read books that discuss the role of suffering in our lives. Pursue resolution, acceptance and peace until you can call them your own. In our own lives, Barbara and I have had to wrestle with the issues ourselves until we finally arrived at some answers:

Sexual betrayal is not God's desire or will; of that we feel certain. But like a loving parent, He gave us the capacity to make our own choices, even if they fall outside of His will. In the case of your partner's addiction, the one you love chose to exercise that will and it led to addiction and eventually to the destructive consequences in his or her life and your own.

Now where is God in all this? Of course, we don't have the ultimate answer to that difficult question, but we suspect He played a role in exposing your partner's addiction in order to protect you from further consequences. Perhaps He played a role in helping you find this book. We know He led us to write it. He might be in the people he has placed around you to help you get through this time. He is definitely there for you to run to with your hurt and to give you comfort. And He is there to love, give grace, support, heal and give hope as you recover and heal.

We've learned over the course of life that God doesn't waste anything, even this. We've watched as He's taken our pain and turned it into passion and purpose, using it to strengthen us and to bring hope to others. He didn't cause it, but He absolutely will use it if we allow Him into the pain and the process of healing our hearts and transforming the loss into new passion and purpose.

What should we or shouldn't we tell the children?

There is no one-size-fits-all answer to this difficult question. Each of us must come to our answers on our own as we consider our children's ages, abilities to understand and our own situations and timing in our lives. *Disclosing Secrets* by Jennifer Schneider and Debra Corely[7] is one excellent resource to use as you struggle to find the right answer for your family. Schneider and Corely interviewed children of sex addicts and report their responses, then provide tips for a variety of types of disclosure.

Realize that your children already know that *something* is going on between their parents—they just may not know exactly *what* it is! They may have all sorts of wild ideas they've arrived at as they've tried to evaluate the risk to their parent's marriage and the continuity of the family they depend on for stability in their lives. Hearing from you that "Yes, indeed there are problems" serves to validate the children's perceptions so they know they aren't crazy, and it models to them that families can talk about difficult topics. That alone is a gift they can take into their futures; one that can help them work their ways through life.

Ultimately, the amount and kind of information you reveal should be based on the developmental level of the child. Young children need to know that even though Mom and Dad are not happy, they will love and take care of them. The older the child, the more information you may need to share in order to provide the child with a structure that enables them to understand what is happening between their parents. Mark Lasser's *Talking to Your Kids about Sex* [8] is another good resource that can help you with this challenging subject.

Ultimately, this crisis provides an opportunity to model to our children that there are healthy, open ways to deal with and talk about difficult topics. It also provides a forum in which to promote healthy sexuality. Too often families neglect discussing sexual topics out of discomfort or embarrassment. Sexual addiction flourishes in secret and dysfunctional views of human sexuality. Learning to talk openly with your kids will provide them with the tools to manage their own feelings and temptations.

Your children don't need details of what the addict did, but they will most likely benefit from information on addiction and recovery. They are sexual beings, after all, who will ultimately—and may already be—struggling with these behaviors themselves! Sadly, we hear that frequently. Addictive behaviors are often passed from generation to generation. If you discuss these issues openly, you may give your children the encouragement and guidance they need to prevent this problem from developing in their own lives.

Disclosure presents another challenge that comes with sex addiction. How you decide to handle it needs to come from discussions between the addict and the partner and from their agreement on the issue if at all possible. We encourage you to use the resources we've listed to help you with this decision.

What is sexual anorexia?
Sexual anorexia and the pain it brings surface again and again, week after week in our work with partners of sex addicts.

"We haven't had sex for ten years." "We never have sex unless I initiate; then he doesn't seem to want me." "I shower, light candles, put on sexy music and do everything I can to seduce him, but he rolls over and goes to sleep." These are just some of the comments we frequently hear. The results of all these comments have two things in common: they produce mountains of confusion and emotional pain.

If you've lived with this painful consequence of sexual addiction, we know you need understanding and help. We recommend that you read a helpful article on the topic written by Douglas Weiss, Ph.D., a sex addiction specialist, and posted on the *Safe Families* Web site. In the article, Weiss helps illuminate the dark and painful dynamics that result from this complicated dysfunction that can develop in a sex addict's life. Weiss defines sexual anorexia as "The active, almost compulsive withholding of emotional, spiritual and sexual intimacy from the primary partner" and goes on to say "It is the consistent sabotaging of any ongoing intimacy in a marriage or committed relationship."[9]

Dr. Weiss shares three causes of sexual anorexia, including sexual abuse, attachment disorder and sexual addiction. The article provides a great deal of helpful information for those who deal with this painful issue. Here we share just one part that we hope you'll find helpful:

> Weiss (1998) contends that the early sexual reinforcement being bonded to the fantasy world (with or without pornography) and being maintained through adulthood can lead a person to primarily sexually bond to the other world. The neurological chemical bonds to the unreal world combined with the psychological ease of a fantasy world can allow a person to conclude the altered state fantasy world is not only easier psychological and sexually but preferred. Once the individual makes this conclusion, whether in their 20's or 50's, the anorexia symptoms will follow.[10]

Sexual anorexia is a deep-seated issue in many sex addicts, and it requires significant therapy to heal. If you live with this devastating twist on sexual addiction, we know the pain you feel. Try to remember that as painful as your partner's lack of sexual desire for you can be, it bears absolutely no reflection on you or your desirability as a sexual partner. Rather, it is another symptom of the intimacy disorder present in your partner. And it's a disorder that requires professional help.

How will I know if it's time to divorce?

This is another very difficult question and one that no one can answer for you. The answer depends on many things, most of them individual to your situation and beliefs. However, over time most counseling professionals have come to agree that it may be a decision to delay for awhile, if possible. Let's look at the reasons.

Any life-altering, major decision (especially divorce) imposes changes and *subsequent* changes and consequences as part of the package. Divorce affects children (whether young or adult), extended family members and friends. It has enormous financial repercussions. And it is yet another loss on top of immeasurable losses you've already experienced. To rush on this decision may invite unintended consequences when you can least manage them, and it may add to your already mountainous pile of stressful situations when your emotional and physical energy is at an all-time low. We suggest you try to delay your decision until you are able to think clearly, then weigh all your options.

However, a huge percentage of sex addicts aren't willing to consider recovery and change *until they are about to lose something they aren't prepared to live without: their family and half of their accrued wealth*. Very often, a partner's role includes the responsibility to take action that can cause the addict to reach a place of brokenness in his or her life *so the addict will reach out for help*. A partner's most loving act can mean allowing the addict to experience the painful consequences of sexual addiction.

In addition, many partners have done all this. They've waited patiently, hoping for change. They've confronted the addict and taken consequence-producing action, only to watch as their spouses refused change. In such cases, divorce may be the most realistic decision for you. As we learned in chapter 5, living with sex addiction produces dozens of consequences in our lives, particularly if we live with continued addiction and little or no change. At some point we have a responsibility to take care of ourselves.

We both know partners who have made this difficult decision and progressed to emotional and physical health after their divorces. We also know many who decided to defer the decision to give recovery and restoration a chance and the miracle of change occurred in their lives.

In the end, only you can determine how long you should wait to make a decision as to whether to divorce or not in the face of continued betrayal or lack of commitment. Only you can decide if the damage is too great for you to reconcile, even if your offender is actively in recovery and committed to change. For some, the only way to heal is to move on. We encourage you to involve those you trust in this most important decision if they can provide supportive input in your decision and life.

We are privileged knowing you've chosen our strategies and encouragement to help you on your healing journey. Thank you.

Appendix

Advice for Counselors, Pastors or Friends

First, we want to say "Thank you!" for your care and concern for those affected by sex addiction. We the authors know only too well the silence, puzzled looks and occasional scoffing we receive when we tell some people we specialize in helping partners of sex addicts. Many people, even many professional helpers, are uncomfortable and significantly unprepared to effectively respond to someone who has experienced sexual betrayal in intimate relationships. Many people don't know about or understand sex addiction and often what they do know is incomplete or ineffective for the partners who walk into their offices, their churches or their support groups.

In this book, we have tried to delve into the needs and feelings of partners of sex addicts. Here we offer some additional thoughts and ideas for helping this hurting population.

- **Don't use the term "co-addiction."** The term co-addiction labels a traumatized partner with accusatory stigma, telling that person that you see him or her as somehow partially at fault for the mess the partner is in. Contrary to the working model of treatment that sees partners as unhealthy codependents or even co-addicts, many partners of sexual addicts have no awareness of their spouses' addictive behaviors prior to disclosure. Upon disclosure, many immediately confront the addicts and attempt to communicate, often imposing appropriate consequences immediately.

    Partners are in a great deal of emotional pain and many are debilitated by the traumatic experience. They also face their spouses' denials and continued deceit as pertinent information continues to be withheld. Others suffer under the repeated wounding of painful sexual information that leaks out slowly over time.

We recommend you view partners just as you would other victims of traumatic experiences. In this book we've discussed how and why such people's pain is like that of victims of debilitating experiences.

- **Provide individual counseling.** Individual therapy sessions for partners allow them to work through their trauma symptoms, focus on themselves and deal with their own issues that surface because of this experience. In many settings, the partner's individual session follows a joint session with the spouse. In these settings, a partner is often given the role of helping the addict recover.

However, we see a partner's needs as requiring separate treatment; at least until he or she's stable, the addict is committed to the recovery process and that person's sexual acting out has stopped. Initially, your work with the partner needs to focus on restoring the partner's sense of safety and empowerment, because the betrayal and trauma it produces strips most partners of those elements in their lives. Until the partner regains those essential ingredients, healing cannot begin.

In addition, a partner's treatment needs to help the partner understand his or her emotional and behavioral responses to the addiction and educate the partner about what can be done to regain stability. The treatment needs to help the partner establish boundaries to protect the person, as well as the many other helpful activities you'll find on the "Pathway to Healing, Empowerment and Transformation Following Sexual Betrayal Trauma" chart in chapter 6.

If in your counseling setting you only do couple's sessions, make sure you incorporate helping the partner with trauma and its symptoms and the partner's need for support.

- **Conceptualize the partner's behaviors as typical responses to trauma and fear.** Among trauma victims, hypervigilance and scanning the environment are normal. Automatic in nature, they are the victims' efforts to avoid further pain and injury. Help partners understand and accept alternative ways to gain the safety and empowerment they seek. Give healthy, empowering tools that will equip the partner to meet that person's very real needs, including (as needed) emotional distance (detaching), boundaries, accountability, self-care, support and others you'll find in this text. Together they enable the partner to exercise some level of control over his or her environment and well-being.

Focus on what traumatized partners *can* do, rather than placing the focus on things over which they have no control. Trauma survivors need to find ways to exercise self-determination and personal responsibility in order to counter feelings of powerlessness to protect themselves. Help equip them to exercise empowering choices in the midst of their personal environments and circumstances. Help partners learn to assess and weigh options against personal values, determine action and then use personal power to follow through.

- **Help the client build social supports**. We have learned through our own professional practices, research and other professionals that trauma survivors do better in recovery if they have positive support systems. Many partners have experienced long-term isolation by the time they seek help. Generally, the isolation is imposed by the addicts and has become part of the dynamics within the relationships. Occasionally, partners hide their secrets out of shame or embarrassment. Breaking that isolation by telling even one other person the truth can be frightening but ultimately liberating and healing.

  As you help partners, remain aware that many of them have experienced long-term emotional control and, frequently, emotional and financial abuse as part of their marriage relationships. As a result, many have difficulty determining just who's safe to tell. Even their closest friends may not know. For these reasons and more, support groups or therapy groups can help a great deal, because they become safe places to share, gain insight and awareness and grow. Seek to help partners identify and develop relationships where they can be honest about their experiences, feelings and circumstances.

- **Help identify positive protective behaviors.** Many partners of sexual addicts do not know how to protect themselves from mental and emotional abuse. Often, they have little understanding of their rights to and needs for personal, protective boundaries. Educating and assisting partners in this area also falls to those in helper roles.

Initially, encourage and assist partners in the need to secure physical safety by helping them understand how essential it is that they be tested for sexually transmitted diseases, no matter what the spouses say they have or have not done. Taking this often difficult measure is a step away from denial into the reality that their partners' actions may have placed them at physical risk.

Boundaries classes or support groups are wonderful adjuncts for partners of sex addicts if you or some other caregiver is able to accommodate that need. If a group is not available, incorporate boundary education into partners' counseling by asking them to read books on boundaries and then processing them. As you do, you can help partners assess their needs for boundary initiation or modification in their interpersonal roles, particularly with their addicted spouses.

- **Teach and inform the addicted partners.** Much effort goes into educating traumatized partners about sexual addiction and compulsion and what it takes for addicts to heal. With your new awareness of partners' pain, help them and their marriages by educating the sexual addicts about the traumatic impact their behaviors have had on their spouses. The trauma recovery model can help encourage the addicts to have awareness, understanding, compassion and patience for the traumatized partners' healing processes, which can take much time. Use the model to help addicts grow in these ways. If addicts are open, your effort can go far toward helping their marriages survive and eventually thrive.

- **Treat the partner as an individual**. Often the partner experiences treatment as an extension of the betrayer's treatment. Traumatized partners are wounded people in need of treatment and care in their own rights, given the traumatic devastation brought about by relational betrayal. Assess the person's mental health needs, symptoms and relational realities and respond accordingly.

- **Refer if necessary**. If you lack the experience, understanding and training required to help someone heal from relational betrayal trauma, we recommend that you refer the partner to someone who has the necessary background. The spouse of a sexual addict encounters realities not found in most relationships; therefore, traditional marital therapy is not effective in the initial stages of treatment. As discussed earlier, marital work should follow individual work after the addict has established a solid foundation of recovery. However, we do believe that couple's educational sessions to assist with communication and crisis intervention can be very helpful in the early stages of healing.

Additionally, if a partner suffers from depression or anxiety, refer him or her to a psychiatrist for evaluation. A large percentage of partners need medication to deal with the shifts in their body chemistries due to the extreme stress produced by trauma. Often, progress eludes them until they are chemically stable again.

- **For clergy.** The Judeo-Christian perspective on the importance of sexual fidelity within marriage reflects the very nature of our relationship with God. For this reason, spouses of sexual addicts often feel confused about and unable to decipher the "right" course of action when sexual infidelity enters their marriages through compulsive sexual behaviors. Add to that the differing opinions about what to label sexual activities that fall short of actual physical intercourse and partners in faith-based communities can feel trapped in a maze of confusion. And if they've been exposed to the disease model of addiction, they feel further confusion not knowing if their spouses have actual diseases over which they feel powerless or if they have sinned by violating the biblical standards of faithfulness.

  Faith leaders vary in their responses to traumatized partners. Some exhort the person to pray for the addict and stay the course. Others tell the person, especially a woman, to fulfill spousal obligations by becoming more sexual. Some step in and immediately confront the addict, strip him or her of leadership positions and dis-fellowship him or her from their midst. And some, like Katherine's minister, tell the partner to never come back. Many partners of sexual addicts feel pulled between a desire to support spouses and a very real need to protect themselves.

As a spiritual leader, it falls to you to help the traumatized partner make decisions based on beliefs and values of the faith. But you, or a caregiver on your team, need to also provide comfort, support, counsel and practical help as the hurt partner navigates the pain, loss and marital upheaval. Here are some suggestions to aid you in responding in helpful ways when traumatized partners of sex addicts from your congregation seek your help in the midst of their crises.

• **Listen.** Most partners who seek help usually do so after discovering evidence of sexual behavior outside their marriages. Their worlds have been shattered and they are in crises, sometimes even shock or dissociative states. They need time and space to explain what has happened and to express their feelings. Listen to the pain, confusion, anger and fear without judgment, without rushing to conclusions and above all, without giving advice.

• **Respond.** Let the partner know that the sex addict's actions and attitude are not the victimized partner's fault. The partner did not cause it and it has nothing to do with the person's value. Let the partner know you will stand with the person and, if open to it, so will others on your staff or in your congregation.

• **Assess.** Ask open-ended questions to assess how the person is doing emotionally, as well as in the practical areas of his or her life, such as at work and in caring for children if they are not grown. Ask about how he or she is responding to this knowledge. Is the partner depressed? Anxious? Fearful? Is there emotional, verbal or physical abuse within the relationship? Does the partner have a backup plan, should one be needed?

• **Offer assistance.** Communicate how you can help. You may aid the partner in confronting the offending spouse and offer support and accountability. Partners need to know that it is not their jobs to fix or heal addicted partners, nor to keep these secrets to protect spouses. Help the partner sort out who can and cannot be turned to for support and help.

• **Refer.** A partner's needs will often surpass your time and ability to meet them, and in actuality, most needs of female partners are better met by female staff members. Ideally, your house of worship will have trained male and female staff members (whether paid or volunteer) available to minister to partners of addicted spouses as they surface in your midst. In addition, know which counselors and other mental health professionals in your community are trained in sex addiction and the treatment of trauma, but who will also show honor and respect to people of faith. A counselor who respects not only emotional and practical needs, but also a person's faith, can offer partners of faith the best help.

• **Be careful what you say!** Unfortunately, some of the deepest, most profound wounds (besides those inflicted by the addict) a partner receives come from those in the faith community. Uninformed pastors, staff members and members of the congregation often create tremendous damage and compound the pain and shame experienced by a partner.

We are happy to serve as consultants to any professional who desires to work with partners. This is very challenging and rewarding work. Please join us in helping partners heal.

Our continued desire and passion is to increase awareness about sex addiction's broad social impact on partners, families, congregations, workplaces and on addicts themselves and to facilitate conversation to address the significant trauma partners experience through their relationships with addicts.

Acknowledgments

I would like to thank and acknowledge those women who participated in support groups where we began to realize and fully comprehend the trauma experienced by partners of sex addicts. These brave women shared their stories and experiences and encouraged me to give voice to their journeys. These women want therapists, clergy and medical professionals to recognize and validate the reality of trauma in partners of sex addicts. They also want other partners to know they are not alone and that there is hope. All those who were ever in "Barb's group"—you are my heroes. I also thank my clients who also shared their stories to encourage others on the journey of healing.

I also want to thank those therapists who "get it" and encouraged the writing of this book. I especially want to thank therapists Valerie Arnette, Sue King, Kent Ernsting, Doug Reed and Mark Laaser for their encouragement, support and training. Your work with sex addicts and partners has helped many and has encouraged me to continue this work through the years. I also want to thank Omar Minwalla and Silvia Jason—we are like-minded in our call to witness, voice and validate trauma experienced by partners of sex addicts. I also thank the Society for the Advancement of Sexual Health (SASH)—this organization exists to educate professionals and society about the issues of sexual addiction.

I also would like to thank those friends and family who have put up with, listened to and prayed for me as I sought to follow what I believe is a call to do this work. What a blessing to have you in my life! I also want to thank my church "family" of Vineyard Church Northwest.

Erin and Emily—I couldn't ask for any better privilege than being your mom. Steve—you are God's greatest gift to me. Thanks for your belief in me. —**Barbara Steffens, Ph.D., LPCC**

Every book writing project owes its conception, gestation and eventual "birth" to many contributors, but this book in particular would never have come to life were it not for the hundreds who shared freely of their stories, their pain or their expertise in helping broken hearts heal after the trauma of relational betrayal. I am indebted to each and every one of you.

Barb, thank you for sharing your research with me and for choosing me to partner with you to transform that research into this manuscript.

Thank you to every woman and every man who gave us permission to use their stories, giving flesh and blood to the facts associated with sex addiction's traumatic wounding. I won't thank you by name in respect of your anonymity, but a heartfelt thank you to each and every one of you. And Katherine and Neal, we are especially grateful to you for your boldness in sharing not only your stories, but your names, as you continue to integrate this painful chapter of your lives into your larger life stories. Along with you, I pray that your sharing will help others experience the amazing healing God continues to do in your marriage and in your lives.

And to every woman who ever turned to me for hope, I say thank you for sharing your stories and experiences with me. I continue to learn from you. We are indeed sisters on this journey.

Michael, thank you for allowing me to be your friend as we've utilized the teachings of Shepherd's House and others to bring healing to the life-altering trauma you experienced as a child and the toll it took in every area of your life. For the last three years I have watched and listened as God has slowly done his agape love miracle as you remained committed to your emotional and spiritual healing. The transformation continues to amaze me. What a privilege it is to participate in that life-changing process.

Gaylie, thank you for sharing your experience with Phoenix Rising Yoga Therapy and the way this spiritually-neutral body therapy enabled you to reach and heal the trauma that had been stored at your cellular level for many years. I am grateful for the addition of this "non-talk" therapy for readers who, like you, discover that words simply won't enable them to release the pain that their bodies have absorbed.

Dr. Milton Magness, thank you for sharing your experience in using polygraph testing in a clinical setting with couples who seek healing from the damage sex addiction has created in their marriages and lives. Though we've only met through e-mail, I hold the highest respect for your work as again and again women have shared with me the caring, kindness and support you've provided during your three day intensives with individual couples.

Silvia Jason and Omar Minwalla, though we've not yet met, thank you for sharing and trumpeting your firm belief that partners of sexual addicts frequently suffer from trauma and post traumatic stress. What a joy to find kindred spirits who share our passion to bring attention and healing to those who suffer these wounds without recognition or help.

Thank you to the many authors (and their publishers) who generously allowed us to learn from your work and to quote from your books. We are grateful for your expertise.

And lastly, I am grateful to a dear friend whose story appears in the pages of this book. Even as she faced her own death as a result of her husband's addiction, she chose to share with our readers her experience with the trauma sex addiction produced in her life. She did so in the hope that it would help point the way toward healing for the millions of others who suffer trauma's pain as a result of their partners' devastating addiction.

—**Marsha Means, MA**

Resources

Steffens Counseling Services (Ohio)
Mental health counseling practice specializing in helping partners
of sexual addicts and those impacted by sexual betrayal.
   Barbara Steffens, Ph.D., LPCC
   www.bsteffens.com

A Woman's Healing Journey
Specializing in offering hope and help through telephone
and e-support groups, individual telephone coaching, an online
community, written resources, healing intensives and training.
   Marsha Means, MA
   www.awomanshealingjourney.com

Healing and Hope (Houston, Texas)
Mental health practice specializing in sexual addiction treatment
and treatment of the partner/spouse. All services available in
Spanish.
   Silvia Jason, LMFT, CSAT
   www.healingandhopehouston.com

Healing for the Soul
Offers telephone therapy and teleconference recovery groups for
men and for wives in recovery worldwide.
   Jayson Graves, M.MFT., Director
   www.healingforthesoul.org

The Institute for Sexual Health
Psychological services, research and training clinic. This institute offers a multidisciplinary integration of cutting edge treatment and clinical services that treats all aspects of the individual and the family system impacted by sexual and relationship challenges.
> Omar Minwalla, Psy.D.
> www.sexualtreatmentprograms.com
> dromarminwalla@gmail.com

Hope & Freedom Counseling Services (Houston and the Canadian Rockies)
Certified Sex Addiction Therapist (CSAT) who specializes in three-day intensives for men and for couples to jump-start recovery. Intensives are also good for relapse recovery.
> Milton S. Magness
> www.HopeAndFreedom.com
> (713) 630-0111

International Service Organization of COSA
12-step recovery program for men and women whose lives have been affected in any way by another person's compulsive sexual behavior.
> www.cosa-recovery.org
> info@cosa-recovery.org
> (763) 537-6904

Phoenix Rising Yoga Therapy (PRYT)
A body-based movement and awareness practice that supports the capacity to hear and integrate traumatic life experiences with compassion and meaning. PRYT practitioners can be found worldwide. Gaylie facilitates workshops or individually as a PRYT practitioner or as a spiritual director in the Christian faith tradition.
> Gaylie Cashman, MA, PRYT
> www.pryt.com
> www.yourstillsmallvoice.com

Notes

Introduction
[1]We define a sex addict as one engaged in compulsive out-of-control sexual behaviors that negatively impact his or her life or the lives of those in relationships with the person, yet he or she is unable or does not want to stop.

PART I: WHEN YOUR PARTNER'S SEXUAL ADDICTION SHATTERS YOUR WORLD

Chapter 1: What is Trauma and Post-Traumatic Stress?
[1]Carter, *Alchemy of Loss.*
[2]American Psychiatric Association, *Diagnostic and Statistical Manual,* 563-471.
[3]Johnson, *Emotionally Focused Couple Therapy,* 182.
[4]Steffens and Rennie, "Traumatic Nature of Disclosure," 249.
[5]Ibid.
[6]Ibid., 251.

Chapter 2: A Study in Contrasts: Is it Co-addiction or is it Trauma?
[1]Borchert, *Lois Wilson Story.*
[2]Carnes, *Don't Call It Love.*
[3]Ibid.
[4]Schneider, *Back from Betrayal,* 45.
[5]American Psychiatric Association, *Diagnostic and Statistical Manual,* 563-471; Carnes, *Don't Call It Love.*
[6]Omar Minwalla and Silvia Jason, "The Sexual Trauma Model: Partner's Reaction," SASH National Conference, Cambridge, MA: 2008.

Chapter 3: Why Your Partner's Sex Addiction Hurts So Much: Attachment Bonds Betrayed

[1] Brooke C. Feeney and Nancy L. Collins, "Couple
    Relationships,"
    http://family.jrank.org/pages/118/Attachment.html.
[2] Clinton and Sibcy, *Attachments*, 22.
[3] Slay, *Counseling Techniques*, 1.
[4] Pretiti and Amato, "Infidelity a Cause or a Consequence," 218.
[5] Glass and Wright, "Reconstructing marriages," 475.

Chapter 4: How the Addiction and Trauma Models Differ in Helping You Heal

[1] ISO of COSA, "More about COSA," www.cosa-recovery.org.
[2] ISO of COSA, "COSA Recovery Tools" and "Letter to a
    Mental Health Professional," www.cosa-recovery.org.
[3] ISO of COSA, "COSA Recovery Tools," www.cosa-recovery.
[4] ISO of COSA, "More about COSA," www.cosa-recovery.org
[5] Ibid.
[6] Ibid.
[7] S-Anon International, "The S-Anon Problem (Long Version),"
    www.sanon.org/Prob.htm.
[8] Doug Weiss, Ph.D., and Milton Magness, Ph.D., are two
    psychologists who specialize in sex addiction and require
    their s.a. clients to take lie detector tests.

Chapter 5: Trauma Impacts on Every Level: Potential Physical and Mental Health Side Effects of Trauma

[1] Van der Kolk, "In Terror's Grip."
[2] Cowley, "Anxiety and Your Brain," 46.
[3] Van der Kolk, "In Terror's Grip."
[4] Ibid.
[5] David Baldwin, "About Trauma," *David Baldwin's Trauma
    Information Pages*, www.trauma-pages.com/trauma.php
    (accessed January 13, 2009).
[6] Van der Kolk, "In Terror's Grip."
[7] Baldwin, "Trauma/PTSD," *Self-Injury: You are NOT the only
    one*, http://www.palace.net/~llama/psych/injury.html.
[8] Van der Kolk, "In Terror's Grip."

⁹Ibid.

¹⁰American Psychological Association, "Effects of Trauma."

¹¹Van der Kolk, "In Terror's Grip."

¹²Sweeney, "Neurobiology of Psychic Trauma."

¹³Van der Kolk, "In Terror's Grip."

¹⁴Ibid.

¹⁵Ibid.

¹⁶Ibid.

¹⁷"Stress Disorders," HealingResources.info.

¹⁸Perry, "Applying Principles of Neurodevelopment."

¹⁹Freyd, Klest and Allard, "Betrayal Trauma."

²⁰Sweeney, "Neurobiology of Psychic Trauma."

²¹Horner, "Damaging Effects of Stress."

²²Cowley, "Anxiety and Your Brain."

²³Horner, "Damaging Effects of Stress."

²⁴Cornish, "Emotional Immune System."

²⁵"Stress Disorders," HealingResources.info.

PART II: YOUR JOURNEY TOWARD WHOLENESS

Chapter 6: Healing from Trauma and Post-Traumatic Stress

¹H. Norman Wright, "Grief and Crisis Counseling: Ministering to the Hurting," *Leadership Seminar November 15, 2001*, CNN Leadership Training Series.

²David Baldwin, "About Trauma," *David Baldwin's Trauma Information Pages*, www.trauma-pages.com/trauma.php (accessed January 13, 2009).

³Sweeney, "Neurobiology of Psychic Trauma."

⁴Friesen et al., *Living From the Heart Jesus Gave You.*

⁵Milton Magness, personal communication with the author.

⁶Levine and Frederick, *Waking the Tiger*, 35, 36.

⁷Australian Centre for Posttraumatic Mental Health, "About Trauma," *Trauma and mental health*. http://www.acpmh.unimelb.edu.au/trauma/about_trauma.html (accessed January 13, 2009).

⁸Levine and Frederick, *Waking the Tiger*, 49, 61.

⁹Ibid., 156.

[10]Ibid., 155.
[11]Van der Kolk, *Psychological Trauma*, 155-156.

Chapter 7: From Crisis to Stability
[1]Slay, *Counseling Techniques*, 11, 23.
[2]Van der Kolk, "In Terror's Grip."
[3]Hannigan, *Ida B.*, 85.
[4]Levine and Frederick, *Waking the Tiger*, 95, 96.
[5]Haines, *Healing Sex*.
[6]Slay, *Counseling Techniques*, 11, 23.
[7]Freeman, *Clinical Applications*.
[8]Bourne, *Anxiety & Phobia Workbook*, 200.
[9]Estes, "Story as Medicine," 7.
[10]Malchiodi, *Expressive Therapies*, 1.
[11]EMDR Institute, "A Brief Description of EMDR," *EMDR Institute, Inc.*, http://www.emdr.com/briefdes.htm (accessed January 13, 2009).
[12]Levine and Frederick, *Waking the Tiger*, 101, 215.
[13]Ibid., 111.
[14]Ibid., 61- 62.
[15]Ibid.

Chapter 8: From Integration to Triumph
[1]Tedeschi and Calhoun, "Posttraumatic Growth."
[2]Levine and Frederick, *Waking the Tiger*, 120.
[3]Chellis, *Ordinary Women*, 2.
[4]Virkler, *Speaking Your Mind*.
[5]Van der Kolk, *Psychological Trauma*, 8.
[6]Enright, *Forgiveness is a Choice*, 25.
[7]Levine and Frederick, *Waking the Tiger*, 194.
[8]Ibid., 33.
[9]Estes, "Story as Medicine."
[10]Ibid.

Conclusion: The Rest of the Journey
[1]Society for the Advancement of Sexual Health (SASH), 2007, http://www.sash.net (accessed February 12, 2009).

[2]Mayo Clinic Staff, "Compulsive sexual behavior," *Mayo Clinic*, http://www.mayoclinic.com/health/compulsive-sexual-behavior/DS00144/DSECTION=symptoms (accessed February 12, 2009).

[3]Marsha Means, "Coping with your Husband's Sexual Addiction," *A Woman's Healing Journey*, http://www.awomanshealingjourney.com/copingwith hisaddiction/index.php (accessed February 12, 2009).

[4]Ibid.

[5]Source unknown.

[6]Holeman, *Reconcilable Differences*, 12.

[7]Jennifer Schneider and Debra Corely, *Disclosing Secrets: When, to Whom, and How Much to Reveal* (Center City, MN: Hazelden Publishing & Educational Services, 2002).

[8]Mark Laaser, *Talking to Your Kids About Sex: How to Have a Lifetime of Age-Appropriate Conversations with Your Children About Healthy Sexuality* (Colorado Springs, CO: Waterbrook Press, 1999).

[9]Weiss, Douglas. "Sexual Anorexia," 3.

[10]Ibid.

Bibliography

American Psychiatric Association. *Diagnostic and Statistical Manual of Mental Disorders.* 4th ed. Washington, D.C.: American Psychiatric Pub, 2000.

American Psychological Association. "The Effects of Trauma Do Not Have to Last a Lifetime." *Psychology Matters.* http://www.psychologymatters.org/ptsd.html (accessed January 13, 2009).

Borchert, William. *The Lois Wilson Story: When Love Is Not Enough.* Minneapolis: Hazelden, 2005.

Bourne, Edmund. *Anxiety & Phobia Workbook.* 3rd ed. Oakland, CA: New Harbinger Publications, 2000.

Carnes, Patrick. *Don't Call It Love: Recovery From Sexual Addiction.* New York: Bantam Books, 1991.

Carter, Abigail. *The Alchemy of Loss: A Young Widow's Transformation.* Toronto: McClelland & Stewart, 2008.

Chellis, Marcia. *Ordinary Women, Extraordinary Lives: How to Overcome Adversity and Achieve Positive Change in Your Life.* New York: Random House, 1994.

Clinton, Tim and Gary Sibcy. *Attachments: Why You Love, Feel, and Act the Way You Do.* Brentwood, Tennessee: Integrity Publishers, 2002.

Cornish, Tarilee. "The Emotional Immune System." *Whole Approach.* August 2008. http://www.wholeapproach.com/ newsletter (accessed January 13, 2009).

Cowley, Geoffrey. "Anxiety and Your Brain: How Living with Fear Affects the Mind and the Body." *Newsweek* 24 February 2003.

Enright, Robert. *Forgiveness is a Choice: A Step-By-Step Process for Resolving Anger and Restoring Hope.* Washington, D.C.: American Psychological Association, 2001.

Estes, Clarissa Pinkola. "Story as Medicine." *O, the Oprah Magazine.* November 2001.

Freeman, Arthur. *Clinical Applications of Cognitive Therapy.* New York: Springer, 2004.

Freyd, Jennifer J., Bridget Klest and Carolyn B. Allard. "Betrayal Trauma: Relationship to Physical Health, Psychological Distress, and a Written Disclosure Intervention." *Journal of Trauma & Dissociation* 6, no. 3 (2005), http://dynamic.uoregon.edu/~jjf/articles/fka05.pdf (accessed January 13, 2009).

Friesen, James G., E. James Wilder, Anne M. Bierling, Rick Koepcke and Maribeth Poole. *Living From the Heart Jesus Gave You.* Pasadena, CA: Shepherd's House, Inc., 2004.

Glass, S. and T. Wright. "Reconstructing marriages after the trauma of infidelity." In *Clinical Handbook of Marriage and Couples Interventions*, edited by H. Markman and W. Halford. New York: Wiley, 1997.

Haines, Staci. *Healing Sex: A Mind-Body Approach to healing Sexual Trauma.* New York: Cleis Press, 2007.

Hannigan, Katherine. *Ida B and Her Plans to Maximize Fun, Avoid Disaster, and (Possibly) Save the World.* San Francisco, CA: Greenwillow Books, 2004.

Holeman, Virginia Todd. *Reconcilable Differences: Hope and Healing for Troubled Marriages.* Downers Grove, IL: InterVarsity Press, 2004.

Horner, Christine. "The Damaging Effects of Stress on Your Health." *The Doctors' Prescription for Healthy Living* 7, no.11.

Johnson, Susan. *Emotionally Focused Couple Therapy with Trauma Survivors.* New York: Guilford, 2002.

Levine, Peter and Ann Frederick. *Waking the Tiger: Healing Trauma: The Innate Capacity to Transform Overwhelming Experiences.* Berkley: North Atlantic Books, 1997.

Malchiodi, Cathy A., ed. *Expressive Therapies.* New York: Guilford Press, 2006.

Perry, Bruce. "Applying Principles of Neurodevelopment to Clinical Work with Maltreated and Traumatized Children." In *Traumatized Youth in Child Welfare*, edited by Nancy Boyd Webb. New York: The Guilford Press, 2006.

Pretiti, D. and P. Amato. "Is Infidelity a Cause or a
     Consequence of Poor Marital Quality?" *Journal of Social
     and Personal Relationships* 21, no. 2 (2004).

Schneider, Jennifer. *Back from Betrayal.* Tucson, AZ:
     Recovery Resources Press, 2001.

Slay, Tana. *Counseling Techniques for Trauma Pain Resolution
     in Self and Relationships.* Nashville: Cross Country
     University, 2003.

Steffens, Barbara A. and Robyn L. Rennie. "The Traumatic
     Nature of Disclosure for Wives of Sexual Addicts." *Sexual
     Addiction and Compulsivity* 13, no. 2 (2006).

"Stress Disorders Including Anxiety and Depression Caused by
     Early Life Experiences." *HealingResources.info,*
     http://www.traumaresources.org/stress_related_anxiety_
     depression.htm (accessed January 13, 2009).

Sweeney, Daniel. "The Neurobiology of Psychic Trauma and
     Treatment Considerations." *Christian Counseling
     Connection* 1 (2007),
     http://www.rachelsvineyard.org/Downloads/Notes/
     Neurobiology%20of%20Psychic%20Trauma.pdf (accessed
     January 13, 2009).

Tedeschi, Richard G. and Lawrence Calhoun. "Posttraumatic
     Growth: A New Perspective on Psychotraumatology."
     Psychiatric Times 21, no. 4 (2004).

Van der Kolk, Bessel. "In Terror's Grip: Healing the Ravages of
     Trauma." *Cerebrum* 4 (2002): 34-50,
     http://www.dana.org/news/cerebrum/
     detail.aspx?id_1490.

Van der Kolk, Bessel. *Psychological Trauma.* Washington, D.C.:
     American Psychiatric Publishing, Inc., 1987.

Virkler, Henry A. *Speaking Your Mind Without Stepping on Toes: A
     Christian Approach to Assertiveness.* Wheaton, Illinois:
     Victor Books, 1991.

Weiss, Douglas. "Sexual Anorexia: A New Paradigm for Hyposexual
     Desire Disorder." *Safe Families,*
     http://www.safefamilies.org/docs/Sexual%20Anorexia.pdf
     (accessed February 15, 2009): 3.